Creative Power

Other Books

By

HUGHES MEARNS

Lions in the Way
Creative Youth
I Ride in My Coach
The Vinegar Saint
Richard Richard
Lincoln Verse, Story, and Essay
The Creative Adult

Creative Power

The Education of Youth in the Creative Arts

By

HUGHES MEARNS

With an Introduction
By

WINIFRED WARD

Second Revised Edition

Dover Publications, Inc.
New York

This Dover edition, first published in 1958, is a
revised and enlarged version of the work first pub-
lished by Doubleday, Doran and Company in 1929.
This edition is sponsored by the Children's Theatre
Conference of the American Educational Theatre
Association.

Library of Congress Catalog Card Number: 58-59929

Manufactured in the United States of America

Dover Publications, Inc.
180 Varick Street
New York, N. Y. 10014

To

WINIFRED WARD

who believes with the author that the natural
creative interests of childhood and youth may
be developed into superior personal powers.

Author's Foreword to Second Revised Edition

One must be reminded in this new edition that the earlier chapters of this book tell the story of my first experimental classes in creative education done several years ago in The Lincoln School of Teachers College, Columbia University. That story is retained in this edition as a picture of the difficulties, and the opportunities, that confront any teacher who, in an alien environment, seeks to bring out and direct the dormant creative powers of youth. Few doubt now that these powers can be made to work for us instead of against us.

In that first year were many clumsy if earnest attempts to understand the new kind of freedom. However, when the novelty of our approach was accepted as reasonable and personally rewarding, our classes conducted themselves, as hundreds of visitors will testify, in the same orderly fashion as any adult groups gathered seriously to perform worthy social functions.

1958

HUGHES MEARNS
Bearsville, New York

Preface to Second Revised Edition

There is a triumphant story underlying the republication of *Creative Power*. It's a story of people dedicated to the belief that every child has something worthy to contribute and should be encouraged to express it.

The story begins with Hughes Mearns. With the advent of the nuclear age and increased scientific and technological developments Mr. Mearns became even more concerned with the need for cultivating the creative and humanistic powers of youth. Students who had studied with him and students who had been introduced to his philosophy by Winifred Ward and other educational leaders felt a similar concern, and out of this came a strong demand for *Creative Power* which soon became out of print. They felt that the teaching experiences of this book were never outdated, for Mr. Mearns' book enforces the belief that the basic philosophy of creative growth is timeless and true to every generation of youth.

The first plans for republication were initiated by the Children's Theatre Conference Division of the American Educational Theatre Association. Many of its members throughout the country believed that this book was needed for those engaged in creative dramatics as well as in the other arts. Kenneth L. Graham, Executive Secretary of the American Educational Theatre Association then took charge and launched an extensive campaign. He discussed republication with, among others, Walther Volbach of Texas Christian University, chairman of the Rare Books Project for AETA. Mr. Volbach and Mr. Graham made inquiries among several publishers finally arousing the interest of Hayward Cirker of Dover Publications, New York City. Mr.

Graham wrote to the Children's Theatre Conference members urging them to write to Mr. Cirker. As a result of the strong interest of this group Dover Publications decided to publish this new edition of *Creative Power*.

The American Educational Theatre Association, particularly the Children's Theatre Conference Division, is grateful that this book is once more available. It offers a dynamic philosophy to parents, teachers, and youth leaders who are concerned with the responsibility of keeping alive and channeling the creative spirit of youth.

Republication is significant. It symbolizes achievement of cooperative effort and it reinforces a belief in the necessity of creative arts for children and youth.

1958   GERALDINE BRAIN SIKS
                                         University of Washington

Table of Contents

AUTHOR'S FOREWORD vii

PREFACE by Geraldine B. Siks ix

INTRODUCTION by Winifred Ward xiii

CHAPTER I. The Beginning of an Adventure 1

CHAPTER II. The Poetry Drawer 10

CHAPTER III. The Voice of the Individual Spirit 19

CHAPTER IV. No Love Without Propinquity 29

CHAPTER V. Wordists 47

CHAPTER VI. Back Talk 55

CHAPTER VII. The Native Language of Childhood ... 64

CHAPTER VIII. Confessions 76

CHAPTER IX. The Play's the Thing 92

CHAPTER X. The Demon of Inhibition 97

CHAPTER XI. Poetry Is When You Talk to Yourself .. 106

CHAPTER XII. The Natives and the Rhymesters 116

CHAPTER XIII. Other Rhymings 131

CHAPTER XIV. Copy Cats 141

CHAPTER XV. A Humdrum Lot 147

CHAPTER XVI. Roots and Absolutes 159

CHAPTER XVII. Creative Business 165

CHAPTER XVIII. Dumppiddyfetchets 171

CHAPTER XIX. Introjection 180

CHAPTER XX. One Food of the Spirit 189

CHAPTER XXI. Putting the Screws on 'em 198

CHAPTER XXII. The Conservation of Youth Power ... 217

CHAPTER XXIII. All God's Chillun 229

CHAPTER XXIV. Newer Types of Learning 242

CHAPTER XXV. Creative Hands 250

CHAPTER XXVI. Youth Calls to Youth 253

CHAPTER XXVII. Each of Us Has a Gift 263

Introduction to Second Edition

When *Creative Power* was first published, in 1929, it carried enough dynamite to shatter preconceptions, prejudices, platitudes — and reputations. Hughes Mearns had been teaching in the famous Lincoln School of Columbia University, as one of a group of practicing artists brought to the faculty by Otis Caldwell, the director. "In five years," wrote Harold Rugg, "he changed that school and produced a body of examples that led a creative revolution across the nation's schools."

While other teachers of English were insisting that, first of all, their students must conform to the rules of good writing, Mearns was freeing them to express their ideas in their own original way. While the sticklers for convention were making imitators of their young people and achieving only commonplace results, Mearns was stirring their imaginations to create such verse as these concluding lines of a remarkable poem called "The Circus", in which the young poet wrote of the acrobats:

> Then bowing when their lauded act is ended
>   And tossing kisses, jaunty and so glib,
> I wonder if they really comprehended
>   They've tickled Death along his bony rib?

and this from "The Door Stands Open":

> I stand by the window and look at the faces.
> I would know what life is, and what the world is,
> Before I go.
> Those who come back are often sad or tired;
> The stories they tell are not always pleasant;
> Yet all who go out are happy; and they hurry,
> Looking ahead at something just beyond.

How Hughes Mearns encouraged the adventurous spirit of his students and developed their native talents is described in *Creative Power* which Robert Frost considered "the best story of a feat of teaching ever written." And though it is concerned mainly with creative writing, teachers of any other subject, especially in the field of arts, will easily see its application to their media and make the translation. The philosophy is the same for all.

Since 1929 the elementary schools have made a noteworthy advance in creative teaching. The extreme freedom of the so-called "progressive" schools has given way to a moderate control in which a child's individuality is encouraged to express itself; though all too often the strong emphasis on group cooperation has tended to stress conformity at the expense of creativity.

Certain it is that the vast majority of educators have not yet caught up with the philosophy and techniques which made Hughes Mearns a great teacher. At best, few people have his understanding of how to reach young students and challenge their abilities to achieve such amazing results as are recorded in *Creative Youth* and *Creative Power*. But the spirit of Mearns' books is contagious, and I doubt if any teacher can read them without becoming a more keenly sensitive guide. One of his early students at New York University predicted that "years and years from now we shall be using the ways that Hughes Mearns is teaching us today."

To me a sure proof that *Creative Power* is a significant and lasting book is the attitude of modern university students who read it. Though it has been required reading for my classes in creative dramatics at Northwestern University since the early thirties, there has seemed to be no slightest diminution of student interest in the years since then. Its style continues to fascinate them, its humor to delight them; and the philosophy of teaching set forth on its pages is as powerful as ever in inspiring them to be the kind of leaders who will set free the creative spirit in the students they teach.

Because of the unique qualities of the book which make it invaluable in creative education, and because in the years since its publication no other work has appeared to take its place, it is particularly fortunate that *Creative Power* has again been made available. New chapters have been added in the revised version which will be welcomed both by old friends and by those who have tried in vain to acquire copies of the first edition. Named by the National Education Association as one of the twenty foremost books in education in recent times, it should have a long and influential life.

1958   WINIFRED WARD
                                                           Evanston, Illinois

YOUTH

I must laugh and dance and sing,
Youth is such a lovely thing.

Soon I shall be old and stately;
I shall promenade sedately

Down a narrow pavement street,
And the people that I meet

Will be stiff and narrow too,
Careful what they say and do;

It will be quite plain to see
They were never young like me.

When I walk where flowers grow
I shall have to stoop down low

If I want one for a prize;
Now I'm just the proper size.

Let me laugh and dance and sing,
Youth is such a lovely thing.

By ALINE WECHSLER

when she was in the
eleventh grade

CHAPTER I

The Beginning of an Adventure

IT WAS IN MY early Army days, when I was about getting used to the smell of saddle soap, that I came abruptly before my first colonel, a full colonel with eagles. By this time one had mastered the technique of meeting an officer, which was, mainly, to center all attention upon the shoulder insignia and then to give a salute, with rising degrees of awe and subjection, from a mock and grinning wave to second-louies up to a solemn, head-up-belly-in adoration to majors. I had been told about lieutenant-colonels, but I had not fallen upon one; and here I was before the eagles themselves.

"Halt!" said I to myself; followed a cracking of heels and a salute that nearly snapped off my garrison hat. He did not even look up from his papers; so I stood there at rigid attention.

When finally he glanced over in mild surprise and gave me a nonchalant salute in release I recognized him — he was just a boy I had once taught in the eighth grade! So I grinned and snapped into it again, with a heel-click of unmistakable amusement; for I saw by his bewilderment that he was slowly comprehending the comic situation: this groveling creature before him had been his one-time master.

"Oh," he said, coming forward awkwardly, "uh — hello. What — uh — are you doing here?"

I saluted smartly again. "Sir — " I began.

"Don't do that!" he exclaimed hastily. "It — it embarrasses me."

"Why should it, Richard?" I asked as we shook hands. "Long ago I had to get used to my pupils' passing me."

"Well — " he fumbled for words — "I can't forget that

you were once my teacher; and I suppose I'm still a little bit afraid of you."

"I never did anything to make you afraid of me, did I?" I asked.

"No," he meditated as he lighted a cigaret, "I don't remember that you ever did. You were awfully easy on us, in fact. Still — Well —" he brightened up and tried to joke it off — "maybe it's because I used to respect you." Then he scanned my sleeve, bare of chevrons, and became even more embarrassed; for he was a full colonel and I was as far removed from colonel as one could get, going the the other way. "I was only a little boy then," he covered hastily, "and you were a big man."

"I was only a little boy myself," I told him, "just turned nineteen, and more scared of that roomful of kids than you would believe."

"We had good times there," he mused. "We used to laugh a lot. I don't know if we ever learned anything, but I do remember how we laughed. All other classrooms I have been in were mighty solemn affairs in comparison."

"Yes," I admitted, "we did laugh. Perhaps that was the best thing we did there. If I couldn't have laughed with you I would not have stayed in the business. But the laugh worked, and I have never given it up. In fact, it was the success of the laugh that kept me in teaching; I learned something about education because of that laugh, something that seemed at times to bring me almost to the verge of a great discovery. I have been on the trail of it for years, and like all fanatics, I am always hoping that the solution of the problem is just around the corner; which stimulates my enthusiasm mightily and bucks me up when I fail. When —"

"What's the great discovery all about?" he inquired, interrupting, as colonels will do.

"The mystery of all living," said I. "When —"

"A large order," he remarked.

"Yes," I agreed. "When this war is over —"

But that discussion was continued later, in the privacy of a hotel room, where a colonel might conceal the treasonable act of dining on terms of social equality with the buck private of a training camp.

II

Then one day, when the war was over at last, two telegrams came offering jobs, one a superintendency in a great state system, and the other a grade position in an experimental school. In our family we never gave more than a passing thought to the superintendency; all our eager discussion was upon the teaching job. What did they mean by experimental school? Could one really work with children without interference from the traditional machinery of supervision, recitation, textbook, examinations, and curriculum, as the telegram seemed to imply?

The next week I was in New York meeting at luncheon with a group of men, among whom, I was told, were members of the famous General Education Board which was providing the financial backing for the experimental venture. I talked enthusiastically about what I believed could be done with children if one were given half a chance with an experiment in free teaching. They listened most intently, but they laughed at my excitement, a laugh in which I joined, for my eagerness and faith were really comic; and I knew from their joking that they had not misjudged my warmth as mere salesmanship in job hunting. "Oh, I believe in miracles," said one. From the heartiness of the laugh that followed I have always suspected that he was a clergyman. Another asked if I could bring a rabbit out of a *very* high hat. And another said, "Tell us the story of your life, but — this is a hard crowd — the only thing we'll admit believing is that you were born."

I did not mistake their fervor either. Their high good humor did not at all conceal their earnestness; they were as eager as I to try out a new way with childhood. And their jokes and their laughter were music to me; long ago I had crossed off the solemn ones as lacking in either faith or judgment. One remark, however, I must not omit. In the cloakroom one of them said, "Don't worry about results. An experimental school is, by definition, a place where courageous parents send their children."

Later in the day, alone with the director of the school, I grew suddenly depressed. I had talked too much, I told myself. After all, I was undertaking an adventure; who could guarantee outcomes? "You don't expect me to show results right off?" I asked. "I may be here months before there is a sign of all this creative power I've been talking so glibly about." He answered me seriously, but with a jesting light in his eye, "We don't expect anything from you for years." At no time did he worry me by premature expectations; for the five years of the experimentation I was given the unmolested freedom of a scientist in a laboratory.

All my conditions were accepted, one of which was that I should begin with the eighth grade. Everyone knew, I argued, that creative activity had almost untrammeled expression in the first three grades of the school; there was much of it still in the fourth and fifth grades, although rapidly diminishing before the demands of school tasks; in the sixth and seventh grades it was found only in wayward spots; but surely it had gone in the eighth grade. Well, had it? My belief was that it had only withdrawn from public view. The world of school did not value its products, had repudiated them, indeed, as worthless and often immoral; hence it became, at about the eighth grade, one of those vices loved in secret but eventually given up and lost to possession forever.

III

Through it all I was buoyed up by a well-founded optimism. Twenty years or more of experience with children and older youth had given me grounds for confidence. In classroom and in groups outside the classroom my interest had never been primarily in subjects of study or in anything taught or studied, but rather in the swirl of wild and often incoherent imaginings that roared continuously in the conscious undercurrent of the mind. Impersonations of grandeur; stories, lived throughout months and never really ended; fictitious debates with authority; daydreams of power, love, and hate; inventions that defied all the laws of everything; practical plans for the next contest in the school yard; phrases of incomparable beauty and often of no meaning at all; this was the sort of mind stuff that I had specialized in. Believing oneself a runaway train rushing toward a river-bridge that is only slowly closing, or walking deliberately down the dark stairway while a clanking skeleton is lumbering and slithering just back of you with long white arms reaching — these are common scarifying thoughts of timid young boys. "If you had an eye in the back of your head —" one lad confided to me. This never-ending current beneath the surface of public behavior was to me something of enormous educational value; and practice and failure in many situations had given me a clue to its use.

To step into this region with a strong presumption of its importance was a game I had often played with young folks; for no reason at first, I must admit, save my own amusement, but that, of course, I never revealed. The overpowering curriculum took up most of the time, but there were always moments that could be stolen from the lessons, with one eye on the door to see that no supervising officer was about; and the after-school group that gathered around and seemed never to want to go home was fruitful in illustration of that world which lies just below the surface of everyday living.

Early I began to note that it was often a rational world where youth brought their elders before the bar of pure reason; and here the absent adults were without their old support from tradition, prejudice, or arbitrary·authority. Many a fine lad is worried over the puzzling question of God's justice; and the evasions of older people, to whom he should have a right to go for answers, are even more of a puzzle to him. He is reluctant to convict them of hypocrisy or of ignorance, but, as is so often the case when his mind functions better than theirs, he is accused of evil-mindedness and is thereby thrown into himself where help is not to be found. Hungry in the search for truth, this type is often eager to unburden, but not until he has cautiously made sure that his fine ideal will not be scorned.

Others had accumulated a store of information from the pursuit of collections, stamps, birds' eggs, butterflies, and the like, or from the strangest readings in encyclopedias and compendiums of fact like the *World Almanac;* so their talk, once it was loosened through proved friendliness, approached that of the intensity of a research student in his special field. Sometimes, I noted, these were the chaps who stood low in "school facts," but often they knew more about equally important things of the world than their instructors.

Inventors cropped up with plans or rough models of their contrivances; one had worked out a simplified Morse code with fewer dots and dashes and therefore cheaper and speedier; another had plans of football strategy that would surely take out opposing players and guarantee an average gain of four yards to a down, which, of course, would be enough to win any game. A girl could make astonishing statuettes out of stray bits of chalk; a pair of imps showed me how to carry on a classroom conversation by wigwagging with the thumb, unsurpassed, they claimed, for all purposes including examinations.

Of course, the deeper rhythm of their minds was not to be disclosed except in private, very private, interviews. In spite of all their familiar chatter they ever commanded a remarkable reticence. When I lowered my standard to count their confidences as right and respectable I learned much, but the more serious stirring of heart and mind I rarely touched; and I respected this side of their lives too much to probe. All I have learned was given freely.

Creative activity comes from this pulsing stream of inconsequential thought and feeling. One must know something about it, therefore, and one must take its crude manifestations seriously if one is to help it to that finer expression which is creative art.

Unaided it does not advance far into the realm of production. The various media are there, language, crayon, color, and the like; and there is always some attempt, however crude, to employ them; but failure to achieve complete satisfaction in the result, or the outright suppression by elders, or the intimidating intrusion of adult standards, something chills the ardor of self-expression along these lines except among those, the predestinate artists and thinkers, whose urge to express is superior to all rebuff.

IV

I must interpolate here an element, of the importance of which I was not entirely conscious at first: I came to youth with little interest in teaching as such, but with a great concern for individual self-expression in writing. I am a writing man and not a teacher of writing; and there is a vast difference between these two sorts of creature.

A word or two on that theme, for it is most important. I have interests in a number of things, teaching among them, but these are not my real interest. I would not give up a meal willingly for any of them. But for my real interest, the fashioning into words of that turbulent undercurrent of my life, of whose meaning and significance I am not fully aware until I have so fashioned it, that is something for which I have gone willingly without food and sleep for days and nights on end. It is so terrible an attraction that one must avoid it when there is other work to do ("Apage, Sathanas!" one cries, as if it were, indeed, the very devil, as I am sometimes persuaded it is); for once it seizes the victim, then he is done for until physical exhaustion denies further effort. Through that travail he comes to possess an understanding of all publicans and sinners and winebibbers generally who have lost the will to withstand temptation.

The temptation would not be so bad if the mere writing were all. Long after the script has been done the thing winds and unwinds through all the waking acts and thoughts; constant mental revision goes on; rereadings must be made; addenda, elisions, expandings, interpolations, all these trouble and torture. Interest dies and revulsion takes its place, but the driving force of patching and remodeling goes on. Oh, those who fashion creative stuff out of the welter of consciousness, they know what an interest is, and, according as they know, they both love and fear it.

The teacher of writing, however, is a much cooler person. One could easily doubt that his interest ever reaches so boiling a point. The shape of the written thing takes his fancy, not the moving power of it; he goes in for classification and definition; he hunts synecdoche and brings down alexandrines and preterites. He believes that a sonnet must have fourteen lines, and if you show him that even the masters have written sonnets that are just two lines too long (see Shakespeare's XXIX), he simply does not understand at all, for he blinks at you and repeats his definition.

"I shall sit here," the Footman remarked, "till to-morrow —"

At this moment the door of the house opened, and a large plate came skimming out, straight at the Footman's head: it just grazed his nose, and broke to pieces against one of the trees behind him.

"— or next day, maybe," the Footman continued in the same tone, exactly as if nothing had happened.

Further, he is sure about the matter of taste, believing that all the good artists in letters are listed in the textbooks; and, worse, that all of these — all, mind you!— should be appreciated by everybody equally. He has no loves and hates in literature, no more than a museum guard might have for dodecahedron crystals. He would not give up a meal for anything.

I cannot leave him so easily, so must give him another paragraph, for he stands in the way of more abundant life and must be so stamped, and for the reason that he must be distinguished from that great band of humane teachers of literature in all the grades through the university who have never confused the letter with the spirit, who believe in life and know that literature *is* life, who have never withdrawn from the world and, therefore, have never refused the cup of the thirsty. But these others, cool and passive and so serene, with their high standards and impeccable good taste! Always they play safe on the side of the heavier authorities. They wait until time has settled the hash of this one and that one; so they must always remain years behind the live appreciations of their own day. One may suspect their complacent Pharisaism but when one has graduated from believing pupil to teaching colleague and has seen them in a corner of the faculty room conning over their marked-up textbook in the thousand and first preparation for the next class — where their exact learning will shine like true wisdom! — one is then quite sure of it. Oh, quite!

I am unfair to him, of course. I cannot be otherwise; for his ways are not my ways, and he has no pity in him. He and his kind have too often denied the crumb to Lazarus. And children are not of his kind either. Children are creative persons, not scholiasts; they use language as the artist the world over and in all ages has used his medium, not as an end in itself but as a means for the expression of thought and feeling. Language in itself, they sense, is comparatively unimportant; if the vision is steady and the feeling true these will find their proper vehicle. The attention is never on the word but upon the force that creates the word.

CHAPTER II

The Poetry Drawer

AN HOUR OR TWO in the school before meeting my first class was enough to place it roughly in its progress toward being a free-activity school. It was still in the noisy, semi-hysterical stage: between periods children were rushing forward at an angle, as if the feet could never catch up with the head; the eyes were intent on a purely egoistic endeavor, so collisions with other egoistic bodies were the rule. Ego called out to ego, commanding, directing, censoring, and receiving no attention at all from other egos. To be heard above the din, teachers in the halls had almost to practice lip-reading, and they were a smiling but brave lot; one third of the staff, I was told, were new on this the third year of the experiment. Obviously the school had unleashed a mighty and valuable force, but it had not been able in so short a time to teach the beauty of order via self-control.

Fortunately I had seen this development before in the first few years of the Shady Hill School in Philadelphia, where once I was nearly knocked downstairs by a rush of boys who warned, "Look out, please!" as they hurled themselves through the air to the landing where I was, and cried, "Excuse me, please!" as each one took me amidship — a polite lot, you see. It was Mary Frazier who gave us courage in the Shady Hill days; she had just returned from a long visit to Bedales, Abbotsholme, and a dozen other places in Europe where the new idea of child-freedom had been put into practice. "They must learn to use freedom," she would say. "This is just the necessary transition stage; they all tell about it; but something new and fine in child-life will be the outcome if we have patience and do not give up and revert to the old suppressions."

During those first few hours in the new experimental school I could look on with more complacence than others of the staff. Some of them were outspoken in their condemnation of the social incivilities all about us, claiming that nothing would come of this selfish savagery until a good firm heel was put down upon it. I watched a child rush to the elevator, which had already closed its door and had gone halfway up to the next floor; she called it to come down; she banged upon the door steadily, then turned with flushed, indignant face to a group of silent, observing teachers. "He wouldn't come back for me!" she cried, and darted up the stairs. A teacher said something we could not hear; so we leaned our heads over while she repeated, "Each child should have a private elevator, of course."

Eventually, all that was taken care of through the machinery of student council, group discussion, town meeting, and the like, until the individual sacrifice that goes with social order was understood and intelligently accepted; and the iron heel was brought down where necessary upon such anarchists or dangerous individualists as temporarily imperiled the commonweal; but even the transition stage was to me inspiriting and full of hope for the future.

There was noise and confusion but no disorder in the usual school sense; each child was intent upon a proper school job: they rushed to the library to get down the books that might help them; they rushed into the rooms to which they were assigned from period to period; they rushed to the gymnasium, the lunch-room, the assembly hall, a complete surrender to the interests which that school had set up. The sneaking about, the loitering, the open or covert resistance to school authority, characteristically present under the old discipline — these were simply not in evidence at all. The faces were often hot and flushed, although the eyes were steady and serious; the physical reactions were nervous and high-strung, obvious signs of overstimulation; but the readiness and the will were all pointed in the right direction.

II

Naturally, then, I was prepared for that stampede of the eighth grade into my room. They came with the impact of a subway crowd at Times Square in the peak of the rush hour; I am sure that for a moment they wedged in the doorway, presenting eager faces, cool-eyed and serious.

The first group cast one appraising glance at me and decided that the front of the room would be the best place to get the most out of that period; the next group, after one swift estimate, decided that the back of the room would give them the supreme advantage; the remainder disputed noisily for the chairs in the middle of the room. In place of the usual desks the room was equipped with movable tables, and they were well named; they moved, caromed against one another, shoved this way and that by grasping hands and darting bodies.

In a matter of seconds the children settled their conflicting differences and turned upon me with startling silence. To this day I retain the picture of those coldly unprejudiced eyes; just, they were, but self-centered and merciless. "Well, who are you," they seemed to be saying to me, "and what, pray, do you think you are going to do with us?" There was no respect for authority, certainly no awe of it, nor was there the slightest warmth of hospitality. Even the silence was their own notion of what to do next. They waited for me to expose my wares — and myself.

One must not think for a moment that I was confident of the right procedure. Frankly I was frightened, as one might reasonably be in facing a strange animal. Twenty years of teaching seemed just the worst sort of preparation. For, consider, I had come among them to touch some of the secret sources of their lives, to discover and to bring out the power that they possessed but, through timidity or ignorance, could not use; to develop personality, in short. Naturally I could not disclose my mission, and naturally I must win their approval for whatever I should do: so, under the disguise of a teacher of a special subject, I must bide my time, wait for propitious moments, utilize whatever luckily came to me, and with nothing to guide me but an abundant faith and the spirit of adventure.

And they never did find out my mission from me. Always I was just a teacher, and, as the school environment was planned to keep the teacher out of any serious position of authority, my treatment was often the amiable condescension of good fellows and self-sufficient lassies who tolerated me as not too much of an interruption. A boy confided that his father — a high official in one of the great railways of the country — had said that all teachers were unsuccessful persons, a poor lot usually, who had failed in life or just hadn't the brains to go out and make something of themselves. He told me, in all innocence, that he agreed with his father! A delicious moment, that! Not unless they read this book will they be aware of the deliberate experiment in creative education that was the motive of my five years' work with them.

III

That steady silence was most embarrassing. I fumbled in my pocket and came upon some manuscript poems which Roy Helton had just given to me. I talked about him as a friend and not as a literary person. They were amused at incidents in the personal side of our relationship, the fact, for instance, that it had always been my bad luck to chum up with tall men, which didn't show me off at all, and made everybody think of — I hesitated purposely. "Mutt and Jeff," someone suggested quietly. "Exactly," said I, and the group and I were immediately in comfortable rapport. Some of the cold inquiry left their faces; they slouched forward in a warmer mood.

I read them *Old Christmas,* then only in manuscript, a bit of the lore of present-day Kentucky gathered by Helton among the mountain folk. It told of that night twelve days after the "real Christmas," when speerits walk and one must stay up and keep the door ajar; for the speerits are a-weary and may want to come in and rest. The author permits me to print it here.

One must know that Sally Anne Barton has been sitting

up all night in her cabin, keeping the ghostly vigil of Old
Christmas, and that in the hour just before dawn she sees
Lomey Carter coming toward her across the snow. Sally
Anne goes to the door to welcome her old friend, but she
does not know that Lomey Carter is dead and that this is
a speerit come a-calling on Old Christmas night, when the
elder blooms and "critters kneel down in their straw."

OLD CHRISTMAS

"Where you coming from, Lomey Carter,
  So airly over the snow?
And what's them pretties you got in your hand,
  And where you aiming to go?
Step in, Honey: Old Christmas morning
  I ain't got nothing much:
Maybe a bite of sweetness and corn bread,
  A little ham meat and such.
But come in, Honey! Sally Anne Barton's
  Hungering after your face.
Wait till I light my candle up:
  Set down! There's your old place.
Now where you been so airly this morning?"

"Graveyard, Sally Anne.
Up by the trace in the salt lick meadows
  Where Taulbe kilt my man."

"Taulbe ain't to home this morning. . . .
  I can't scratch up a light:
Dampness gits on the heads of the matches;
  I'll blow up the embers bright."

"Needn't trouble. I won't be stopping:
  Going a long ways still."

"You didn't see nothing, Lomey Carter,
  Up on the graveyard hill?"

"What should I see there, Sally Anne Barton?"

"Spirits do walk, last night."

"There was an elder bush a-blooming
  While the moon still give some light."

"Yes, elder bushes, they bloom, Old Christmas,
  And critters kneel down in their straw. . . .
Anything else—up in the graveyard?"

"One thing more I saw:
I saw my man, with his head still bleeding
  Where Taulbe's shot went through."

"What did he say?"
"He stooped and kissed me."

"What did he say to you?"

"Said, Lord Jesus forguv your Taulbe;
But he told me another word:
He said it soft when he stooped and kissed me.
That were the last I heard."

"Taulbe ain't to home this morning."

"I know that, Sally Anne,
For I kilt him, coming down through the meadows
Where Taulbe kilt my man.
I met him up on the meadow trace
When the moon was fainting fast;
I had my dead man's rifle gun
And kilt him as he come past."

"I heard two shots."

" 'Twas his was second:
He shot me 'fore he died:
You'll find us at daybreak, Sally Anne Barton:
I'm laying there dead at his side."

With one movement those movable tables swung closer around me. No sound was made either of approval or disapproval, but the unanimous gesture was unmistakable. Some of the hot excitement had faded from their faces. The spell of the poet, as I read on from other Helton manuscripts, worked upon them; it gave rest to their minds, stilled the fierce incitation which the school in that stage of its growth had unwittingly brought out in them. A lovely, awkward friendliness appeared among them, touching the faces before me with that grotesque grimace and look of wonder which only hobbledehoy youth shows when completely off guard.

Then suddenly I came to the end of my manuscripts. They waited; I had nothing more to give them; and somehow speech and idea had left me a blank. Thirty minutes to go and no more material; any teacher knows the terror of that situation! In the embarrassed silence, which the children did not seem to mind, a deep boy's voice spoke slowly, "What are *you* gonna teach?" I shrugged and looked at the class. "And just when we were having a good time!"

I said in mock pathos. That set them up with a shout. It was most sporting of me, their bright eyes showed, but that is not what interested them. They valued my verbal return for its swiftness, for the surprise in it, and for its utter lack of truth. That is part of my own equipment, of the utmost importance to me in molding the tricky stuff of personality.

Almost immediately a girl asked abruptly, as if disaster threatened, "Are we going to have grammar?" The tone was menacing, and I knew right off that we were not going to have grammar. At least not in the way they had experienced that subject. Some years later this little lady was to write *Before Cliché* and receive not only the tribute of many reprintings, but, as well, the appreciation of hundreds who were grateful for her keenly humorous invention. "Are we going to have grammar?" There was humor in the question, and irony, satire, criticism.

She took the whole class with her by sheer dramatic power, which I noted with excitement, for it was the very thing I was after. Three years later Margaret Holz was to discover this gift and present her in two scenes from the Joan plays, Schiller's and Shaw's, each in its own tongue. At that time the youthful actress gave a power of dramatization which, I safely claim, was superior to the then current best; she made the audience wholly unaware of the barrier of language. After that performance I leaned to her mother to say, "Astounding, isn't it!" She nodded but was unable to do more than whisper, "I do not — I do not recognize my own daughter."

While I rejoiced — to return to my eighth grade — in the young lady's gift, I had to admit that for the moment her dramatic genius had shattered the little friendly hold I had made with this class. Luck stood by me, however, as it did throughout this whole period, but the disaster drove me back upon my one sure resource when in trouble with children — I tell the truth.

Of course, I know the proper traditional procedure when, meeting one's first class, an impertinent question like that intrudes. Incipient revolt must be crushed; the rebels must

feel the swift stroke of the master: one levels that group
with a commanding eye and, arms folded, says, "If in my
judgment this class needs grammar, this class will have
grammar!" And that usually is that! But I had been three
years away from the classroom; the very day before I had
been in Army uniform; so perhaps I had forgotten the old
technique.

In silence I rested my eyes on the view outside the window
and visibly meditated the question. "Grammar?" I spoke my
thoughts. "I don't know . . . I never use it myself." (A quick
laugh from the group, but I went on unmoved.) "I have
studied it, of course; and I have taught it, and enjoy teaching it. But I don't know what good it ever did me. . . . Really
I don't. . . . I speak and write the language I have heard, in
my family and among my friends. It is important, of course,
to have the right kind of family and the right kind of
friends. . . . My speech is probably full of blunders; I don't
know; it doesn't seem to bother anybody. They laughed at
me up in New England, where I went to school, because I
said thawt for t-h-o-u-g-h-t, instead of thot, but they didn't
like me or respect me any the less for that. I know that my
written language is far from what it should be, for I can't
write a page that does not need revision; and even after I
have done my best work upon something that I want to
publish, the copyreader in the editorial rooms makes corrections. And this same story is told by everybody who writes
for print, not excluding teachers. Grammar? I suppose it is
like good manners, or friendliness, or unselfishness, or
sportsmanship; it's something one lives and therefore cannot get satisfactorily out of a book."

Over that we had a spirited debate — the truth always has
that power of stirring up things — leading to some equally
frank truths about teachers and teaching. The grammatical
methods of foreign-language teachers came in for some
bitter scoring and for some equally strong defence. I listened. Here I was at once tossed into the undercurrent of
their usually unexpressed thinking and feeling. Power of
language they undoubtedly had, I mused, terrific power; but
no one had apprised them of that gift, I suspected, for it is

not the sort that would pass as creditable among teachers generally. It was the clipped, colloquial idiom of youth, hot, prejudiced, rebellious; ungrammatical, and impolite; highly absurd from an adult standard; but beautifully fitting as an instrument to convey genuine feeling.

This, I considered while the battle raged, is the gift which I must bring out for my own purposes through friendly appreciation, through a slow building up of courage in its use. I must convince them of my belief in it; I must rid them of the fears in its use that adults had everlastingly cast about them; then I must teach them how to eliminate the elements — really unimportant! — that give offence to others.

Later in similar scenes, when strong feeling had seized them, I would copy swiftly their vibrant phrases and confront this and that youth with his success, especially that youth who had rooted unbelief in his linguistic powers. "Just listen to this," I would say to him; "you said this so well that I copied it down. Powerful stuff! Boy, you certainly can swing a mean sentence! It fairly makes the hair stand up!" Or, "Did you know that you were really eloquent just now? Let me read what you said. Almost poetry! Grace and beauty and wonderful feeling; really, a perfect thing!"

There is not anyone who cannot be stirred by proof like that. Flattery they hate, these children; and praise they are apt to suspect; but their own ability thus put to them is something that they themselves can appraise as worthy. "And here I've been speaking prose all my life," exclaimed Monsieur Jourdain, "and never knew it!"

IV

Record was kept of these contacts, bits of dialogue, the summary of opinions, remarks made by vistors, suggestions of colleagues, and even the complaints of parents, for this was a research job in a region where data had not been hitherto captured and standardized; therefore it is easy to present here a fairly complete picture from the concluding minutes of that first period with the eighth grade.

CHAPTER III

The Voice of the Individual Spirit

"EVERYBODY WRITES POETRY NOWADAYS," I was saying. "I write poetry myself, but no one enjoys it but me.
I used to think my family liked my poetry, but — one day
I found out it was only politeness. After the excitement of
making a poem I usually couldn't rest until I'd captured
some members of the family. Then I'd read my poem. 'Wonderful!' they'd say. 'Splendid! Has James heard this one?'
'Well, no,' I would reply, quite laid out by the reception. 'I
just finished it, you know.' 'Oh, James!' And James would
amble in, lean against the door jamb and listen in marvelous
imitation of complete, idiotic absorption. After I'd done,
James would wobble about with excitement and say, 'Gee!
That's swell! A swell poem that!' Always he said the same
thing, with the same wobble every time.

"Then one day I stopped reading my poems to them. That
was years ago. And, do you know, they've never noticed that
I stopped! . . . So that's how I found out. . . ." The children
seemed stricken into silent sympathy. "But everybody writes
poetry now," I hastened to change the subject, "even boys
and girls. So," with an exaggerated gesture to cover the intimacy of my recent confession, "will you please pass up
your poetry?"

My intention was to joke them out of their intense and
pathetic absorption in my story; they had hung upon it as
if they knew all about family indifference, as if, indeed, it
might have been their own story; but the uproar that set
loose in that class at my abrupt conclusion convinced me
that I had hit on something funnier than I had intended.

Suddenly they swayed with laughter, put their heads

down on those movable tables, and let themselves go, or looked up weakly at me as if to inquire how in pity's name I could be so devastatingly comic. One lad in the rear of the room stood up, leaned against the movable table, and slipped to the floor; he stayed there in helpless merriment — I see why they screw down the desks in most schools; it is to prop the children up — he waved a hand back and forth aloft and murmured again and again, "Pass up your poetry!" as if it were the very height of the ridiculous.

Long after this they gave me the answer to the puzzle. A substitute teacher, one of the old disciplinary type who simply could not manage youth once it had had a taste of freedom, used to scold for the whole period, they said, but invariably she would end with a screaming command to "Please pass up your papers!" These youngsters passed up every paper they could find, even scraps picked up from the floor, all of which, to their daily delight, she accepted! The very phrase "Please pass up," therefore, had become dangerously explosive; and when I, a teacher, had tossed it at them so unexpectedly, it had acted like a bomb.

"So will you please pass up your poetry!"

But while they writhed helplessly, gasping out their merriment, I noted three girls who had not joined in the excitement at all; erect as chimney stacks in that moving throng, they were smiling at one another in a most secretive and knowing way. Instantly I knew that I had caught my first clandestine poets! I visualized the very type of blankbook, perhaps carefully hand bound, in which they wrote! There would be a romance, unfinised, of course; a diary, kept for a week and a half; much doggerel verse; imitations of Robert Louis Stevenson and the favorite poets of their early childhood; and, perhaps, that rare good thing on which my search was bent. They would not be aware that it was good until someone had told them.

The bell rang for the end of the period. The class gathered themselves together and began the rush out. They waved to me as they sped by; all were smiling, and the eyes were gay and alert; from some came a happy, "See you to-morrow!"; sure signs, all, of the right sort of friendliness without which I could not work.

As the three girls began to leave, however, I stretched out my hands and said, "But *your* poetry in particular I want." How did I know! That exclamation was immediately written large on their faces. For they had been writing secretly; not even their mothers were aware of it; and they were confident that not one of the three would have told a single other human soul. How did I know? They never did find out. That was my secret, divulged here in print for the first time.

They locked arms immediately and began to sway; two of them giggled, and I knew I had them; but the third looked at me steadily and said, "I have nothing — for you."

The pause after *nothing* was too deliberate to miss. It was a blow — how may one doubt that youngsters can use language! — and I recoiled visibly from its effect. Sensitive to reprimand of any kind — perhaps that is why I never use the weapon against children — I felt that this was, without any doubt, a rebuke to my impertinence.

Fortunately, in that emergency I knew some of the strategy of retreat. I turned away from the embarrassing position of facing them and began to open and close the top drawer of the empty teacher's desk, making it bang considerably each time. Looking children in the eye is, seemingly, the way for authoritative persons; it must be so, for they prate so much about it; but it is never the way, so I have discovered, to achieve the private relationships essential in the pursuit of things of the creative life.

She made quick amends, sensitive undoubtedly to the effect of her unintentional thrust. "If I have done anything," she said ("She *has* done something!" I noted to myself, my head turned in serious contemplation of the drawer), "I don't want it made the subject of that laugh." That great guffaw, she meant, which had burst forth at my phrase "Please pass up your poetry."

"Don't be afraid of that," I replied. "When you get to know me better you'll find I wouldn't do anything like that. I am a writing person myself. There's nothing in the world I like better to do. I've been writing all my life, ever since I can remember. . . . This is the poetry drawer." Sudden change of subject, always a good trick; much banging of the drawer amid laughter at nothing at all. "Just drop them in here and I'll guard them like the queen bee's jewels."

"Oh, we're late for gym!" a shout from one of the gigglers, and they were off at a mad tilt.

Some of the technique of approach I knew, but not much. Of one thing I was sure, however: place must be provided for the reception of material. One cannot say, "Give it to me." It requires a special kind of courage, which the creative life does not cultivate, to walk up to any person and present the things of one's private endeavor. There are those, of course, who can do this thing; but they are the ones who have received all the credit in the past; they are the bold, insensitive ones; and, in my judgment, they are not those with the greatest creative gifts. Artists are fearful of judgment; they know too well the inadequacy of their efforts; they are tortured by experiences with misunderstanding — by failure, in short. It takes a special courage, even for adults, to take one's manuscript to the corner mail box; painters do their three years' toil of paintings and quail before the detail of packing and shipping to the exhibition. In the artist's life it is the hard-boiled business or literary agent (or the thrifty wife!) who has the strength to perform these essential functions. Much more are these fears operative among children.

II

The impersonal drawer worked. The next day two bulky volumes were dropped into it; then a laugh and a scurry of fleeing feet. But there were only two, note, at the first catch. The third of the trio waited to see what sort of reception these would obtain. Evidently I handled them with the right kind of appreciation, for on the fourth day she approached my desk slowly; under her arm she carried her precious book. This was the one who "had nothing — for me."

I remained very, very still. She looked at me steadily for a moment as if to say, "I know I'm a darn fool. I don't know you and I don't see at all why I should give this to you." Then slowly she opened the poetry drawer and tenderly laid

her book with the others. I hadn't the heart to say a word
as she walked slowly away.

In those three volumes I found only two things of the sort
for which I was searching. All the doggerel and splay attempts to find language for fugitive imaginings were there,
but only two were, in my sense, good and really creative.

One was a lullaby, done the year before — no wonder
there was hesitation in exhibiting it to a stranger! — but
nothing in the pages that followed showed anything worthy,
a fading off, rather, into the usual imitations of standard
rhymings. The lullaby was the real thing, but the youngsters themselves did not know this; they had inadvertently
tapped the very source of creative effort, but without someone to show them the value of their find it is natural that
they should pass it by and succumb to the demand for standardized materials, especially when they are the only ones
that secure public approval.

Let us examine this lullaby, which is common enough as
an expression of young-girl interests, but not by any means
commonly expressed:

THE WIND IS A SHEPHERD

The wind is a shepherd;
He drives his clouds
Across a field of blue.
The moon puts her face up
Behind them now
And sings a song to you.

So sleep, my baby.
And the wind will keep the clouds,
And we'll look at them tomorrow,
Me and you,
As he hurries them through meadows
And they lay them down to rest
In a field of blue.

The situation is old — all genuine life situations are old!
— but the language design that pictures it to us is unlike
any other in the world. Even the verse form is not a standard pattern. This unique quality of individual freshness is

always present in the outcome which we call by the name of art. Nothing just like it has ever appeared in the world before! There is a criterion to start with. If one is able to recognize this outstanding distinctiveness one has opened a world which the world itself often ignores or notes only to reject.

Because children have not been too much molded by the prevailing taste for the copied article, it is easier for them, I suspect, to produce their own individual and preciously private art; and possible because they have a more ready access to the source of all creative activity, that inward world of unreality; but if their product is not received with the appreciation and respect which are its due, it may never develop; and if it is not allowed to grow through its natural stages, something of personality dies. For the individual spirit — I am stating my faith — is itself something that never appeared in the world before; if allowed its fullest development it would transform the world for the world's good. My own belief is that the creative spirit was given us for just that purpose; but we have always missed its perfect manifestations because of our devotion to another faith.

The general approval goes to the imitators. We set up models for everything. We dress so much alike as to lead one critic of manners to suggest that we had practically reached the stage of a common uniform, one sort for each sex. In one year we stand stiffly erect or bind ourselves in whalebone or Piccadilly collar; in another we slouch and go in for looseness generally, But whatever we do, we do in unison, each fearful of showing a sign of the unique individuality with which we have been spirtually endowed. We think, and even pretend to feel, in the prevailing mode.

The demand for one form of standardization is supplied by the publication of millions of copies of books of etiquette. A few of these, of course, have a higher purpose than to supply the proper phrase for all occasions of living, but, in the main, their great sales represent the universal hunger to conform, to annihilate one's individuality of thinking and feeling. Perhaps the greatest humiliation, this side of criminal conviction, comes of a knowledge of having failed in social conformity. Thousands said, "Pleased to meet you!" and were unaware of their ridiculous confession of social inferiority until William Lyon Phelps placed it on his *index expurgatorius* whereupon they all began a hysterical practice of the equally ridiculous "How do you do!" But there is no rest to the pleased-to-meet-you group. They are fated forever to be always just a little behind the times. Before they have all learned their "How do you do's!" there will be a new convention of greeting.

One learns early in life that the expressing of ones' unique individuality does not pay. The sure way to become disliked is to express one's real self. Disliked? Hated, rather. If one disbelieves, an easy proof is near; for one may at any time, with a little practice, reach into the sure current that runs quietly within us, wherein flows our honest reactions to the life about us. The truth is always there, the truth as we see it, contradicting all the polite agreements that are voluble on the surface of daily living. Reach within and pluck it out for a single day and see what the world will do to you! Now it is the cultivating of this individual sense for the truth which is the beginning of wisdom, even though one declines to be so impolitic as to try it on a conventional world; but to wall it up so that it is beyond any possible reach, until, indeed, the possessor is finally unaware of its existence, that is the Great Stupidity. It is those who thus immure their birthright, however, who teach the young that its naive self-expression is an unholy thing.

The artist, of course, has just never conformed. He dresses the way that suits him, and, unless he is a portrait painter, he need not bow the knee before even the powerful gods of society. He lives in despised neighborhoods, not because he likes dirt, but because he thereby slips out of the clutches of that merciless conformer, the Price of Mere Living. Of course he appreciates the beauty of the tawdry, but he dwells where he does mainly to escape the enormous price exacted of those who are compelled to live between the proper numbers on the proper street.

I have proof enough that *The Wind Is A Shepherd* would have been ignored by the standardized adult. And the reason? Very simple; the rules were broken: the verses are in partial rhyme, using the forbidden "identical rhyme" at that; they do not conform to any regular meter-plan; and — unforgivable! — they harbor an undeniable solecism, an illegitimate case relationship between appositives!

It may be that you never noticed all that as you read. Perhaps you caught only the picture of the little make-believe mother sheltering her own as they watched together the shepherd and his flock in that far-off heaven. But the effect of the thing — and the feel of it — do not concern the standardized person, who is essentially a law enforcer; feeling, sympathy, pity, emotional understanding, these are not in his pack. He believes, and with good conscience, too, that in all cases the woman taken must be stoned. Is it not the law?

Painters will recognize this as the typical academic point of view: there are rules of art; if one does not conform to the rules the outcome is failure.

The other attitude is to inquire what the art effort does to the recipient. If it affects him in a fine way, then it is art; if the rules have been broken, then the rules will have to be changed. At this hour of writing, for illustration, very few persons would question the position of Cézanne or Matisse, at least not openly, for these two artists have become the vogue. To be sure, they have in their time broken all the rules of the academy, but the rules are now being revised to fit their cases. And what an old story that is!

The adult governors of youth have always been great sticklers for the rules; they do not trust their own individual sense of appreciation, nor do they try to cultivate it. Of an art product they do not ask, How does it affect me? but, Is it conventionally right?

III

The poem *Youth,* with which this volume opens, has a history which illustrates the point. In a chat with the author as she left for college she said, "Do you remember the first day I ever gave any of my things to you?"

"Oh, very well," I replied. "You were a little toddler from

the elementary school, a new pupil with us, and you came all the way up to the third floor to see me. You gave me your little bit of paper and hurried off without saying a word."

"You were being tested that day," she said mysteriously, "and you never suspected it."

"I'm sure I never did," I rejoined. "Tell me all about it."

"You didn't know what a terrible thing it was for me to go all the way up to the third floor among the huge high-school pupils."

"Oh, yes, I did."

"My first week in a new school, too. Well, the little verses I gave you, I had offered to my teacher in the old school. I was vain enough to want to see them printed in the school paper. She read them coldly right before me. I felt myself congealing. She didn't like them; I could see that before she was half through. She handed them back without a single touch of feeling. 'They are not up to our standard,' she said. . . . Then I came here."

"And you tried them out on me."

"Yes. She said they were not good. And I *knew* they were good!"

"Of course you did!"

"I was testing you, to see if all that they said here was true, to see if you were just like all the others."

"And I wasn't, was I!" I exulted . "Do you recall what I did?

"Yes. The next day you came downstairs to see me; and you talked about the verses excitedly, and we laughed and enjoyed ourselves; and you printed them. And everybody who read them said they were good. And they *were* good!"

"They probably didn't rhyme," I joked, for even after many years she was still vibrating from that first cold contact. "And," I whispered, "they probably had a misplaced caesura in the ante-penult! But what did we care about that! We liked them, and that was enough for us!"

Of course, for all the years of her sojourn with us, she went on producing steadily, editing the school magazine in her senior year and presenting the astonishing lyric *Youth* as her farewell to childhood. Turn to it now and read it. There is the beauty of reminiscence in it for those of us who still cherish the things of youth, and all the more because youth has gone from us forever.

CHAPTER IV

No Love Without Propinquity

MY EXPERIENCE WITH THIS unusual and distinctive manifestation of the creative spirit, as illustrated by that rare find of *The Wind Is a Shepherd* among the mere imitations in those childish notebooks, had not been sufficiently extensive to make me sure of the next steps. It is quite clear now that our initial procedure is, at least, one of the right ones. Since the publication *of Creative Youth,* whose aim was to depict a school environment that fostered creative activity and to present some of the concrete outcomes, I have traveled thousands of miles visiting and conferring with others who have made similar finds. Rich artistry among children is simply universal; and teachers and administrators in encouraging numbers are already awake to its possibilities for personal education. In many a conference we have shared experiences wherein I have received confirmation of the general application of those first adventurings.

In judging the worth of these intimate and personal offerings, we generally agree, one must rid oneself of all the customary technique of literary criticism. One is in a region of new forms and, possibly, of new laws. Of course, this is hard, for all teachers have been trained in another tradition. They are sensitive to abnormalities in script, in punctuation, spelling, verse form, and particularly in grammar. Well, they must teach their eyes not to see such things at all, to regard them, indeed, as comparatively unimportant.

There is a rhetorical error in our own Constitution but only teachers of syntax would be disturbed by it. School grammar and school rhetoric, in fact, lag many years behind

the continuous changes in good usage. In my school days —
long ago, my dears! — we were compelled to use "thou" in
the second person singular when conjugating verbs, for
example, "I stay, thou stayest, he stays, I am, thou art, he
is," incredible, but it is simply a common indication of the
sturdy resistance to inevitable language development, a denial of the facts of experience, when not recorded in the
school books. Such worship of the dead past is characteristic of the old-type pedagogue and text-book writer. This
comic obsolescence, still with us today, I illustrated recently
in a bit of light verse which *The New Yorker* permits me to
reprint here.

GRAMMARIAN'S CHILD

When looking out I see a car
Of friends come calling from afar,
I cry to Mother right away,
"Oh, that is they! Oh, that is they!"

When in my room with girls and boys
I hear, "Who's making all that noise?"
I step outside and cheerfully
Call down, "It's we! It's only we!"

When Teacher asks, "Who has, pray speak,
"A birthday in the coming week?"
And *I* have, then I'm mighty spry
To say, "Please, Ma'am, it will be I."

But pounding on a bolted door
With bears behind me, three or four,
If I should hear, "Who *could* that be?"
I'd scream, "It's me! It's me! It's me!"

We seem to be in accord, further, that one must beware
of regarding as important only those themes that adults
believe in for children. Moralizings about being good and
silent and obedient, even certain types of imaginative
stories, and, in fact, much of children's outward show of interests, have possibly been put upon them. Social expectation is a terrific force. As yet we do not really know what
comes up naturally and unbidden from the deep sources of
the creative life and what is summoned to appear by the
overpowering convention of "what every nice child should
be thinking about." An openness of mind here and an ability

to stand some shocks are most essential. But of that theme more later; it is too important to dismiss in a paragraph.

Most of us would admit, in addition, that having uncovered a bit of the genuine creative stuff one must begin the cultivating of a liking for it in the child who brought it forth. Strange as it may seem to the uninitiated, it is not often a thing the children themselves would prefer at first among the many offerings of their mind or hand.

Outside approval is here most important. You, their friend, like it and show them that you like it. "Oh, that?" they say in surprise. "If you like that—" and proceed to produce more for you, but usually this is not "that" at all, but just the old conventionalizings; so you say nothing, reserving your approval for only that rare thing that "never happened in the world before"; although you may, when the time is just right, talk to them about this astonishing and unique quality. You wait; and when the individual voice speaks once more out comes your approval, the most potent of weapons to fight the battle against the general liking for the commonplace. "That's it!" you say warmly. "Just no one ever said this before, or in this way. That really is *you* speaking!"

For a long time I waited, refusing to be genuinely moved, until one day the following lines came fluttering into my hand from one of the early group who had begun in marvelous confidence to bring me their most private imaginings:

DEEPEST MYSTERIES

A glorious cloud bounds through the sky;
  I follow and peer, far away,
Where the deepest mysteries lie
  Beneath a mass of gray:

Gorgeous courts and castles rare;
Many knights are resting there;
A prince his princess doth adore
With music never heard before.
Night comes; her darkness brings
  A host of butterflies
With brownies on their wings—

Then the dreams of night arise!
Hark! A silver bell doth chime:
    Silence time!
    Silence time!

The oak tree bows low
As fairies go,
  Floating onward—onward—
Leaving behind a nightly, silvery glow.

  I shoot like an arrow
    Back to To-day;
  The land of my vision
    Is swept quite away.
  Dreams fly fast!
  The gray cloud has passed.

Conventional ecohes are here, of course; for, remember, these are children with years of reading back of them and with no one to praise their true unusual lines; but there are also here the clear notes of individuality; it is indeed remarkable that this exquisite child quality should have persisted so long.

II

During that period of waiting one receives some of the worst possible products. They are often so bad that nothing but superior courage and faith could carry one through. The former standards of language set up by the school drop down, down, farther down than went the famous *Royal George*.

This should give some cheer to those mothers and teachers who try the new way and succeed in stirring up little less than the mud at the bottom; for it is a necessary stage in growth that has not been sufficiently advertised. The creativists have been to busy celebrating their victories of the spirit over the machine; presenting their best accomplishments so gaily, they have been innocently at great fault here, for instead of encouraging they have been well-nigh depressing. Let me make amends for my share of neglect in too often forgetting to warn against the slow movement upward in this important nonproductive period. We must face this slough of despond frankly and with understanding. Transition periods play the very devil with every reform.

The phenomenon is general, then, that while children are learning to find their more perfect native notes they seem to slump temporarily into ineffective croakings. The collection of good specimens is, therefore, incredibly slow. Those who work with children on the creative side are compelled to discard or ignore a hundred attempts while they are getting a mere half-dozen "good ones."

Just one "good one," however — painting, poem, clay figure, song, flash of clear thinking (for thinking, too, is creative art of the very highest) — just one is worth several months of searching. That is a common agreement among us. We know that it will beget others. And two is more than twice as effective as one. A half dozen is treasure!

When visitors were admiring the fifty paintings in the annual exhibition of the work of The Children's School of Acting and Design, in New York City, one of the directors was heard to say, "Oh, but you should have seen the two hundred awful ones we threw away!"

The creativist, however, likes the bad stuff, if it is the right sort of bad stuff. He gets to know that it represents one of the stages upward and rejoices and admires and pins it up on the wall. Smudges of inconceivable comicality one finds him adoring, to the mystification and disgust of the conventional person who has been taught that the only admirable result is a perfect pattern. Even those attempts which he eventually "throws away" have a quality that is really worthy of admiration — artists who drop in know what it is right off and talk about it understandingly — but it takes time and much experience before one learns to see this good side of the bad ones.

Here is one of the visible differences between product-education and creative education; the former turns out really good patterns in large quantities, seemingly every hour on the hour; the other brings forth a continuous mass of low-grade stuff. Another visible (and audible!) difference is the degree of interest and sincerity: the most splendid absorption of the workers in the standardized product-manufactory cannot hold a candle to the fierce self-motivated stirrings of genuine creative activity. But, granted a superior personal urge to do, the creative systems, we all freely admit, turn out a comparatively ragged product; one must pick here and there with care to uncover a "find."

Another vast difference between the two systems, we agree, is that each has its own notion of the use of time; and one must regard this difference, or disappointment and depression are sure to follow those who set up to practice the new way. The standardized curricular education requires "results" each day, each week, surely each month, with an accumulated measurable outcome at the end of each semester; creative education thinks in terms of years, and even in spans of years. The creative school cares not how inept and slovenly a lad may be this whole term if it sees something personal and fine taking slow possession of him. During the past twenty-five years the older school has reformed its method considerably in the face of public criticism; in my boyhood it used to expel youngsters each month, out of school and into the job, with the regularity and efficiency of an electric cherry pitter.

One may err sometimes in trying to mix the two systems. After reading an enthusiastic book on the creative side, or after hearing a modern school lecturer, some teachers go forth to their classes, rap for order, explain the idea, and then, with the best intentions, assign a lesson in "creative work." They are most disappointed when they do not get a roomful of results the next day. "Fraud!" they are apt to cry, and give up forever.

Once upon a time a determined visitor came swiftly into my ninth-grade class and objected because the boys and girls were absorbed in writing. She stalked up and down between the movable tables, examined the childrens' work, greatly to their amazement (and to mine), and then announced, "I see no reason why this work should be done now."

I hurried her to a distant corner of the room and begged her to lower her voice. Fortunately the children were far away in their own land of Make-believe; for a moment they looked up dreamily, as if drugged, and then fell back to their work.

"I have come from Illinois," the visitor said, in a tone of almost benumbing authority, "and have only a few hours in New York. I sail for Europe to-morrow morning. I came here to see creative appreciation, and I think I should be permitted to see it!"

"Do you expect me to turn it on and off — like a faucet?" I asked, trying my best to warm this lady's professional hauteur.

She said, "I am Professor of the Methodology of the Teaching of the Language Arts in the Blank Normal College" (I paraphrase the titles, but, my word for it, the original was even more comic), "and therefore I know enough about the practice of teaching to request that you stop this written work and demonstrate creative activity."

"But, my dear Professor of Methodology et cetera," I told her quietly, "though I should do just that and you should stay all morning you would see just nothing at all."

"My own thought exactly!" she snapped back. "Because exactly nothing would happen!"

She was a most forthright person, but, as I heard later, and suspected at the time, she was really ill, poor thing, and had been sent off on a year's leave of absence. (Overwork, they said, but I diagnose Too-much-methodology.)

I lowered my voice still more, so as not to disturb the children. (They were really engaged on a creative job that had absorbed their complete attention, creative appreciation in abundance if the visitor had had any educational vision at all.) "I have a good stop-watch in my desk," I whispered and pointed out the window to Morningside Park. "Do take it and go out, right away, into Morningside Park. Sit down on the grass for an hour and time the dandelions. As the seconds tick away, watch their growth and then come back and report to me. Do you know what you will say? Exactly nothing has happened."

I found the watch in my desk and tried in dramatic whispers to press it upon her. She edged away from me. I stalked her. "Do go out and time the dandelions!" I begged. But she would not. She did not speak. She would not even stay. She went quickly away from there.

The creative educationists have a different notion of the use of time, and they have a different notion of results, but give us our own time and we promise to more than match the old school in even its own conception of "results." A high-school principal has just presented me with the report of an extensive examination of the work of his pupils in school subjects and in social, athletic, and other extra-class activities. We were both interested in seeing how pupils trained in a famous "free activity" elementary school had fared in comparison with those who had been subjected to more controlled school procedures. This "free" school is almost wholly a creative education school: it has no curriculum, no "subjects of study," no textbooks, no recitation, a total absence, in short, of the usual machinery of lessons and assigned tasks.

In this report the pupils from the "free activity" school were found among the leaders in every phase of school life, including what was to them the strange and novel experience of academic subjects. Their trained resourcefulness had carried them everywhere to the top.

One of the girl's colleges has recently made a similar report upon the work of students whose preliminary training has been creative rather than predominantly college preparatory.

III

Those rare offerings which are superior, because they are expressions, either partially or wholly, of the mysterious life of the spirit, should be given the advantage of a conspicuous setting. Here, let me admit, is where my fellow workers meet me with strong if friendly antagonism. They would display all without discrimination, the good — in this special sense of good — and the bad; for the sake of encouragement they would even admit the faithful but ununknowing copiers.

Our disputes are most fruitful, but upon this point we remain at the end each of his own opinion still. Our difficulties are irreconcilable, because, I think, each has a different educational aim in view. Should children be led to believe that creative activity is natural to all and, therefore, that it is not to be stressed as a gift of the special few? Then, of course, one should draw no attention to it by this isolation of the unusual ones. But if the aim is to raise the standard of all, so that even the creative activity heretofore accepted as good may be discarded by the children themselves as inferior, and, further, so that even those superior ones may reach forward to a higher and unsuspected superiority, then, discounting the risks, the leaders must be given their conspicuous positions of distinction.

We must be always reminding ourselves that the rare expression of individuality is not only ignored by the world or rejected as inferior, but that even the child-creator must be taught to recognize its outstanding character of worthiness. Therefore he must be given many opportunities for companionship with it; it must be advertised constantly to eye and ear. Mixed with both good and bad it is lost, and, as is usually the case, evil is easily dominant and characteristically corrupts good manners. Remember the first law of mating: No love without propinquity!

"We produce excellent creative work," my friends tell me often, "but it reaches a certain stage and stops. We do not touch the general high grade of your output. Tell us why."

My invariable answer is that I so manage the controls that the highest approval goes solely to that work which bears the mark of original invention. To be sure, one must perform this office so adroitly as never to be suspected of controlling at all. No matter how crude the product, judged by the usual standards of adult perfection, the work with the individual touch is given the place of distinction; and there it is kept for all to see. Not that other contributors are neglected or made needlessly to feel their lack; there are many easy devices for the encouragement of those who have not yet found their native tones. Experience with the better brings, not contempt, as the proverb foolishly avers, but affection; and a real knowledge of the good will always drive out a taste for the inferior.

In some instances, however, I have come upon an experience which seems to contradict the notion that a liking for the strange output of the creative spirit is an acquired taste; although it does mightily back up the argument for distinguishing the good and ignoring the conventional. It often happens that a few pages of fine work, printed well and distributed for all to contemplate at leisure, will bring an instant and sincere general appreciation. I have seen a wave of approval sweep quietly through a group, touching even those inarticulate ones who have never heretofore given the slightest sign of possessing artistic standards. The power of the thing has struck them; separated from the mass it has had its opportunity to work upon them.

I speak of the linguistic art because that is the field in which I have done my main work; but it serves here merely for convenience of illustration. Workers in other media will instantly recognize the application of their materials and will have no difficulty in making the translation. There is little difference between us, as a matter of fact. We have none of the absorption in our special field, nor have we the insurmountable barriers separating one another, so destructive to childhood education among the "subject" specialists.

A teacher of eurythmics, who had been a most encouraging listener in a series of discussions of creative activity, writes:

You rarely speak of the dance, because, I suspect, you have had little experience on that side of the creative life, but that is all I see. "All I see are periwigs!"

She is quoting from Helen Elizabeth's *His Excellency's Maker of Periwigs,* which we give in full on page 186.

"However (she goes on cheerfully), every poem and picture and clay model, every invention even, and all the wise thinking of these children are just eurythmics to me. I go away each time fortified in my conviction of the value and importance to complete living, of self-expression through mind-and-body-release. You and your group are giving me hourly proof of the infinite resources of my own special field; they confirm my own experimentations; they show me the way to further and unsuspected gains and possibilities. For fear that this may worry you as criticism, let me hasten to remark that I prefer it this way. *Most talks on my own subject bore me; they all say the same abstract things in the same abstract manner.* Your 'child-stuff,' as you call it, those concrete crudities in language, color and what-not, help me to think in terms of body, mind-control and movement. It stimulates me to make the translation, gives me a sense of inventing and creating myself; and I have no difficulty at all with it."

IV

One must be patient, but eventually the childlike quality of the real thing gives courage to many silent ones who have in the past been benumbed into repression by the overpowering vogue of the impossible adult thing. The work that they see us admiring is, after all, their own language. That, indeed, is the main reason, in my opinion, why it works upon them so powerfully. Into their silent hours it plays its spell, evoking similar secretly familiar music. The friendly welcome, which they know will greet anything of theirs, does the rest; and soon another gift joins the collection, to take its place for general admiration, and to work, in turn, its own powerful contagion.

The control of the guide is here all important. He must know instinctively by feel, as it were, the texture of the native offering. At the right time he must be able to say, "This is the real thing!" That probably is his greatest bit of teaching, if one call it teaching. Mere talk about it, without the experience, is often misleading, and results in bringing forth at times the bizarre and the silly.

Listen to the words of H. Caldwell Cook, who in England was finding ample illustrations of the creative life in young boys, his "littlemen," as he calls them in his books, long before we in America had begun to think seriously about the matter:

"The development of personality demands freedom of expression and every opportunity for the exercise of originality. . . . For such work as this the teacher must sink himself

in the needs of his class as a group of individuals; must take
care not to thwart natural inclination, and yet at the same
time insure that the efforts of his pupils do not run away
into fantastical conceits, blind imitation, affected novelty
or sheer tomfoolery. He must know a good thing, actual or
potential, when he sees it, and must neither let pass unchal-
lenged any work which the author could improve, nor reject as unfit anything which has life in it and a true inspiration, however feebly showing. He must be ready to set
aside all convention in method, all blind rigidity or discipline, and pin his faith on no stereotyped formulae. There is
a different way every day."

V

Those teachers who know how to keep their praise for
the good thing just a step in advance of the moving group
are agreed upon one other interesting and puzzling phenomenon. The results of each year are better than the year
before. A new class arrives; seemingly one should begin at
the beginning; on the contrary, the immediate product is in
advance of last term's beginning. This goes on from year to
year; the whole output continues to grow in an upward
gradation of superiority.

We thought at first that the explanation lies in the improved skill of the teacher. That is a partial element, no
doubt, but we have much evidence — in teachers moving to
other schools, for instance, where they must start at the
very beginning again — that something happens to the exact *locus,* making it a place, like improved ground, which itself produces a better and better crop.

Some of the improvement may be due to the spell of the
fine work of previous classes decorating wall and shelf.
Some comes from the spread of interest and enthusiasm
which reaches the lower group in daily social contacts. A
certain expectation is set up in advance. The changed personalities move about among the younger ones and evoke
desire. Or those younger ones who have the urge in their
secret hearts become conscious of a possible future fulfilment and begin thinking about it early. This "spread" is

notably obvious if the school uses the assembly period as a natural outlet for the presentation of child-engendered projects. Dramatic work, for instance, will improve from year to year if the younger children have been touched by seeing, hearing, and feeling the advanced skill of their slightly maturer mates. Of course I am referring to guided child-initiated work in drama, not to memorized patterns of adult construction "coached" in the adult manner.

The really mystifying side of the phenomenon of "spread" is that new pupils are absorbed swiftly and do not become retarding laggards. At first their work may be conspicuously far below the natural standards all about them; but they soon step into the unusual region and are at home. Once we moved into a larger building and thereby doubled our enrolment. The new fact-taught and memory-drilled group, motivated largely by fear or by the dangling rewards of "marks," exhibited for the most part the rawest manners in matters of the spirit. We had anxious moments while they frankly laughed at our verses and at our other manifestations of creativity, and even more anxious ones when they innocently displayed their own uneducated taste. "Even in the art and science of jokes," said one of our own, "they are in the primary class." Then they dismayed us further by making honest demands for changes; our refinements were understandingly annoying. But we postponed and waited. They came around eventually and without really being aware that a magic influence had been working upon them. Propinquity once more overcame indifference and scored a mating.

Another fact, not so puzzling, is that the "spread" may often radiate from one spot and influence a whole community. I have in mind the work of a high school teacher of biology who was so much more than a biologist that all forms of creative invention, of scientific urge, of active regenerating living, had gradually become characteristic of other classrooms besdes his own. When he left that school the life went out of it. For a while it traveled forward on its own momentum; then it slowly retarded; finally it stopped and became just a place where boys and girls learned things from books and teachers.

It had taken many years to make that school conscious of the illimitable powers that lie hidden within, to build up a faith in self-education, to overcome the fears of clumsiness, to stir up, by right praise, a knowledge of the enormous value of self-discovered wisdom; it took but a short time to lose all those gains.

Administrators should be aware of this slow progress and should know that class growth and school growth, measured in terms of superior accomplishment, are possible through a long range of years, although a new set of children are arriving in each classroom. In one elementary school I have watched the tempera painting mount slowly from infantile daubs to high-grade expressionism. It took eight years to arrive at its present stage, but the work, done now so easily and naturally by children of the primary grades, has values, in color, composition, and imaginative idea, which make their pictures not inappropriate for framing and hanging as decoration for one's own home.

This gives us another clue to the difference in method between the education in information and the education in taste. The fact master can get only so far in a given year; his work, therefore, is easily measureable for grade-placement. Taste is a matter of living; and no bar has yet been found for its expanding power. In the range of the development of creative ability grade-placement and grade-expectation are almost meaningless terms. Very young children in my presence have hit upon Emerson's theory of the oversoul, upon Fichte's demand that *deus* must of necessity create an objective world, and even upon Kant's general conclusion concerning the limitations of sensory experience. In their own language, of course. Permitted, the creative mind will go far.

Further, fact education has always insisted upon drill; education in feeling comes through experience. One appeals mainly to memory; *creative education demands an exposure to an influence.*

One sees, therefore, why the modern teacher, when he would explain his unique effects upon the personalities before him, insists so much upon "environment" rather than upon courses-of-study-the-same-for-all. He means all those influences — art product, child performance and group performance, constructive materials, physical organization that permits freedom, administrative attitude toward control, teacher attitude toward the creative life, teacher suggestion that provokes creative activity, and information from every available source — which, acting directly upon individual desire and individual appreciation, stimulate the forces of the creative life and stir them to continuously superior activities.

These journeyings about the country have brought me a surer knowledge of the ways and means of enticing the creative spirit to expose its unsuspected powers; but mainly they have shown me that the schools everywhere are putting on the latest styles in education. With characteristic hustle America has suddenly adopted "creative work." Undoubtedly two great natural urges of childhood, to draw and to write, have been allowed gratification. The results in a better developed personality are good, but I seem to notice among teachers and administrators a satisfaction with the natural products. If a child punches clay, splashes paint, or writes a rhyme, that seems to conclude the educational obligation of the school. School officials show me the primitive work of children, announce with pride that there has been no instruction, and end with a satisfied, "Yes, we have creative work."

My sympathy is wholly with the attempt they are making to give a chance to the individual personality, so in all kindness I ask: Is it not the business of education to improve ability, to add to strength, to secure superior results?

At the risk of erring in taste I should like to emphasize the fact that in this chapter I have suggested a way to increase enormously the potential power of the creative product, or, rather, to draw more powerful achievement from a greater depth in personality. The picture is that of the teacher playing her special kind of admiration upon the best work of a group, skilfully and unobtrusively drawing attention to it, deliberately permitting it to stay in the mind like a well-placed advertisement.

The presumption is that the teacher shall know what is the best work of a group. Unless she does, much is lost. One may have "creative work". and present the results for the world to see; it will remain in a definite and interesting infantile stage unless genuine creative education has a place in the classroom.

Wherever I go I see splendid work of children ignored, even in the most liberal modern schools. The pattern copiers too often win the larger approvals; the crude attempts at individual expression are passed by.

To secure teachers who know the good from the bad will take time. We cannot adopt a national creative program and have success overnight. One should be aware of the slow nature of our undertaking and be cheerful about it, nor demand too much at the start. The first outcomes, in enlarged freedom, are most worthy. Here and there we shall have a superior result. At first we shall credit it to gifted children or to social advantages or even to the I. Q., but eventually we shall find as a constant factor a teacher who understands some of the mysterious ways of the creative spirit, one, too, who appreciates and approves its crude and original manifestations.

VI

The versifying of the three youngsters, luckily captured on the first day of adventure into the region of creative education, would have gone the way of other unencouraged child-artistry, we suspect, had we not deliberately brought it forth into the warming influence of our best praise. The mere assumption of interest in these early scrawling attempts to express the emotional side of their lives was enough to stir them to a continuous making of verse and prose which lasted the whole five years — and still continues; but conviction of its worth was made doubly sure, in my judgment, when the distinguished setting of print gave it its frame and its wall and its fine picture-light.

I watched the stately responsibility of leadership come imperceptibly upon them; eventually they became the center of a group of equally free spirits, boys joining early and soon outnumbering the girls. That experience in leadership they

carried with them to the colleges as a possession more valuable than learning.

Without seeking or thrusting forward, that tiny band of
creative artists were accepted wherever they went as natural guides and counsellors; in a short time we began to hear
of them, from Yale, Harvard, Michigan, Vassar, Barnard,
whatever the place, as the chosen representatives of their
own contemporaries for high position in student literary
activities.

At the end of the five years with us, some of their youthful work in verse was placed for all to see in the pages of
Creative Youth; the results, in the approval of their own
generation, judged by letters alone, would seem to indicate
that the expression of their creative lives, brought thus
from obscurity, has been heard and welcomed, literally,
round the world.

Poets say that no form of application gives them the
same inexpressible thrill as that which comes from children.
To the general anthologist these writing men and women are
often cold, but a request for reprint in books for the young
brings an unfailing warm response. "Our books will fade out
of the public mind," one of them expressed it, "but if some
scrap of our work is handed on to the young we may continue
to live. That would be one of the desirable forms of immor-
tality!"

Today I turn over the pages of a splendid series of modern
readers for the elementary grades, and, here and there, side
by side with the poetry of Edna Millay, Eugene Field, Sara
Teasdale, Holmes, Rossetti, Frost, and Robinson, I find the
verses which were made by the boys and girls during those
experimental years. This, really, is an astounding thing.
The composings of their private hours, contributed casually
without much thought of their worth, a waste product of
education, really, for which no value had hitherto been
found, these have been judged worthy of a permanent place
in the lives of youth. And later I found the verses of still
others of them set to music, along with the best work of our
major poets, in *New Songs for New Voices*, illustrated by
Peggy Bacon and edited by Louis Untermeyer and Clara and
and David Mannes.

To bring the matter up to date in this new edition of *Creative Power,* The World Publishing Company (New York) is preparing a collection of noteworthy humorous verse over the centuries and wishes permission to print light verse of my own along with some of the work of the boys and girls published in *Creative Youth.* Teacher and pupil in the same authoritative collection! Let me share one of those happy, child compositions with you, but do not think that it is just a humorous poem, for it is basically a keenly observed satire on parents, teachers, older sisters, all those who disturb the joy of living by continuously reminding youth of its natural and proper immaturities.

JOHNNY

Johnny used to find content
In standing always rather bent,
Like an inverted letter J.
His angry relatives would say,
"Stand up! Don't slouch! You've got a spine!
"Stand like a lamppost, not a vine!"
One day they heard an awful crack—
He'd stood up straight—it broke his back.

CHAPTER V

Wordists

ONE OF THE EARLIEST of our discoveries was that of a youth with a remarkable facility in clear-cut phrasing. His product bore no resemblance to the primitive free construction that has been illustrated here; in fact, it was so sophisticated and mechanically expert as to suggest adult editing. The following contribution was held up for some time until many casual interviews convinced us that this eighth-grader was an advanced student of words:

FROM A MINARET

Scarlet skies, purple palms,
Ragged beggars whine for alms.

Orange glow on roof and dome,
Caravans returning home.

Temple, mosque, minaret
'Gainst the sky in silhouette.

Scarlet skies turn maroon;
In the east a crescent moon.

Faces veiled, sparkling eyes,
Shadowed streets in purple guise.

Lanterns gleam here and there,
All is silent everywhere.

Hark! a lute now is played;
'Tis some lover's serenade.

Soon the lute sounds no more—
All is silent as before.

The form is strictly conventional, the verse monotonously end-stopped, and the thematic trappings are just what one would expect of rhymesters who write with no experience at all of their subject. The general effect is that of insincerity; one is not moved by the piece; but the words, one sees, are put together with the care of a devoted workman.

After our first chat I classed him as a "wordist," a term for those chaps who become enamored of words in themselves as an interest aside from meanings. The only reason that I know about this group is that I was one myself; to this day a word or phrase will stir me when the context may not interest me at all; indeed, I must be on guard lest this vice lead me to sacrifice sense for sound. Writing men and women know all about this; perhaps the absorption in the symbols as such is the beginning in them of the flair for the craft of writing. Authors tell me of their early fascination for the signs of the zodiac, even; of their porings over hieroglyphics; of a playing with words as other children play with blocks.

I tested him by my own experiences, and he matched up instantly. "Have you ever read a dictionary?" I asked him.

"Yes! Have you, too?" He was alert in an instant, for up to that moment he had fancied that he was the only person in the world who had ever had such a silly interest.

"I used to mark the place," I confessed, "and turn the page down, reading it just like another book."

We talked of our finds. *Abracadabra* was a mutual favorite. I used to go over the house muttering *Abracadabra!* (Still do.) He gave me *festinate,* which I had missed, and aired his liking for *fanfare, sequin, demoniac, sesquipedalian,* and the like; and I swopped with *hobbledehoy, provocative,* and *predestinate,* which I always manage to get into my writings somewhere or I could not be happy.

Once he brought me four lines called *The Moon.* They began:

Withered harlot of the night!

I must have been visibly stirred; certainly it was a shock. He noted that — with eerie enjoyment.

"Aren't words powerful!" he said.

"I'll say they are!" I agreed.

"I meant that white moon you see in the daytime. Pock-marked. Sickly pale. As if she'd been out all night and was just tottering home."

I stared at the lines.

"Are you going to print them?" he grinned.

" 'Withered harlot of the night!' " I repeated softly. "Boy," I said, "you've spoiled the moon for me for life!"

He understood the social convention, so he soon found a synonym that fitted; it was "wanton". When the revised quatrain was printed in the school magazine he said to me quietly but with real conviction, "The first word was stronger, much stronger, and — it was more honest." I agreed, but I also understood the necessity of the social convention.

II

It is difficult to say whether it was due to our encouragement or to a native gift that would have survived even the coldest of schoolroom environments, but his muse grew increasingly prolific; he learned somehow to subdue the word for the idea, in consequence of which his work began to take on a flavor all its own — the hall-mark of the individual once more! — until one April day two years later he gave us a spring song — and *there's* a theme to test one's originality! — which, I judge from its constant reprintings, must already have given satisfaction to thousands:

SPRING VENDERS

Oh, blessed be the venders in the street
That flaunt their jaunty splendors in the street:
    Violets and daffodils,
    Whirligigs and windmills,
      Bright balloons,
      Rusty tunes,
    Doughnuts strung on spindles!
Yet the doughnut-vender never sells his crullers;
Just the odor serves to make the children sigh;
While balloons and toys sell only for their colors—
    The flimsy stuff they're made of who would buy?
No one wants the music or the flower;
    Who flings a coin to hear machinery start,
Or pays for blooms that wither in an hour?
He only buys the April in his heart.

This lad had been playing with words long before we became acquainted and was aware that he could fashion aston-

ishing effects out of them; so he would not be the one to
give up his gift because of discouraging elders. To be sure,
he was still practicing in secret in those early days, for no
teacher had ever become interested. His school exercises
had required from him none of that fascinating game with
words which would keep him up at night in sheer interest
in the play; in fact, and this is the remarkable thing, I think,
his school writings were rather dull, and certainly they were
full of blunders; no one could have guessed from reading
them that the author was a wonder-worker with words. So
he lived two writing lives, as all fated writing men and
women have learned to do since Eve held her first dame-
school, one for the pedagogues, pale and undistinguished,
and one for his own hours, alive and really brilliant.

It was my luck to find out about the other life outside of
school — probably because I could speak his language. So
I admitted the gift to the schoolroom and saw it grow and
grow until shortly I was to hear important figures in the
literary world wax eloquent in his praise. And that came
about in this way:

Secretly I had sent some of his work to a national poetry
competition, and, out of the thousands of poems entered, his
verses took the attention of one of the judges, Witter Byn-
ner, a distinguished poet and critic, who wrote, "There is
not one of his poems in which I do not feel a touch of something more than talent. He seems to be a genuine and exciting discovery. In fact, I have not heard so interesting a new
voice since Countee Cullen and George Dillon."

III

This, understand, happened when he was still a boy in
school. Naturally, I was delighted, but there was one person even more thrilled, and she had a better right to her
thrill than I to my delight. That boy was pretty far along
in the practice of his gift when I came across him; but she
had known about it long before that, at a time when it must
have been a very tiny gift indeed, perhaps not visible to the
ordinary eye. But she was his mother.

She told me that almost from the beginning of speech he had shown a kind of interest in words which, to her prejudiced eyes, seemed unusual, but that she was reluctant to admit even to herself that it was a gift at all. "You know how mothers are!" she smiled at me. "But I liked everything he did, naturally, and I let him see that I liked it. Perhaps I shouldn't, but I did. That's all I did; and — that's how it happened."

At another time she said, "But there were many things that I didn't do. I never interfered, for instance. Perhaps I am not a good sort of mother. He would stay up half the night to scribble and draw and write music; I let him. He was most prolific when in the bathtub with a board rigged across for writing, sketching, and composing songs; there he would splash for hours singing an interminable melody; I let him!"

This same story I have come upon many times, of a mother's wise interest in what must often have seemed a silly thing; invariably it tells of strange liberties permitted when the creative life swings to the surface and takes possession, becoming so urgent in its demands that lessons are neglected, food is not eaten, and even the necessities of sleep are forgotten. "I often thought I was doing wrong," this mother admitted, "to let him go on and on that way without stopping him, but, somehow, I had an unreasoning faith that I should not discourage him in the thing he most wanted to do, and therefore, that I should permit nothing to stand in the way of it."

In this case, of course, the mother was right, as the sequel proves; but she was an exceptionally wise and self-effacing mother. (That was her gift!) She is one of those who recognize latent ability early, encourage it with interest, and give it a chance to grow. That's nearly all there is to the process; but that is a great deal.

Whenever I speak of this kind of manifestation of the creative life I stand braced for the protesting questions that follow. Mothers and fathers want to know if I would let children be guided by every silly whim that seizes them. Of course I am setting up no such rule of life. Some silly whims are not at all silly; the point is that one must be able to discriminate among them.

The personal problem here is of enormous importance: how to tell the foolishness from a kind of genius! Because the first signs of the creative gift look surprisingly like foolishness. A boy makes caricatures on scraps of paper, puts eyes and noses on all the big O's in his books, copies carefully all the cartoons out of the newspaper, draws airplanes crashing in midair, paints sunset scenes in orange and red that would make the cows stop munching, and in the meantime lets all the real work of life go to smash.

Perfectly silly. Of course. It is always silly in the beginnings. And even comic. So is the beginning of a cold. There is nothing funnier than a sudden, unexpected, and devastating sneeze. And nothing sillier.

An all-powerful, all-absorbing, duty-defying interest is an important symptom; it should never be ignored or belittled by those, parents or teachers, who presume to the difficult office of maturing young life.

IV

The poem that follows is taken from a page of later published work. Truth to individual feeling is here, as of old, touched with a balancing and rectifying humor, but it is an astonishing truth that takes us by surprise, and a humor so deft as to be there only for those who have the wit to catch it:

FUGITIVE AT DUSK

I must seek ambush in some deep recess,
  And flee the jurisdiction of the moon,
  Or I will be attired in livery soon—
A lackey to her regal loveliness!
  There lodges something servile in us all
  That lives to run at beauty's beck and call.

I must take flight before the sun is down,
  Before the garden grows too arrogant.
  The meanest tree, the most downtrodden plant
Will soon be wearing silver like a crown.
  In this increasing hush I quail to see
  Presagements of a fatal tyranny.

During his high-school years this boy wrote an enormous amount of material, every day yielding its contribution of work self-imposed and required by no rule of the school. Included in this mass are poems for occasions, too personal and local for anything but the moment's enjoyment, plays of all sorts from vaudeville sketches up, and everything musical from songs to operettas, one of which was given before the school with a success for that audience equal to a Broadway hit.

This was his workshop period; therefore little of the output is worthy of final preservation. Nor had he nor had any of us any thought at this time of making contributions to the world; he was living and working, and was encouraged so to live and work, with an intense interest in the moment, careless of ultimate effects, sincerely not trying to please any other group than that of his own contemporaries. In his senior year, for instance, he turned out the *Four Edens*, presented here on page 224, as merely a gay illumination to the study of medieval history in Daniel C. Knowleton's class.

If his hours of toiling could be pictured in a graph, day, night, summer, winter, on foot, in bed while sleep is held off, free in solitude or racked in the midst of polite chatter, then one might be able to convince the formalists in education that there is no drudgery like that which the creative life compels. "But you don't teach them to do disagreeable things!" they continually do cry. How little they know about us! When one binds the law willingly upon oneself, as the artist, the craftsman, the thinker and the leader must do, one needs no artificial work assignment!

The defect of the creativist argument is that we conceal all evidences of the weary toil in presenting our final and life-consuming results. We charm our opponents with our art and lull them deceptively into a sense of easy workmanship; and there is something of sportsmanship in us, too, we hope, that disdains boring others with our purely personal and private troubles. We see about us too many asses braying how much they paid for things.

Here are two widely circulated illustrations from the young man's later muse:

REHEARSAL

I heap my palms with sand,
   And let it all sift free
In order that the hand
   May learn passivity.

(He must have practice young
   Who ever would be trained
To leave some songs unsung
   And many cups half-drained.)

I turn from each embrace
   Before the fire is spent,
That I may make with grace
   The last relinquishment.

THE CONTRACT

I must stop to heed the dusk,
   For I have signed;
Industry and peace are for
   The blessed blind;
I could coldly waive it off
   If it were just
Moral obligation or
   A sacred trust . . .
I must heed the terms of earth,
   For I have signed,
And the clause concerning dusk
   Is underlined.

CHAPTER VI

Back Talk

MY GRAVEST PROBLEM WITH earnest teachers who wish to learn how to reach helpfully into the creative life of their charges comes from a lack on their part of any memory of their own childhood that would make them compatriots of the young. They have surrendered to the adult tradition so long ago that all vestiges of individuality have well nigh disappeared. It is only with those who retain, in some part of their being, an egoistic celebration of the unusual and unique self of their younger days that I am able to work, with hope of conviction and understanding.

To these I often present that part of my personal life, naked and unashamed, which is still alive and as irrepressible and foolish, therefore, as any of my self-centered youngsters. Communication with children on the level of their secret and private imaginings is comparatively easy for me just because, I fancy, I have never considered that that sort of thing is unimportant. The story of my own revelings among words as a child has been of such help to others in getting them into rapport with similar rhapsodic, and perhaps idiotic, creative activity of children that I use the excuse to tell one part of it here.

II

Words were my first important interest, my mother tells me, the strange words of a newspaper, but by its means I inquired myself into a knowledge of reading and the mystery of word signs at a very early age. And that interest has never died down. Since I have written for the popular magazines as well as for technical journals, my work has traveled to every part of the world — as letters prove often enough — and my circulation — magazine and book not personal! — is numbered in the millions.

I say this just to prove that my job is respectable, for my former teachers emphatically did not think so. Many times I was "on the carpet" for it and twice came within a hair's breadth of expulsion. I can safely say this now without offense to anybody, for that type of teacher is practically extinct.

What hounds they were on the scent of misspellings and wrong capitalizations! And they were the world's champions of neat penmanship, and clean paper with your name at the upper right-hand corner (where no one else in the world ever desired it to be).

They said that we would never get a job and that the world would not love us if we did not put a heavy stroke on the downward slant of letters; and if we pressed too hard on the pen, in the endeavor to have the world love us, we spilled a blot; and two blots on one exercise equaled one visit to the caning establishment of the principal, where we got a job immediately and were a screaming success at it.

To this day I can remember the courage it took to bear lightly on those downward strokes while that grim teacher walked the aisles; and the far-off yells of unsuccessful compatriots caused the hand to tremble. The World War was won in the composition and penmanship drills of the public schools of yesteryear.

Courage? For training in courage there is nothing like it.

"There's nothing like eating hay when you're faint," the King remarked to Alice as he munched away.

"I should think throwing cold water over you would be better," Alice suggested.

"I didn't say there was nothing *better*," the King replied. "I said there was nothing *like* it."

III

But, in spite of teachers, words were my earliest passion and continued to be dominant in my life. I read random pages of the school dictionary for the strange sensation of

discovering unheard-of words; I spent my little money for
works in foreign tongues, getting indefinable comfort in
looking at the unintelligible jargon, learned German script
for the sake of writing secret documents, bought a second-
hand polyglot Bible, and contrived a dozen secret written
and spoken languages.

The only reason I speak of these things is that I know
that I am merely telling the hidden story of all word-minded
boys and girls. They would instantly understand the following cryptic line:

    3 15 13 5   1 18 15 21 14 4   5 1 18 12 25
    20 15 14 9 7 8 20.

And they would laugh, because that is the very first attempt
to maintain secrecy in code, and it is the very easiest to
guess. After a few of these messages have fallen into the
hands of the enemy, creative invention suggests more involved and difficult schemes. A chum and I used to write to
each other with Greek letters spelled from right to left like
the Hebrew, with the lines from bottom to top like the Chi-
nese. But we did not write many letters after the first.

Secret spoken languages do not usually advance much beyond "hog Latin," like "Ill-way ou-yay o-gay ith-way
e-may?" for "Will you go with me?" but after many trials
with complicated spoken languages I finally hit upon one
that is quite simple and always mystifying. Strangely
enough I used it only for private conversations with myself,
talking aloud as I walked along unfrequented roads; but once
I blazed away in it before an astonished group, of which I
shall tell later.

Reading the sounds of a word backward had always been
a habit of mine. I do not know when it began. In school the
words of irritated teachers fell backward in my mind and
there they were silently vocalized; my lips may have moved,
but I knew better than to speak aloud. Nor did I wish to let
anybody in on what was a very private and secret pleasure.
So the oft-uttered word "attention!" became instantly
"nushnetta!"; "stop that!" shifted to "pots tath!"; and
"close books!" was "zohlk skoob!"

When an older person talked too much in my nine-year-old presence I had no right to say aloud, "Shut *up!*" but I often got great satisfaction by whispering to myself, "Tush puh!" At those times the tension in my mind was relieved. "Tush puh!" administered at the height of tedium, was what psychiatrists today call good mental medicine. Certainly it increased my boyish cheerfulness.

To myself I called my language "Cab Caught," which, translated, means simply Back Talk. Remember, if you care to practice it, that it is the sounds and not the spelling that are made backward. For that reason it led me into a study of sounds. I found that the letter Y was just the long sound of E, and that W was the u-sound in "Coo." So "you" became "oo-ee" or, shortened, "wee"; and "was" turned into "zuh-oo." Also I found that X was only KS, and realized that initial H could not be sounded when put at the end unless you gave it a little "huh" (like "tay-huh" for "hate").

Once in the quietness of a public travel talk I astonished the meeting by blurting out, "So do I!" and was silenced by laughter from the audience and by a quick "Ssh!" from my astonished grandmother who sat by my side. The traveler had remarked that the natives of one part of Africa formed their plurals by putting a clicking sound in front of their words, instead of employing our belated custom of adding the sibilant.

My penetrating "So do I!" was the subject of much inquiry afterwards but, you may be sure, I had nothing to offer in excuse or explanation. However, in Back Talk the plural of "loof" (fool) is "zloof"; and the plural of "koob" (book) is "skoob," and the plural of "cham" (match) is "zitcham."

IV

Only once did I break loose and pour forth my pent-up soul in Back Talk. For reasons unknown to me my family had sent me to board in the country for a short period. This was a pleasant enough if ignorant family, and I quite understood, with the unerring clairvoyance of very young children, that they were desirous of keeping me happy and a source of income, but I also knew at the first glance that their ways were not my ways nor their gods my gods. Things that my family believed in, like talking, writing, and reading, this alien family called sins. Writing and sketching in blank books were sins because they were wasteful of time and paper, but the reading of fiction was an almost unforgivable sin, especially when done lying flat on the floor.

I argued for my rights and was instantly guilty of the sin of disrespect and disobedience. I became silent but unconvinced and was condemned for the sin of obstinacy. Other sins accumulating, my beloved book *The Count of Monte Cristo* was taken from me. Nothing was left but to announce that I would write to my mother and insist upon being brought immediately home.

They blanched at that, I noted, and I figured that I had them, but they startled me by placing their notion of righteousness above their obvious interest in money. For the sin of ingratitude, therefore, I should be made to go to my bed on the third floor without an attendant and without a light.

Now I had peopled every corner and twist of that crooked stairway with lions, hobgoblins, and demons rare, and each night as I had braved them I had put them one by one to rout, but on this dark and unprotected journey I knew I should be no courageous and valiant conqueror.

In the doorway I turned on those people whose ways were not my ways and whose gods could never be my gods. Ordinary speech left me, but in one blast from my good old trusty Back Talk I annihilated them and sent them hurrying for the village doctor.

"*Mad* wee!" I cried in my rage. "I *tay-huh* wee! Dna *wee!* Dna *wee!*" pointing to each of them vindictively. "*Law* vuh we! Mad zloof! Mad zloof! Mad zloof!"

"*Damn* you! I *hate* you! And *you!* And *you!* And *you!* All of you! Damn fools! Damn fools! Damn fools!"

"Damn fools!" was a favorite phrase of my father's to sum up his notion of all persons who disagreed with him.

They took me quickly in their arms and soothed my hot brow and comforted my torrential tears. The doctor was seriously impressed and ordered a sweetly pleasant drink.

And they all accompanied me up those perilous stairs —
"Mad zloof!" I whispered to myself joyfully — and they
stayed by me with a shaded lamp aglow.

My last remembrance of that night is of a sudden sitting
up in bed and of a victorious shout, "Mad zloof!" followed
by a hysteric shriek of happy laughter.

My mother came the next day and took me home. I
drooped and smiled faintly, told them how sorry I was to
leave them, extracting, in short, all the dramatic comfort
I could from the pathetic situation.

Always in a group of youngsters I discover those who
have similar experiences with the fascinating plaything of
language. And I have found no child who is not interested
in the story of my own adventures with it.

V

Somewhere in the files of an old magazine is an article
entitled "Berkshire Gabble" which recounts the attempt of
three girls to add necessary words to the English language.
They needed a word, they thought, for the place where the
cloth goes when it wears into a hole; and one for the ending
of roads which you never see but wonder about, and one for
the silence that comes that is silenter than the silence before
it; and one for what you are feeling when you are obliged to
say polite things you do not mean. They accumulated a list
of several hundred such words, slipping them into their
secret talk along with common English words.

And, of course, everyone knows about the portmanteau
words in *Alice in Wonderland*. There must be a great variety of such languages that have never been recorded. One
little friend of mine, whose delightful name is Happy, had
a complete language of her own before she spoke English at
all. English she understood, of course, but her replies would
be in her own invented language. Later she spoke English
for ordinary uses, but for private talks with her mother and
father and for those sleepy words just before slumber, she
spoke low and earnestly in her chosen tongue. William T.
Schwarz, the artist, knows this language, which he learned
in many loving hours spent with Happy, and should some

day write an account of it. I have often listened to Happy. The language is complete for every need, and it has abundant seriousness and delightful humor.

While in the Army, Mary Louise, Captain Watson's eight-year-old daughter, introduced me to "Face Talk," a language which we perfected during many happy breakfasts together. It is not much of a language for speedy communication, as each letter is spelled out by a special turn or twist of the face, but it is marvelously secretive and can be used without detection under the very noses of family and distinguished guests. And it is absolutely soundless.

I used Face Talk in the novel *I Ride in My Coach,* which I was then writing, but as so many persons have asked me for the whole alphabet this seems a good spot to place it in print for the first time. The capitals in parentheses show that this slow-moving speech used the letters also as word signs.

FACE TALK

A—Alligator-snap, a silent bite. (AND)

B—A slight bow of the head. (BEAST!)

C—Cheek-puffs (good round ones). (CAT!)

D—The sleepy dormouse. (DON'T GO)

E—Monkey face — E being the sound the monkeys make — the tongue thrust directly back of the closed upper lip, forehead wrinkled in the highest.

F—Frown. (FOLLOW!)

G—Grief, the mouth shaped like a croquet wicket. (GO)

H—Horror, whites of eyes showing, but mouth closed thin and cheeks sucked in. (HAVE)

I—A slow closing of the eyes. (IS NOT)

J—Joy, the eyes rolling up and almost disappearing. (WOULDN'T THAT JAR YOU!)

K—Kiss-pucker. (CAKE; ANYTHING ENJOYABLE)

L—Lower lip protruding. (LIKE)

M—Make-a-face, the tip of the tongue showing disdainfully. (WAIT A MINUTE)

N—A delicate, noiseless, inquiring nose-sniff. (NO)

O—Mouth open as if saying "OH!" in mild surprise. (ON THE)

P—Pride, the chin thrust forward. (PLAY)

Q—Question-face with plenty of forehead wrinkles but with mouth closed. (QUICK)

R—Roll of head on neck, as if the collar bothered. (ALL RIGHT)

S—Smile. (SPEAK; SHOUT; SING; SNIGGER; SAY SOMETHING)

T—Teeth-showing-in-a-snarl. (THANK YOU)

U—Underlip tucked-in. (UNDER THE)

V—Vertical toss-up of the head, like a horse trying to loosen a tight rein. (VETO; SAY NO)

W—Slow wink of the right eye. (YOU ARE WELCOME)

X—Kiss-pucker and smile together, since X is just KS. (EX-CUSE)

Y—Yawn. (YES)

Z—One look at the exact zenith. (ZERO; SAY NOTHING)

A single negative shake of the head marks the end of a word; several negatives, the end of a sentence. Rapid blinking of the eyes means "Message coming," which is kept up at intervals until the answer is received, a roll of the head (R) meaning "All right!"

VI

This public exhibition of some of the secret undercurrents of my own mind will not increase my standing with certain of my contemporaries. They will depreciate me lower, however, when they learn of another fancy of mine —so many intelligent young persons share it with me as to make me believe that it is not just imaginative foolery— which pictures these certain ones of my contemporaries as not contemporaries at all but senile persons, the young life in them long since dead, a trembling great-grandsire in incompetent charge; their dignity, then, becomes just stiffness of joints; their silence, inability to think; their serious conservatism, simply fear of discovery. For a youthful mind, at whatever chronological age the body, is still living on the fresh and boundless current of the creative life, it has never denied its own turbulent and incoherent spirit; it has

never admitted as folly its wilful imaginings and its surprising and ever-new reflections on the world, the flesh, and
the devil. Age begins with a denial of the spirit of youth;
with some it comes surprisingly early; with some it never
begins at all.

To those who keep the spirit alive, communication with
youth is easy, for genuine companionship is possible among
those only who confess the same follies. Perhaps that is
why the learned, the perfect, and the wholly good are never
much of a success in soul-winning. I have yet to find the
dominie who would sense the marvelous personal confession
in the Master's, "Neither do I condemn thee."

CHAPTER VII

The Native Language of Childhood

I have a secret from everybody in
the world-full-of-people
But — I cannot always remember how
it goes.

Hilda

AS SOON AS CHILDREN begin to speak they attempt
the language of literature. During those early months and
years, when they are struggling with the difficult medium
of language, come occasional flashes of achievement. Parents
have always known about this; but outsiders make it the
subject of their jokes. Anything under the heading Bright
Sayings of Childhood is always good for a laugh. Our jokes,
however, exhibit our natural antagonism; or, rather, our
lack of understanding. Literature is simply unique self-
expression; yet at the start we strive for conventional self-
suppression and laugh away, or scold away, that individual
utterance without which literature is not.

In a short time, under our living but ignorant drive, the
native gift of language may hide itself away in private dialogue with doll or toy, or carry on solely in the spirited
domain of silent dream-life — out of which the child comes,
stumbling and awkward, to receive our chidings for stupidity — or it may die out and seemingly be lost forever.

Mothers have been aware of this more surely than teachers. Each mother knows that she has a wonder child, one
who talks to her in a language adequate for every need, who
inquires with intelligence, whose reasoning is direct and
well-nigh miraculous. She cherishes the startling beauty of
every casual utterance, but she learns early not to speak of
her wonder aloud. That bored look, the smile of cynicism,

the jest that labels her as "proud parent," these and other manifestations of an unbelieving and prejudiced world soon silence her.

Lately, however, an international interest in the unique contribution of childhood has brought courage to mothers; out of secret drawers have come the precious baby-books which record questions, fancies, soliloquies, indignations, and protests even. I have only to mention this in public and then, when the lights are being turned off warningly, they wait in the darkening hall to tell me, with a wistful and timid eagerness — so few there are who will listen to mothers — of this and that startling expression of their very own. I urge them to keep careful notes. "The child," I tell them, "is now expressing his real self; so you may find out much about him now which will serve later. Later he may not believe in himself; you it is who must give him the strength of self-faith, for you know — you have seen and heard."

My mail is full of such records. One night, just before tucking-in, Bunnell says,

> Mother, did you see the sun go to bed? . . .
> He pulled the wooly white covers
> Up over his head . . .
> Are his blanket soft and white and warm
> Just the same as mine?

"At another time," writes Bunnell's mother, "he asked me if the clouds in the sky were the people who had gone to God" — this in a family where there is no attempt to inflict any theological theory, grewsome or otherwise.

To childhood the life within is one of the sure realities. Gretchen, thinking of clouds, says, very, very slowly,

> I see the white clouds floating low
> As though sheep in a meadow
>
> I see a man wave his crook
> In a deep blue shadow
>
> I see the house
> Where the shepherd lives.

This, of course, is literature. What else? All the elements are here: rhythm, design, unique insight, and the perfect picturing of thought and feeling. Some of us have tried to teach these children language! They already possess a language adequate for all the purposes of their little lives, but we do not often discover it; nor do we always recognize it when it appears right before us.

In the high-school classes Sandy had begun suddenly to weave a strange pattern of words; it was, really of course, an old gift that had disappeared into the depths of personality until aroused and brought to the surface by a school environment which welcomed and paid high prices in social approval for genuine self-expression. He surprised himself, I think — for the voice of his inner spirit was unlike anything that he had ever sounded before — but he must have drawn strength and confidence from the delight of those around him; he seemed to grow visibly into manhood before us.

There was another result, however. I may be wrong in tracing it to Sandy, but I have always felt that the strong home interest in the boy's new development was caught up by the little brother Jack. In those confidential hours at eventide he began to talk to mother in a new way. One day she came to see me with the story of the awakening in Jack of a self-expression totally different from Sandy's but like Sandy's in that it was all his own.

Although it was winter and the family were in the city Jack talked exactly as if he were back in the summer home, in his bed beside the open window. Children, of course, do not give titles to these quiet pictures but when the mother wrote it out for me she called it

SUMMER LIGHTS

I love to see how many kinds of light
I can find on a summer's night

I love the white spots of phlox
In the gardens
With the moon shining on them

I love the white spots of stars
Twinkling in the black sky

I love the white spots of fireflies
Sparkling
On the edge of the woods

And then, besides,
When my brother goes out to see that the chickens are in bed
I see his lantern
Bobbing in the garden

And when I go to bed
I like to see the light, way off in the woods,
That comes back from the windows
Of the old stone house

And, last of all,
I love my mother's candle light
On the little table
Beside her bed

Mothers have given us our best revelations of the creative spirit in the young. I pay my tribute here, as I have done elsewhere, to one mother who listened to the beautiful voice of the child artist and had the fine courage to give the result to all of us. Hilda tells us much of the reality of that inner life when she says, in one of those quiet moments beside her mother,

I have a secret from everybody in the world-full-of-people
But I cannot always remember how it goes;
It's a song
For you, Mother,
With a curl of cloud and a feather of blue
And a mist
Blowing along the sky.
If I sing it some day under my voice,
Will it make you happy?

II

Most of the speech of children that we hear is not their own language but the imitative forms, thought and imagery of their elders. The adults that surround a young child go in eagerly for teaching their own speech; they ignore the native gift or drown it out with doggerel rhymes, set phrases, adult polite idiom, verses and prose made for children by adults. School readers, *Mother Goose,* and books such as the exquisite *Child's Garden of Verses* have their place in childhood education, but these excellent materials, wrongly used, may really deprive the child of certain valuable experiences in self-expression.

So children talk like their primers — saying, "See the," for instance, an infantile idiom that is purely bookish to Americans whose phrase is "Look at that" — or they bang out bad rhymes that obstruct their clear and beautiful thinking, or they force their language into imitations of adult poets. Now, imitation, however excellent, is never art; and proof is ample that even very little children have a language of their own whose outcome is undoubtedly art.

For, notice, in the illustrations already given, that children speak naturally in a form that we adults are accustomed to call poetry; and without any searching for appropriate use of the medium. That is because their minds are wholly intent upon something real within them; the language is instinctive and really of secondary consideration; they fashion it to the significant form exactly as other artists handle their medium, swiftly and without disturbing thoughts of standards outside themselves. The child poet — without ever knowing that he is a poet — "weaves to his song the music of the world and of the clouds," as little Elizabeth so wisely phrased it when she wrote of

THE PIPER

The sun shines on the brook and makes it look like silver
And in a cave where the winds are all asleep
A piper plays a tune;
He weaves to his song the music of the world and of the clouds.

Elizabeth has other lines which I never read without thinking that she, all unwittingly, is giving us the picture of the real voices of youth which are lost because of the storms we elders set up in the name of education!

The sun is leaving the heavens and the wind is waking
And the music of the piper
Is fading
Like a shadow.

The younger boys and girls who compose Camp Van Daal at Woodstock in the Catskills put their energies continuously into creative activities and for the sole reason that that is the way they prefer to spend their summer. The range is enormous, from boat making to poetry. A printing press seems to be the center of camp life. The authentic note of the real thing is there, I found; and it is so natural and to-be-expected-of-anyone that it really flourishes. On a rainy day a boy writes — and you must know exactly how to read this or you will miss some of the joyous "magic of discontent" — and then, of course, he proceeds to set up and print:

> What is the magic of discontent
> Which sows the seed so wild and sweet
> Of rain, of rain, of rain, of rain,
> Of rain upon the roof?

In the camp notebook of one boy were found these strange but altogether serious lines; they were written late on the day when death had come swiftly and unexplicably near him:

THE LILIES AND THE ROSES IN HIS GARDEN

Death passed by my door
And left me with a chill
So that I sought the fire.

Death passed. I saw him:
He was tall, and mockingly robust;
On his head was an opera hat and on his feet a dirty pair of shoes.

For a moment I found myself wishing that when Death went by
I might hug the fire and the fire's warmth, with the door close locked;
That I might leave the pavement to Death.
I hoped that I would not become intimate with Death until I had
  exhausted Life's friendship. . . .

What matters it
Whether I dwell with the lilies and the roses in the parlor of the
  House of God
Or with the lilies and the roses in His garden?

Only the artist may appreciate the work of an artist; and adults are standardized persons without the gift of language that marks one's speech as unique. Our chief aim — reflected in textbook and curriculum — is to become expert copyists. It is the public demand that has forced the telegraph companies to supply us with the wording of the only seven ways to express our congratulations or seasonal wishes!

Yet, sad thought, the unstudied naturalness of the early "poetry" of childhood will thrive among those only who have ears to hear and judgment to approve. *It is a terrible law of training that we shall have whatever we approve.* If our standards are conventional the artist-child in our care will surrender his most valued possession with hardly a misgiving. Only through constant exercise in a favoring environment will the artist nature survive. The rare rebel, of course, is of different mould; he fights and suffers but remains an artist, mainly, I often think, because he refuses to give up his gift of seeing and thinking and feeling as a child.

Quite often, however, he does not rebel; outwardly he conforms, but about his real self he is forever silent except before someone who has comprehended. A teacher tells me of an Italian lad whose work she found and was about to proclaim before all when she caught his protesting face and was mercifully silent. Their friendship lasted for years, and he continued producing all that time, but no one else dreamed of it. In a sort of pagan world he lived, translating all the cold science about him into myths of his own. After a thunderstorm had been explained to the children he wrote:

> One day Thunder
> Wanted to play a song,
> So, taking his bugle,
> He let out a mighty blast.
>
> Thunder's friend, Rain
> Wanted to join in the chorus
> But Thunder wouldn't let him;
> So Rain wept!
>
> People on Earth said,
> "What a storm!"

After he had gone up to the next grade the teacher inquired cautiously if the boy had been writing those strange individual fancies and received the assurance from the teacher above that nothing of the kind had happened. All the while a notebook was filling up, and later he brought them down to the only one who understood. Here is his reaction to the complete theory of earthquakes and volcanos as presented by the course of study:

A real stomach is Earth;
It gobbles and gobbles
And never seems to tire.

But every time the Heat is too great
        It bursts,
And the things she has eaten
Creep upward from the bottom of her huge stomach

But when Heat has gone away
Nature has repaired Earth's stomach
And again she starts to
        Gobble, gobble, gobble!

One must not here bring up the question of poetry. From an educational standpoint we are interested solely in the persistence of an individual language, in its adequacy for the child's purpose, and in the child's demand that it shall be a secret from "everybody in the world-full-of-people."

III

I had taken upon myself to find that lost personal voice of childhood in the eighth grade, but Nell C. Curtis was finding it abundantly in the third grade. Hardly a day passed in those early years that we did not contrive meetings to show each other this and that discovery of the strange, powerful speech which children rarely disclose to others but which they have "under their voice," as Hilda tells us so unerringly, "a secret from everybody in the world-full-of-people."

But one day she met me with disconsolate brows. I believe she had just come from an informal conference of teachers and parents. We walked along the halls in silence until she said with a kind of mournful humor, "They have called me — a gifted teacher!" It was an accusation, and she took it indignantly, as she knew I would. That is the excuse they give for not finding what we experience daily. "Gifted teacher" always ended the argument, we knew, and sent them back with renewed strength to their everlasting struggle to make inartistic and conventional adults out of children. We hated the phrase.

"I want you to come with me," she said firmly, "right

now; I am going into the third grade for about thirty minutes. I want you to stay with me and watch me, to see," she smiled, "if I have anything up my sleeve, any 'trick' that anyone else couldn't have."

I agreed to go and to watch. She turned to say at the door, "Thanksgiving will soon be here. They may tell me about it — in their own way; and, if they do tell me, it will be good — because their own way is always good."

She walked in thoughtfully but did not once eye the class professionally or call it to attention. She seemed really to be looking out of the window while, musingly, she let fall the word Thanksgiving.

Then she wondered — really wondered — as if to herself, what she, Nell Curtis, should be thankful for. It was so well done, the simulation of genuine inquiry — so different from the conventional mastery of a class by means of the drawingout question — that it took me completely off guard, stopped me in the awkward position in front of the group, where I had not meant to stay, and set my mind wondering, too; while one could almost feel the thinking going on in the little bodies before us.

Then she just said nothing at all, while she continued to gaze thoughtfully at the bare trees and grassy hummocks of Morningside Park. With the children who knew her she was not afraid of silence; rather she comprehended its great value for little bodies. They thought slowly; and, so great was the spell of the moment, I thought, too.

I was thinking, I remember, how thankful I was that at last I had reached the age when I could afford to be honest with my own thinking — when a boy spoke thoughtfully "under his voice"; and another followed, and another.

They were not using the accustomed classroom speech, I noted instantly, that high-pitched monotone of children reciting before other children. They were conversing in the low, contented, slow-measured syllables of self-communion. Miss Curtis could do that to children; cause them to lose the conventional pose of being other than themselves — if that be a gift, make the most of it! — but I hasten to say that even she could not do it at the first meeting. Many previous hours had gone to make them accustomed to her; little by little, as she accepted (and so approved) the voice of their secret and seldom-heard personality, they lost their fears of alien standards, strengthened the deep feeling of contentment with their own sure ways of speech. And then one day, as on this day, her casual appearance in the room would be a sign for the shy self to speak out.

She had moved so shadow-like to the blackboard that no one was disturbed; they continued to speak on slowly with easy long silences in between, while, with her back to them, she scribbled an illegible shorthand of her own.

During the fifteen minutes or so that followed she hardly ever turned to face them. Once she grimaced over her arm to me, a brave attempt, I guessed, judging from my own feeling, to stay unaccountable tears; and then I turned my back, too, for those mites would never understand how the simple beauty of their speech could affect us olders.

A whirr of buzzers off somewhere in the school, and she stopped and moved quietly away from the board. "I shall need guards," she said. Two girls came forward understandingly and stood beside the welter of unintelligible chalk marks. In another moment someone appeared at the door and the class filed out for the roof playground. The guards produced apples and munched them; they knew they were to keep watch over the blackboard until Miss Curtis could have time to get a notebook and make a complete copy.

The next day, according to agreement, I went in to watch for "tricks." In clear manuscript writing Miss Curtis had placed all their statements on the board, naming the author in each case. Among repetitions they proceeded to choose the best; decided which should be combined with others; elided and amended here and there. Hardly a word from Miss Curtis. In an exercise in taste she was not one to impose judgment. I wish I had space to record their quiet acquiescence or cool disagreement and final compromise.

Eventually it became the following Hymn of Thanksgiving. The phrases are the work of children unaided by adult suggestion but, on account of time, the parts that belonged naturally together were combined and grouped by

Miss Curtis and two other teachers, the whole being used by the third grade as their contribution to the Thanksgiving Assembly.

A HYMN OF THANKSGIVING

I

We give thanks for the beautiful country that lies around us
We give thanks for the grains and vegetables and fruits
    prepared for us
And we give thanks for the growing trees and flowers about us

II

We give thanks for the rain that falls and the sun that
    shines down upon us
We thank God for the mountains that tower above and for
    the rocks that give us shelter and beauty
We give thanks for the sky above us and the earth below us
    and the birds that fly between earth and sky

III

We give thanks for the cloth to make sails and the wood to
    make boats that sail on the water
We give thanks for the little streams that flow
We give thanks for the tide that rises and lets us go out in
    our boats
We give thanks for the sea with fishes in it
We thank God for all the living creatures on the earth

IV

We give thanks for the fire that warms us
We give thanks for warm clothes and beds and houses to live in
We give thanks for the schools to learn in

V

We give thanks for the beauty and love all around us
We give thanks for all the things that the Lord has set
    upon the earth

A week or so later, in the elementary school Thanksgiving Assembly, two tall candles burned at each end of the curtained stage, otherwise bare of ornament; a selected group from the third grade came up one by one and told us these their own words of thankfulness. It was powerfully effective, religious, if you will.

IV

Childhood will have no difficulty with literature if it has a chance to develop its own native gifts in language. This, of course, is not the whole story, but it is one of its most important chapters.

CHAPTER VIII

Confessions

A YOUNG MOTHER HAD been driving me to the station each afternoon following the lecture, but while she admitted having a boy of five she contributed nothing about him. It was obvious to me that she had little else in the vivid undercurrent of her mind but the daily manifestations of the wonder and the power and the mystery of him; but she was a young mother and proud; she would not be classified as one who thought much of her own. The fear of the consequences of exposing her love was in her careful eyes, for she was intelligent and knew all about the illusions of motherhood.

Then one day she grew less guardful, sensing in me, I hope, a trusting spirit, and said, slowly and watchfully, ready to withdraw all confidence at the slightest false move from me, "Of course my boy says things. And now that you are advising us to copy them down . . . Well, here's something he said last night, just before he went to bed."

With interest I listened to the delicate phrases; it was the authentic language of the spirit. She glowed as I quietly talked of the perfection of the thing: there was not a word that one would wish to change or to omit; it had all the marvelous economy in the use of material and the swift impact of the sure artist. Before her I recopied the words, placing them in the irregular lining of free verse. "For it is poetry," I said.

The word with all its masterful associations thrilled her, as I knew it would, but she kept to her mood of smiling indifference. "Poetry!" She laughed softly. "But it doesn't rhyme."

"Oh!" I affected surprise. "Are you one of those who believe that poetry should rhyme? Don't you know that rhyme was invented only day before yesterday, as the centuries go; and only by a thoroughly sophisticated people who had arrived at an advanced intelligence? For thousands of years the races of mankind gave forth their finest utterance in the powerful medium that this lad uses so naturally. The Psalms of David are written in the poetry of the ages. Rhyme is a marvelous but unnecessary ornament; a great thing, no mistake, when done by expert artists, but a weak thing and an obstruction of the spirit oftentimes in the hands of any but the technician."

At another time she showed me others, among them these intimate lines,

> Do you know what the stars are, Mother?
> They're the lights God puts out
> So I won't be afraid
> Of the dark

"He told me that just before he went to sleep," she confided.

By this time we were well acquainted. "That's when they all do it," said I, making playful fun of her absorbing interest. "Just before they go to sleep. And that is your hour, my fine young mother. Now you have him. You will know it because he communicates to you his most precious thinkings. But you will not always have him, unless you are very, very guardful of your present possession. Boys and girls slip slowly but surely away. The boys are gone at eight often; the girls may linger on until ten. They must be off to their own affairs, the boy to take on the compelling man-things, the girl to her own individual privacies of womanhood. Mothers should prepare for this from the beginning and accept it, for it is the way of nature. But he is yours now. At the hour of going to sleep. When he ceases to share his inmost imaginings with you, then you will know he has gone."

We talked of this, she a little fearful and not wholly believing. I did not frighten her with too much of the truth, but I was thinking of mothers unaware that their little sons and daughters had already slipped away. I have watched them at times when an unreasoning fear would seize them; they would draw the little boy quickly to them, press cheek to cheek and whisper, "You still love Mother, don't you, darling?"

In half wonder at the truth, but not even admitting it to the upper surface of consciousness, the lad would struggle and give up. "Yes, Mother," he would say, a phrase without feeling.

"Then kiss Mother," she would beg.

Dutifully I have seen him perform the unintelligible ceremony and, released from the mad pressure, rush away to the real affairs of his own life. Love, alas, may not be compelled, and youth may not be stayed.

Having gone so far I am under obligation at this point to warn mothers against a misinterpretation of this matter of securing the confidences of their children. I would give much to be able to shirk my duty here, for what I am now about to say will be resented with all the fierce resistance to facts by which nature has mysteriously endowed motherhood. My obligation, however, is not to mothers but to children. I would save them from the devitalization, physical, mental, and spiritual, that always follows when strong mothers give over their whole lives to the greedy possessing of their offspring. The story of *The Silver Cord* is alarmingly common.

Boys and girls must live their own independent lives. It is right and morally important that they should. She who interferes with that right unduly is wronging her own. Opportunity, of course, should be given for the confessional relationship, but it must never be forced; nor must one pry for the sake solely of one's own personal enjoyment. My fear is that in presenting this method of keeping a healthy relationship between mother and child I may be simply putting a weapon into the hands of those who would sacrifice their own for the orgy of selfish and unbridled mothering. I know too well the devastating effect of their work upon the whole existence of their children.

It gives me a kind of horror when I think of their creep-

ing in at the bedtime hour and, possibly because of my revelations here, subtilely coaxing confidences. It is a relief to
feel that I may be making some amends by writing these
two disagreeable paragraphs, and I hasten to close this part
of the subject.

Needless to say, I must add, that this topic did not come
up at all in our conversation with the mother of the little
poet; she was too well schooled in modern thought to require it; her danger could easily be that she might, because
of her superior knowledge of the subject, swing to the extreme of aloofness and avoidance of intimacy.

There are mothers, I told her, who keep their own through
life. The little sure links of confidences have been forged
and strengthened during the years, so that in manhood and
in womanhood those children still come back to gain once
again the strength of spirit which may be had only from
those who enter without conflict or indifference into the
region of their private living. These are the mothers who
reserve the hour of confidence as one into which neither chiding, nor admonition, nor even teaching, is ever allowed to
enter; and at no time, though their own soul cry out for
relief, do they refuse the listening ear.

I reread the lines. "What do you think of them?" I asked.
"They are beautiful, of course," she returned.
"Is that all?"
"They are poetry, I suppose."
"Oh, yes, they are that," I said. "They quite satisfy my
notion of poetry. But they are something else; and you,
his mother, do not know it?"
"What is it his mother doesn't know?"
"He is confessing something to you," I said. "He is too
much of a proud man to admit in other language that he is
afraid of the dark. If you asked him about it — and you
must not, if you wish to preserve these confidences — he
would probably deny it. But he is telling you, just the same.
When he speaks thus in his native language it is important.
Some children pass through this fear without harm; to others
it is a memory that persists to defeat them later in life. So
if he needs you near just now, your voice in the next room

or a distant light for protection, see to it. But — if you wish him to stay with you a little longer — you must do it without comment or the slightest sign of knowledge that he has told you."

II

Children's art at its best is always something in the nature of a confession; it admits one instantly into the privacy of personal thinking and feeling. Most good art is confessional, I suspect; therefore it fails when it imitates or poses or attempts concealment. The child knows that his world — the world of home and the world of school — gives its praise to imitation and to posing-as-someone-other-than-self, and he discovers early that it is best to conceal.

Wherever creative work with children flourishes I seek the one who has opened up communication with them on the side of their secret unexpressed selves. She is usually a person who has no objections to anything that children tell her seriously; so she gets nearer and nearer to them, as one might become acquainted with birds; and as the communications develop into confessions she secures the astonishing results that are so often called gifts.

Much of this material may not be printed or exposed in any way. How often even among senior high-school pupils have I received sealed documents marked, "Private! Not to be shown to a soul!" Here is a conflict with the usual school requirements which presume that not only will the pupil's work be exposed but that it is a proper object of public criticism. If the creative life is to have its legitimate sustenance, it must be permitted at times to graze in its own private grounds. A confidence cannot be shouted to the crowd; and the first important creative activities of youth are confidential and confessional.

Even with the communicating doors open the ultimate in self-expression, using the word literally, will never come through. Rather, it seems that there are grades of intimacy, each more intimate than the last — and each with its own language — and that beyond the last are others that must forever remain inarticulate. In my own close relationship with pupils I was forever coming upon astonishing material that had not been shown to me at all: a verse sequence made for a birthday present to a chum; a book of love poems, too personal, of course, for anyone but the other one; and all that type of writing that comes under the heading of diary and commonplace books of private reflections. Sometimes this material would be no different, seemingly, from that which had been shown without hesitation to others, but to the authors there was a tragic difference which one was bound to respect.

III

Probing the depths in this way for the good ore that always lies far beneath the surface, one is always facing possible dangers. The laws of the hidden are never to be quite understood. A confidence may beget distrust, or it may arouse lasting remorse. One of the pictures I should like to forget is that of a sorrow of a youngster of six, which, in spite of our best endeavors, remained with her a frightening experience for months, and only because we had printed her name beside her tiny verses!

The value of my collections of creative activity is due, in my judgment, to the fact that they are not imitations; they have their firm root in the inimitable personal life. About each one I could tell a confidential story. By this time I have learned better to sort out the spurious from the real; and, while so learning, I have come upon personal experiences that make me aware of the delicate nature of the search.

One of the best poems I have ever found in these adventures came to me not from the author at all but in a copy sent in a letter to one of her dear friends. However, I believed I had her approval to print, but the outcome was more serious than I may explain here.

The stunning power of the poem, its swift direct recital of a story, unlike anything that had been told in the world before, made me know that I had come upon a rich find. One may guess that by this time I had taken on a collector's zeal in searching for new revelations of the creative spirit, the which I may use as an excuse for any mistake I may have made in handling the volatile material. In my excitement when I encountered the young woman in the halls the next day I talked of the remarkable character of the discovery and neglected to watch the effect of my words upon the real owner.

She was silent while I talked. She said only, "You liked it?"

My sincere praise did not seem to affect her, which was not strange because she, above others of her age, was gifted with poise and control. But she was moved finally to say, by my warmth possibly, "It seems not my own . . . and yet I know it is all of me. It was written in the night after I had awakened suddenly; it was written rapidly and without consideration; then I went swiftly to sleep. There was little change to be made in the morning. I cannot get over the strangeness of it."

I assured her that while it was not common the phenomenon was known. I told her of instances of the same sort of writing which I had in my collection. "The spirit is communicating without the trammels of everyday living, I suspect. Perhaps that is why the effect is so striking; it is the self speaking and revealing itself."

"It is just that," she said. "I know."

I spoke of printing it.

She looked at me in astonishment, but I was stupid enough to take that steady gaze for acquiescence, especially when she said slowly, "I leave that to your judgment," and turned abruptly away.

In a few weeks the magazine came out with the poem. I still think that because of that contribution it represented one of the highest achievements of our adventure in creative writing. But she was there in the hall to greet me with, "You printed it!" Amazement and indignation were blazing upon her face. "I did not think it of you," she said simply but with a finality that was stabbing.

Before I could say much in my bewildered defense she told me that of course she would have to leave the school.

That gave me a chance to collect myself. "Wait," I said. "I do not comprehend a single thing you are telling me except your evident distress. But believe me when I tell you that it has no foundation whatever in any existing fact.

Why, I remember now; you yourself agreed that I should print it! You said —" I searched my memory — "right on this spot you said, 'Use your own judgment.' "

"I thought you had judgment," was the reply I shall not easily forget. "But it is done, and I must go away."

"Go away for a few days if you wish." I tried to calm her. "And then let us see if what I predict will not happen. These powerful verses may have some source in your experience which you fancy is apparent to every reader. You think they give you away. Well, they simply do not. I have been reading them almost every day for weeks, and I have no notion of their personal application to you or to anyone else."

She was incredulous. I talked on to cover her diminishing fears.

"I know nothing except the marvelous impersonal story you tell us here on these pages. Don't you know that that is the way of all really fine art work? Personal suffering is often the source but the product itself is a thing of art, free from even the touch of its secret origin, a universal thing, and all the more precious because it was wrought out of blood and nerve. Go away for a day or so if you wish, but believe me when I tell you that you will find this whole community ready to welcome you back. You have achieved a supreme victory in the art we have all learned to love and respect."

To this day I do not know what the suppressions were that found their outlet in those remarkable lines; and I doubt if any reader has even thought to guess. She was soon reconciled to the belief that her secret, whatever it was, had been safely kept, for she watched my predictions come true and had the unique satisfaction of the maker of verses in seeing her work a loved thing in the hearts of others.

A year or two later, just before graduation, the seniors had voted that her poem *You Stand on a Mountain* should be printed in the Class Record to represent one of the best creative efforts of the group. I came by when she was absorbed in reading the galley proof.

"So you are printing it," I taunted her; "and not so long ago you were scolding me for doing that very same thing."

"Oh," she looked up smiling and waved a hand off airily, "that was when I was a *very* little girl!"

Her calm pride in the verse as she bent to her task proved to me that she had at last acquired the protective armor of the accomplished artist. We may create our work, verse, painting, or whatever the media, out of secret experience, but none may know the source when the product is impersonal and universally valid.

Hundreds later have admired those youthful lines and have accepted them as a satisfactory imaginative picture of the unattainable ideals of human kind. (In our maturer years we gain courage from our discovery that the vision and the striving are all-important and in themselves necessary and sufficient; they pay their own peculiar awards.) But there is more to the poem than just that prosaic summary; the mysterious voices of the spirit are often beyond the full comprehension of even the artist who expresses them.

The poem could be improved, no doubt, by a small amount of editorial pruning but I prefer to present it here as she wrote it and loved it.

YOU STAND ON A MOUNTAIN

You stand on a mountain.
Behind you the sun rises earlier each morning
Because it cannot wait to worship you.

You are outlined against the brightest light that men can know
And you shine brighter still.
The glory that men need
Can only lightly touch your golden hair,
Bring clearer into view
The straight, strong, supple grace
The tiger's quickness, and the gentleness
Of a yearling buck in your limbs.

Humbly, adoringly, the sun passes over your glorious head
And when at last she must leave you for the night to love
She sends her loveliest light to where you stand;
And the rays of red gold
Deepen the steadfast purpose in your eyes
Warm and strengthen even more
The quickness and keenness of your mind
And make the mystery of your heart
More unfathomable still.

And you stand on your mountain and look out, always out
Over the towns and Cathedral spires
To where the sea is tearing at the land
Impatient to kiss your feet;
When at last it reaches its goal
You will still be there to welcome it,
For you are changeless.

Sometimes you look up toward Heaven,
It is not very far from you,
And the inhabitants of the Holy City
Lean over the wall of pearl and call to you.
Sometimes you will look to your side
Where a wild bird will nestle on your shoulder
Or a doe with her fawns
Will nibble unafraid at your hand
And always find friendship and protection there.

But you never look down
For I am there, kneeling at the foot of your mountain.
From my heart springs a never ending flow of clear water
And I catch it in a crystal bowl
And hold it up to you
Until your radiance has absorbed it.

Then I fill the bowl again.
Day after day, year after year, I have knelt there
Looking up through the dark pines on the mountain.
I cannot see you. But the forest is never dark to me
And the mountain is never unfriendly
Because I know you are at the top.
Aeon after aeon I shall kneel there
Offering to you my never ending flow of living water
And you will always accept it.

Perhaps I shall wonder, sometimes,
Whether, if my offerings ceased,
Your beauty, your radiance would fade.
But I know that they will never cease
And that your beauty is a changeless thing:
So in an aeon or two I shall wonder no more
And only hold my bowl more steadily toward you.

Some day a traveler will pass through the glade where I kneel;
He will ask for a bowl of my water,
Which is all any man would ask for,
And I will smile and shake my head.
He will beg for a little sip of it,
For no other water will quench his thirst.
But no; he must go away with dry tongue,
For my heart-spring will at last be dry;
You, who stand on a mountain, have taken it all.

The line of communication opened by a sharing of the fruits of the creative life brings one into a storm area hidden serenely from the outside world. One gets to know, after a longish experience, to read some of the barometric signs: to know, for instance, that a smiling face may be a perfect mask of defense for defeat within, for despair even; that anger is not always the proof of indignation but of suppressed love, rather; that arrogant self-sufficiency may be woefully weak and timid within. One comes upon a child psychology that just never has been put in the books, where yawning may not be a sign of sleepiness at all but of alert and fearful aniety (at the critical moment of a tight basketball game, for instance), where nonchalance may cover a crime and where blushing may be the outcome of innocence.

After a period spent in my room — the class had been singing original airs most lustily — my supervisor asked, "What subject of study *do* you teach, pray?" My answer, given jocosely at the time, is, I believe, the right one: "I teach no subject of study," I said; "I practice psychiatry." Perhaps I have been helped to my viewpoint about child life by the fact that for nearly two years, as military psychologist, I walked the psychiatric wards under the daily instruction of Arthur Herring.

Let me say swiftly, so as not to stress the matter to the point of alarm, that when one has come many times upon these concealed storms and has seen the occasional tragic outcome, or the determined attempt at tragedy, one learns to take with the utmost seriousness any disproportionate dramatization of life-affairs which is bringing suffering or distress to a child, and to count oneself lucky to have found out about it in time. Psychiatry here is of great help, for its first business is to gain the confidence of the sufferer by complete sympathy and understanding, then, slowly and adroitly, to show the relationship of the tiny causing incident to the whole of life, its place in the scheme of the common troubles of man, to belittle it, in short, and so take away its importance.

IV

The psychiatrist learns from cases as all good practitioners do. There is much to be discovered about the ways of life and living which is not yet down in the books! In everything that concerns human relations, from taxation to social welfare, we are coming down to cases. How children react and grow under given conditions is discovered, not by studying books, but by studying actual children. The book psychologist and the book sociologist are almost in the position of the physician who never had a patient — or whose patients have all died! Though he write a textbook on the learning process or on "the sociological reactions of the herd in preadolescent groups," to quote the title of an astonishing bit of recent nonsense, his word is not taken so seriously as in yesteryear.

The practice of education is something to be observed and recorded; and only long and fruitful experience in a free school environment may give one the skill to observe and record usefully. And the educational environment is changing so rapidly in these happy times that a five-year absence even — in, let us say, the business of administration — may unfit a person for understanding the wise observations and recordings of those who really know.

The sure sign of ignorance in this important matter — a notable defense reaction of the ignorant — is to announce, apropos of some exciting revelations of the new creative education, that one does not believe in permitting children to "do what they please." To those who know what is really happening in the newer practice of setting free creative powers, that remark is most disheartening. For just nothing can be done about it. The man who talks like that confesses that he does not know what is going on, what, indeed, has been going on in child education for twenty-five years or

more; and further more he will never know. When he occupies a high and safe administrative post, it is torture, alas,
and daily frustration for those who see the light but are condemned to work under him who so confidently walks in
darkness. Oh, so confidently!

My prophecy is that our successes will come mainly
through those who know cases, who do the work with children themselves, the authorities in the field, or through
those who watch wisely and have eyes to see and mind to
comprehend the educational significance of the work when
it is well done.

V

Illustrative cases from my own notes beg for admittance
here, but my difficulty is so to disguise the picture as to preserve the privacy of the individual.

A play was in rehearsal, just a fairy tale of a princess
and her lords and ladies. It was moving along in stilted
fashion, comically clumsy and awkward to those of us who
were sitting in the darkened empty theater; but at one
moment, in a procession about the throne, the bobbing
clown swung to the front and delighted all by his panto-
mimic fooling.

The stupid rehearsal came alive for just that moment;
everyone felt it, the few of us who were directing the performance and the players themselves; the latter indeed,
took on life immediately and really lived, for a flashing minute, in the stately and graceful years of Long Ago. The
princess turned as she mounted the three steps of her throne
and smiled, itself an illuminating thing. Motionless the
clown bathed in that royal approval, then with a few swift
steps, still droll and in character, he moved forward, bent the
knee before her, and raised his face in loyal adoration.

In the few seconds of silence that followed I said quietly,
"Boy, that was *fine!*"

The rehearsal went on. Nothing else happened save the
dull, lifeless movement of players walking through parts
and stating their unbelievable lines.

Nearly everyone had left when one of our group said,

"There is someone over there in the dark on those benches, a boy, and he is sobbing his heart out." In a second I was there. It was the clown; but he fled at my approach. I followed him back stage and down a black stairway to the vault under the stage, the storehouse of props and theatric odds and ends. There I found him lying on a pile of discarded costumes and burlap rags, in the pitiful agony of unsuppressed weeping. An electric light burned dimly above us.

For a long time I stood over him in silence. Once I said, "Have it out, old fellow. Things like that we all have to get out of our systems somehow or other. I don't know why. But we all do it. You wouldn't believe it, maybe, but grown men go through it. Only they wouldn't own up. There are times when I have done the same thing. And not so long ago either. But I'd never admit it to anybody else. It comes sometimes when you are quite happy, too. Funny thing. I've gone off somewhere and cried my head off. Then I felt better. Everybody does it, I guess."

This is again the psychiatric approach. You confess to the same weakness yourself, and thereby prove that it is quite normal and to be expected. Nothing, you see, to be much alarmed about.

When the paroxysm began to die down I said musingly, as if talking to myself, "I've been wondering what caused it, and, by George, I think I've guessed it! Do you know yourself? Try to think. It often comes from the absurdest things. You tell me your guess and then I'll tell you mine. . . . I bet I've got it!"

After a quiet moment he said, "It was when you praised me."

"Right!" I cried. "That's just my guess, too! Now isn't that a funny one: If I'd gone for you hard you might expect something, but praise! Life is just the funniest thing that ever happened."

"That knocked me out," he said. "I'd 'a' been all right if it hadn't 'a' been for that."

Psychiatrists speak of this breaking up as the "crash." Bad treatment may bring it on; in this instance it had come because of sudden and unexpected approval.

We managed to have a laugh or two as we sprawled together on that mound of smelly rags. He told me of misunderstandings, of the attempt to find his place, of a desire to be sporting and no whimperer, of failure. "They always choose me to be the clown," he said. "Elected unanimously. Always. ... When I ask a question in class, they laugh. And then I laugh as if it *was* funny. When I propose something, or have an idea about anything, they laugh. And, of course, I act up then and pretend. I'm supposed to be a funny man. Sometimes they laugh when I get up to recite, before I've said anything. And I grin and play the fool, just — to fool them. Teachers send me from the room — for being funny!" He almost broke down again; and then came this astonishing and pathetic revelation, "And I was never funny in my life!"

Here was the supreme wit of the school, the keenly intelligent satirist, the lad with the swift ironic tongue; why, he had already made an enviable reputation; teachers and pupils alike admired him for his native qualities of humor. And in his own mind he had never been funny in his life! Every laugh had been a misinterpretation of his serious desire. They name him clown as an honor, and it nearly breaks his heart! His funny faces, his inimitable gestures, his devastating quips, all were bluff, a defense reaction purely! Unbelievable, but indubitably the fact.

We talked about that. And as we talked his old spirit came back. Again and again he started a laugh. "Boy," I said, "you *are* a funny man! You are the darnedest funniest man I've ever come across! You've got a great gift and don't know it! It's so easy for you, but you don't realize how rare it is in the world and how the world yearns for it. Don't despise it, for you have the great companion gifts, without which humor is just folly: you have seriousness and nimble intelligence. That pair, matched with humor, will win the world for you. I'll lay my little bet here, at any odds you choose, that it will be your serious intelligent wit that will open the hard doors of the world for you."

A problem might be set here for those who are desirous of learning the next step, clearly indicated in this case. Consider it, then, before I give the answer that worked. It was already tentatively formulated before our interview had ended.

It was to search carefully for some product of his that would not only be serious and intelligent but which would bring from others, particularly his own age-group, the reward of approval. In a little while it came, a quatrain of striking individuality. I pounced upon it with my praise and soon got others admiring. More came; and more; eventually a new reputation was made for him. Later I saw him a leader in the magazine group; the upper school had received him as an equal, the under school was giving him the deference due to acknowledge superiority. And *then* how his native humor bloomed!

His four simple lines gave a pleasant and unusual picture to carry in one's mind but they illustrated also a vast symbolic truth of which the boy was not wholly aware, from timid youth facing the dark future, to the fearful situation of humanity itself in its "lonely, rocking darkness of the night". To be sensitive to such unconscious symbolism is part of the necessary equipment of the successful guide. Superior literature abounds with it; no good art can exist without it. Here is that quatrain:

LANTERNS

Oh, smoky lantern with your unwashed chimney
As you sway in halting rhythm
To the jolting of the wagon
In your lonely, rocking darkness of the night.

CHAPTER IX

The Play's the Thing

ALL THE ARTS COMBINE in the theatre, decor, the dance, impersonation, effective speech, the song, pantomime, the projection of personality, the art of suppressing self, and even ill will, for the sake of unity of effort. Hundreds of other arts could be listed including the art of living together and the art of creative imagination. That is why the play can never be omitted from child education.

With young children the most obvious outcome of dramatization is a releasing of good natural powers hitherto suppressed or unexplored and therefore lost possibly forever. In a simple dance an awkward, undistinguished girl becomes transformed into a personality of charm, like caterpillar to butterfly; and she may remain permanently the well-poised, airy creature. Even a boy with hesitant speech, under the releasing power of the play, may break down the inhibitions of years.

This will be telling nothing new to the children's theatre group nor to those of us who have used these possible transformations in appearance and in behavior for planned educational purpose. In even the very young players, we have observed, new vision is added to interpret the world of people, and — this is not so generally known, I think — it is always on the side of the good. The fine playing of even an evil role can be done only by those who are at the same time indwardly repudiating evil. We know, if others do not, that the play, better than precept, establishes permanently an allegiance to the moral life.

Before writing and other engagements took up my spare time the play was always a part of my educational program. My superiors thought, no doubt — one of them brought me sternly to account — that those hours after school were a frivolous waste of energy, but I noted early that the enthusiastic communion stirred up in shaping an idea into a living dramatic presentation broke down the barrier always present when the young and the old confront each other in an education program.

What I had to teach in the classroom became, therefore, more acceptable. In my younger days I have taught grammar, cube root, Latin, Philosophy, and a dozen varieties of pedagogics but always with the unique advantage of possessing that camaraderie of my student fellow players. Any teacher who, for the love of it, takes charge of outside sports or other extra-curricular activities, knows about the value of these personal relationships. It is an element of teacher power and teacher influence that should be more publicly stressed.

Of course my notion of the play as a fruitful educational implement was strengthened by my own experience, years before, as player and producer of plays in the days and nights I had toiled *con amore* as a member of *Plays and Players* in Philadelphia. We had a snug playhouse of our own and a select and stimulating audience of non-playing members. Often we rehearsed all night on a Saturday, stopping only at dawn for a breakfast of coffee and buns, to go on rehearsing the better part of Sunday. Sometimes we performed outside our clubhouse in a regular theater for the benefit of some local charity or we would go off gaily with our repertory to out of town stages. As our small family of three often played together I can recall fewer happier moments.

The consequences, however, not at all appreciated at the time, gave me an important part of my professional equipment, for, in teaching youth later, the dramatic performance became a natural accompaniment of my educational program. It was then that I discovered that the best plays for us were those that all of us working together had invented ourselves.

For example, I started out one group of older youth with a simple idea, the psychological discovery of the time, that everything that one did or said held deep implicit if unconscious meaning. A professor of the new psychology was needed. An older looking lad took naturally to the part. As a beginning I contributed a verse of my own, a quatrain of pure nonsense; the professor was invited to disclose its hidden meaning. He did. With others contributing he showed that it had significance that touched a dozen of our concealed aspirations amatory and otherwise, mostly amatory. My job was largely as editor and censor. The outcome was a local amateur hit.

Even after many performances the script was still changing and developing into a superior unity. And those young persons were developing, too, and they knew it. They loved the success of our cooperative invention. Within themselves they were discovering new and undreamed of capacities. Also it was undoubtedly a learning experience for their teacher; my future work in education was pointed here, although I was not aware of it at the time.

Another amusing and curious outcome was that my nonsense quatrain, which started the whole thing, got into print in Franklin P. Adams' famous *Conning Tower* and thence traveled, by continuous quotings, literally around the world. This was many years before Bernie Hannighen turned it into a song hit as *The Little Man Who Wasn't There*. You may have read those four lines somewhere:

> As I was going up the stair
> I met a man who wasn't there
> He wasn't there again today —
> I wish, I *wish*, he'd stay away

The technique of these group playlets became standard with us for many years later. We called them Impromptu Plays. When asked by a visitor one day why they were so named, a young wag in the company explained with mock seriousness, "Because nobody prompts you."

One illustration from a senior high school group much later will show the almost miraculous power of the play in bringing out unguessed gifts. As we prepared in November to start a possible Christmas offering for the upper school some girls had whispered to me amid excited giggles, "Get

Anna to do her dance!" Serious protests from Anna. "She does it up in the girls' locker," they confided. "It's a scream!" Anna's half-frightened denial made me cautious but I did whisper back, "Let's go down to the assembly room after school and try it out." In the midst of all those free young persons Anna had always seemed to me to shrink shyly into nothingness. "There'll be nobody else but us?" she begged. I agreed and she insisted upon girl monitors at the doors. "So no boys will see," she explained. A girl friend was pulled along to perform at the piano.

Anna's notion was that she was presenting a take off of the modern dance of Martha Graham, Hanya Holm and others to whch she had dutifully gone with her elders, but what she gave us was not a caricature at all but something of her very own, youth released in rigidly controlled action, swift changes of movement, beauty in motion. Her previously subdued figure loosened and extended itself. I had thought she was small. Before me as the music rippled, she seemed to grow in height.

At the end when she came down stage in excited laughter I waited and then said, "Anna, you were wonderful! This is not at all a mere take off of the modern dance but something of your own, gay, careless, yet marvelously refreshing. Let's do more."

As the rehearsals continued Anna, by general agreement, was given the spot of climax. The boys gathered around her, helped to spangle her gown with Christmas tree ornaments, and voted her tops in the show.

Some weeks later when I saw her, erect and confident, amid a group of admiring youngsters I spoke quietly to a leader among the older boys. "Anna is beautiful, isn't she?" He agreed. "I had hardly noticed her before," I said, "she was so obviously shy and withdrawn. How do you account for it?" I asked. "The dance did it," he replied quickly. "She became somebody after that play."

Of course this is education. What else? You would not find it named in the usual curricula but it is a worthy outcome of the opportunity offered for encouraged self-expression; a person, hitherto withdrawn and seemingly defeated, sloughs off suddenly the gaucheries of youth and becomes mature ever after in step, posture, and speech.

Whenever I have met stern rebuke from well-meaning but unimaginative colleagues because, as they say, I have been wasting my hours in these frivolous ventures with youth, I think to myself, "If when you were a youngster I could have had you in one good play and could have gradually unloosed the traditional cords that at present so hopelessly bind you, you would now be more sensitive, more appreciative, and more tolerant toward what we are doing with the young." Just to be — really *be* — another person in an undistinguished play is to make one immeasurably free forever. For some of my stern friends, however, just one play would not be nearly enough.

CHAPTER X

The Demon of Inhibition

POETRY HAD BROKEN LOOSE IN Caroline Zachry's junior high school classes. It was something more than a classroom assignment guided by a successful teacher; it was a spontaneous and genuine poetic outburst which really seized the interest of everyone. Of course Miss Zachry had laid the long train whose premeditated outcome was this very general explosion. The poetry crop had suddenly burst into bloom; a mimeographed magazine appeared; business managers and editors assumed command. Every member of the junior high school seemed suddenly bitten with the virus of serious poetic composition.

Almost every member. One keen lad remained aloof. With detached humor, noting the excitement about him, he scribbled the first nonsense that came into his head, copied it carefully and presented it to the youthful editors. To his secret glee they read it and accepted it with enormous seriousness, and the lad went off to have his private laugh.

We learned the detals later, so that I should not omit the fact that he had worked a long while over his first rough draft, twisting and turning it this way and that to bring out its delicious silliness; it was really in his mind for several days before he was ready to let it go as a perfected hoax.

On the day the mimeographed magazine came out he watched the absorbed readers. The joke would be on the self-consequential editors this time. In a moment or two, he thought, someone would read his stuff, look up, and laugh. They read, but they did not laugh. They read and they looked over at him, but their glances and their clatter of speech were all of approval for the fine poem he had written!

"One of the best things the class has done," was the general verdict. And the teacher agreed with them!

Again he had his private laugh. The joke was now on all of them. Including Miss Zachary. Why, he had scribbled away with hardly a thought in his mind. Poetry! They didn't know the difference between poetry and hash. This whole poetry craze was pure bunk. Oh, listen to them gush! (We heard all these arguments from him later.) He "had" them and he could prove it now (I believe he had admitted one boy into the conspiracy to use as a witness); but their excited admiration of his work was too serious to give him an immediate chance. In fact, they took his first protestations as just silly modesty and shut him up.

He read the so-called poem over to himself. He could hardly conceal his desire to laugh in their faces. It had practically no meaning at all! But as the days went by he had to listen to parts that began to be quoted on all sides, lines that readers had relished and must say aloud over and over. One phrase in particular gave great satisfaction; it was repeated openly in the halls as the class skipped along and it was whispered secretly in many a recitation room:

> Tum . . . tum . . . tum . . .
> On the back of a hollow bamboo drum.

The poem tells the story of Akib, King of Egypt's son, who

> Lay by the river Do Dum Dun,
> Lay on the gray-green sands
> Of Egypt land,
> On Egypt's gray-green sand.

As he lazily stretched himself out beneath the oily palm, Akib hummed

> . . . a song to the Ukeadahm
> Till he fell asleep, in the middle of June,
> Singing away to the crocodile's tune,
> To the tune of the ugly crocodile,
> As it beat its tail in the river Nile,
> Tum . . . tum . . . tum . . .
> On the back of a hollow bamboo drum.

Then follows Akib's dream of the Ukeadahm coming "with stealthy steps and cautious looks, washing his face

in the cool of the brooks," . . . "crushing the soil and mash-
ing the sod"

> As he sifted the grains through his hoof-like hand,
> Sifting the grains
> To the wind that blew over Egypt land.

And Akib, the sleeping King of Egypt's son, dreamed that
the moon broke out in the sky above

> . . . and tossed about
> Like a ship on the sea in the trough of the storm,
> Fighting the waves as the night went on;
> And he saw the moon shiver at the crocodile
> As it thumped its tail in the river Nile,
> Tum . . . Tum . . . Tum . . .
> On the back of a hollow bamboo drum.

Those who are interested enough to follow the mysteriously uncanny story may find the whole poem in *Creative
Youth*. It has taken the fancy of many other boys and girls;
they see in it the free play of an astonishingly vivid imagination. That it was done rapidly and without much planning has nothing to do with its value; and that its author
thought it worth little is only one more proof that our best
work is often not appreciated by ourselves.

The real fun of the episode came when the Seniors, looking for material for their printed magazine, fell upon *Akib,
King of Egypt's Son*, in the mimeographed periodical and
gave it two full pages with their hearty endorsement. Now,
thought the young author, the laugh is on the whole school;
and it was then that he came out with his own story and his
statement that they were all fooled.

As Sam was able to convince several others, something
like the start of a revolt had burst amid that poetry group.
A real fight was on, no doubt. If someone had come along at
that moment and proposed a discussion of What is poetry
anyway? it would have met with unanimous interest. Intense moments of that sort were characteristic of the atmosphere in Miss Zachry's literary projects. At times
nothing in the world seemed to those children of greater
importance than the differences of opinion that cropped up
naturally out of her work; she was a master in the art of
planting materials that seize the whole life of the child. But

here she was somewhat fearful that the excitement might become too hot to handle for the right progress of that group along creative lines; so we went into private conference on ways and means of meeting the difficulty to make it tell for the good of all.

In consequence, I was invited to go before the class with my side of the story, in order to prove to that youngster that he had really, if unwittingly done a superior thing. I read the poem to the eager young people and then explained why we older persons believed that it was one of the outstanding accomplishments of the younger poetry group. It was most amusing to think, as we debated back and forth, that here were two teachers seeking to convince a student that he had done well in his school work and practically begging him to take a high grade for it! A striking picture out of the new education.

After the reading, a steady and continuous applause came spontaneously from the youngsters, obviously meant for the young author.

I smiled at the youth as the applause continued solemnly.

"Doesn't that affect you," I asked him quietly, "their approval?"

He was slumped low in his chair, one elbow on the table in front of him. "Yes," he admitted honestly. "It does. They like it, I guess. You read it — as if it has some sense. But — it hasn't any; no meaning, I mean."

"I agree with you," said I. "But we don't always like a poem for its meaning. The fascinating thing about *Akib* is its pictures. It is a procession of weird, even grisly pictures. That ugly crocodile! It gives me the shivers. And continues to, long after I have read it. I see him at night

> Tum . . . tum . . . tum . . .
> On the back of a hollow bamboo drum!

Just like *The Ancient Mariner*. I doubt if anybody really knows what *The Ancient Mariner* means; I am one of those who believe that even Coleridge, the author, didn't know! But his pictures are enough to give a body delightful and permanent horrors."

Suddenly a large girl rose near him and said, "Sam, you *know* its good!" and slumped with a bang into her chair. The class applauded again; and that seemed to settle the matter.

II

There is no doubt that something has a grip on our real self. Something there is that does not love our best. Every artist — painter, writer, or fabricator generally — knows about this unseen, unknown enemy; and every artist has at some time or other discovered a trick to throw it off that seemingly eternal guard. Some will smoke endless pipes and pretend to be thinking about nothing at all; and then, presto! they turn suddenly to work and have a lot done before the Thing (who is really a little stupid) can discover what's up. Others walk up and down; or must use a rocking chair; some find places of magic where he cannot always enter — bathtubs, for instance; and there are those who must work in bed (Mark Twain was one of these) ; or go hiking, or, like Mary Roberts Rinehart, take an office in town away from any suggestion of normal living.

Hours are important, too. Some cannot work until after midnight. Others begin at dawn.

The experience of those who awaken suddenly at night and find nothing to interfere with almost perfect self-expression has already been put before us; Sam's *Akib, King of Egypt's Son*, is, I believe, just another instance of an unconscious scheme to divert the creative inhibitions. He thought he was only fooling, but he succeeded in fooling himself. If he had seriously attempted to write, the chances are that he would have had to struggle, and then, in all likelihood, his free-flowing imaginative pictures would not have been forthcoming at all. Not to try is one of the ways of succeeding in the creative field. It is not the only way, of course.

Not to try! How the creative life fights all the precepts of the virtuous ones! The good little boy is one who gets up at an exact hour, does always what he is told, listens to others, and disregards any promptings of thinking that might suggest themselves from within, strives all the time to do his best, never loafs, eats his meals on time, including two hundred calories of spinach, never speaks unless spoken to, assumes an interest in everything worthy, prepares all his lessons with exactly equal interest in each, and goes to bed on the dot without a single original human whine.

The picture suggests clockwork. Well, we elders have tried our best, for our own comfort largely, to arrange a world with only this sort of youth in it; but our success, if any, was only with the uncreative; our failures were with those self-assertive rebels struggling to be free spirits. My own belief is that we should not have failed if we had had a better understanding of their unclock-like make-up.

The aim of this book is to help in that understanding, although it is written in the assurance that many will not think that any of our fine distinctions are important. But it is just through the attention to distinctions of the sort we are recording here that humanity has made its progress. We used to duck poor old trembling women and beat the terrified feeble-minded.

III

My belief is that our serious consideration of Sam's creative ability brought to him a practical knowledge of the workings of his own mind. If that is true then it was one of the best pieces of teaching that the school did for him. We noted that he wrote a considerable amount of material, very little of which he permitted us to see; undoubtedly he got a deal of personal satisfaction out of these scribbling reproductions of the figures in his mind.

Religious experiences absorbed him at one later period; not that he said anything about it; we learned it from others. He wrote a great deal at that time. Obviously the stark reality of Judgment Day had worked upon his imagination, for among the very few contributions that he permitted to circulate was one on that theme. I give it in these pages to show that we were not wrong in attributing to him a strikingly imaginative personality with a gift for condensed and pictured language:

THE COMING OF THE LORD

I

The clouds broke forth
In a mighty ray
Lighting the glory
Of the new-come day.
Angels chanted
And people cheered,
The cattle ran
And the horses reared.
All was havoc
In hell-like fire,
And the old cross glowed
On the steeple spire,
While all around
Grew fiery red
With sparks and lightning
And thunder dread.

II

Christ stepped out
On a crimson cloud
Amidst a roaring
Shouting crowd,
With an ivory crown
And a love-worn face
And a bleeding heart
Of flowing grace.

III

The Devil peeked out
Of a corner cloud
And grinned at the Lord
And mockingly bowed.
And the people yelled
Like a braying bull:
"Begone, you devil!
You goat-horned fool!
Begone to your hell,
Your brimstone and fire!"
And the old cross glowed
On the steeple spire.

IV

Then rich men rushed
To their hidden wealth,
And drunkards drank
To the foul fiend's health.

Some were afraid
And tore their hair,
Doing penance for sin
While full unaware
How beside the cot
Of each good man,
An angel played
On the pipes of Pan.

V

Of a sudden the saints
In double pairs
Came riding forth
On brown-gray mares.
Onward, forward,
All day they marched
O'er the burnt-up earth
Forever parched.
Up the golden ladder!
Through the golden gate!
Others followed after
But were too late.

VI

The earth shriveled up,
Went hurling through space. . . .
The Lord had come and gone in His grace.

How may one doubt that the above effort was performed under the stress of genuine moral feeling? Well, certain stern moralists do doubt. When we permit children to think, they cry anathema upon us and blame us for all the evil in the world. Then they give us a sample of their own type of thinking on the subject of education, and while they protest that they are most modern, they seem unaware that they are opening themselves to the suspicion of what the psychiatrist calls regression.

Defeated by the present, regression turns against it and defends a past that had always been hated. There is a regression period for each of us, perhaps, so one cannot afford to be uncharitable: old age exhibits it, present frustration will bring it on at any age, introverts that have been denied leadership find eventual solace in regression.

The most dangerous socially among the regressives are old leaders of new thought who have been defeated by newer thought or by the crowding forward of younger leaders. The old cheering crowds have gone, but a new cheering crowd may be summoned instantly. How? By shifting to the conservative stand of the ignorant. To start that roar of acclaim the regressive has only to say — as they do — "What this younger generation needs is a good old-fashioned strapping to put the fear of God into their bodies!" A gathering of intelligent mothers, however, would greet that declamation with silence. They would be aware that no help can come from such an undiscriminating generalization, but much harm, for it will fortify the stupid and arm the cruel.

To keep the respect of the intelligent minority the regressives protest that they are not regressive; but an analysis of their proposed school program shows it to be simply a hark-back to their own admittedly hated school regimen. Here is a sample. Look at it and judge: one course of study for all, because we shall cease to be Americans, they rationalize, unless our school-possessions are exactly alike; a hard course at that, because one's pedagogy must not be "soft"; jammed with facts to be committed to memory, because the world is lost, they reason, unless each child knows (verbally!) all that ever happened in the world.

To them the business of education is not to save a child but to stuff him.

Sometimes, however, the regressive knows exactly what is going on about him but simply refuses to admit its existence. This type I pictured in a quatrain which *Collier's* permits me to reprint here:

THE PERFECT REACTIONARY

> As I was sitting in my chair
> I *knew* the bottom wasn't there,
> Nor legs nor back, but *I just sat*,
> Ignoring little things like that.

CHAPTER XI

Poetry Is When You Talk to Yourself

THIS IS THE STORY of an accidental discovery of one way to introduce children to their own creative potentialities. But before that story is told, I must explain an important matter in the teaching of the creative arts. We have learned, by many trials and more than many errors, that a good device is simply one that works. If we treat children like mature little persons, for example, and there are no bad social consequences but many good results in art appreciation, then that is a good attitude to take with children. If approvals bring a better and better output, if displays of the work of all the children lead to a desire to make a better showing next time, if struggle, without helping instructions, teaches where direct assistance would postpone insight, if all these and a hundred other techniques prove their worth as practical devices, then we call them good.

So a group of us working together came upon a mere phrase that seemed to do more to stimulate the writing of original story and verse among very young children than anything we had hitherto employed. It was the one used as the title of this chapter, "Poetry is when you talk to yourself." If one should offer objection to that definition of poetry his position would be unassailable; if one should reject the language as not that of a completely literate person, the author of it would have to agree. Our interest in teaching literature and the other arts is not primarily in either literature or art but in teaching literature and art, two quite different areas of human aspiration. That semi-literate inaccurate phrase worked! It brought results; so we labeled it good.

But to our story. I had conspired with a group of superior

professional teachers to see if I could awaken a dormant creative interest in a particularly inexpressive fourth grade class. It was agreed that it should be a short talk and that it should last not one second longer than that class thought it worth listening to. Knowing the group, we admitted that from four to eight minutes would be high accomplishment; it turned out, however, that we held them on a high level of attention for fourteen minutes.

We had no plan other than an agreement that I should read to them the work of other children who had found their own world to talk about. I began with Hilda Conkling's poem about "Mr. Moon." and then I told them the story of how Hilda used to talk to herself about her lovely world of butterflies, snails with shell umbrellas, flowers, old bridges that groaned when folks walked on them, and clouds, and far-away hills. I told them that often Hilda's mother was by, a very silent and companionable mother; and that sometimes she wrote down what Hilda had been saying out loud.

"Have you ever talked to yourself?" I asked, in as careful a tone as I could summon. I was prepared for a laugh but to my surprise there followed a solemn silence until one deep-voiced boy said an authoritative, "Yes." Smiles and murmurs of acquiescence and a general nodding of heads led me to say, "Of course. Everybody does," but I surprised even myself by adding something that I surely would not have used in addressing a mature group, something which I could not wholly believe to be true, "Poetry is when you talk to yourself."

Instantly tension seemed to leave that small group of youngsters. They were glad, no doubt, to have this difficult mystery cleared up at last.

In language suitable to their years I suggested that they might get a good friend, teacher or mother, to write down what they said the next time they talked to themselves; or they might write it down themselves.

Then, with a wary eye on evidence of fatigue or lack of interest, I produced, one by one, other poems written by boys and girls of about their own age.

I read them a boy's poem on "How Worms Walk". His

teacher had taken down what he had told her and had printed it herself in the Class Book of Our Own Poems. Dicky had been watching a garden worm crawl a long distance. He remembered it and thought about it often, so he told his good friend, his teacher, about it and this is what she wrote down:

HOW WORMS WALK

Some worms don't have any feet.
They pull themselves out,
And they pull themselves in,
And they pull themselves out,
And they pull themselves in;
And that's the way they get along —
Because they don't have any feet.

Then I told them the story of Jenny. When Jenny was seven years old she was overheard talking to herself as she swayed back and forth in the school-yard swing. They were glad when I told them that her teacher, looking on from a nearby window, had taken down what Jenny had said and it had made Jenny very happy when she read it back to her. That encouraged Jenny to continue to sing to herself. Some years later, when she could write down her own words, she made everybody happy and patriotic by something she had been quietly singing to herself. It was while she had been looking at the school-house flag as it flew sturdily in a strong breeze.

"It is a very strange singing," I warned them. "No one else in the whole wide world has thought these words about our flag, but everybody has felt glad and proud as Jenny did. Here is her song:

RED, WHITE AND BLUE

I saw a cow,
Red.
Where? All over?
No; in the hide.
What is the reason?
Mild milk.
What is the reason?
Milk.

I saw a grain of corn,
White.
Where? All over?
No; in the kernel.
What is the reason?
Bread, bread.
What is the reason?
Bread.

I saw a bird,
Blue.
Where? All over?
No; on the wing.
What is the reason?
Happiness! Happiness!
What is the reason?
Happiness!

Jenny's poem is like the flapping of Old Glory in a sprightly summer breeze. "Look up the next time you see it," I told my little fourth graders, "and you will hear it singing, 'Happiness! Happiness!'"

Little Marshall thought and thought about something but it was not anything in the world around him. He kept saying to himself, "Hold on!" Then he told us why,

I keep on walking;
I know there's always an end.
My knees are weak,
My feet are tired,
But my lonely heart keeps saying,

"Hold on!"
The dusty road!
The muddy streets!
People jeering,
Laughing at me.

I think of the castle
At the end of the road
As I keep on saying,
"Hold on!"

The youngsters liked that; so I could tell them that I thought it wonderful that Marshall had stopped with the words, "Hold on!" They are strong words. You can't say them fast. So they stay in your mind and you remember them better because they come at the very end of the story. "Hold on!"

"Sometimes, when you talk to yourself," I told them, "the words sound like the very thing you are thinking about. George, for instance, talked to himself as he lay on the sand and listened to the noises made by the sea. He had said it so often that he remembered it later and told it to a good friend. And that's how I got it. Don't ask me what it means. I doubt if George himself knows. But doesn't it sound just like the waves on a fine summer day, rolling up, breaking into surf, and then hissing back to sea? Listen for all the sounds, especially the strong sound of the s's.

> My mind a sea is,
> Is, a sea is;
> Ships are there, too far to see,
> And fish below
> I'll never know.
>
> And now I'll watch,
> And now I'll hear,
> I'll hear the sound the sea makes,
> Makes, the sea makes;
> No one knows but me
> The sound the sea makes,
> Makes, the sea makes.

My little audience was very interested in what a good listening friend had just taken down when five year old Caroline was talking to herself. Caroline had grown so fast that her mother had to buy her a new pair of shoes; but Caroline loved the old worn ones. This is what her friend heard her saying. "I think it was her mother," I suggested, "don't you?" There was a laughing chorus of, "Yes!"

GOODBYE, MY LITTLE SHOES

> Goodbye, my little shoes,
> I won't see you again;
> You hurt myself,
> I've grown so big a girl.
>
> I wore you when I went to school,
> I wore you when I played,
> I scuffed until great holes came through,
> And now — I won't see you again.
>
> Good-bye, my little shoes,
> Good-bye!

We changed the mood quickly by telling them of another fourth grade class who were studying about Africa. The exciting part told about the war drums; the far-away drums, miles and miles away, which gave quick warning of the coming of enemy tribes. One of the pupils talked to himself, but he talked loud enough for all to hear. What he said made them all stop whatever they were doing and listen. It is called

THE WARNING

In the distance — boom, boom, *boom!*

A tall, strong African man
Playing weird music on a mirimba;
The women gossiping gaily,
Making baskets of reeds,
The little dark babies playing.

Stop! Listen! *Listen!*
In the distance — boom, boom, *boom!*

"Pretty frightening, isn't it?" I suggested. They agreed.

There was as yet no outward sign of fatigue but I knew that they could not stand much more, so I brought one which Shirley Meek had given me; I had saved it for the conclusion. First I reminded them that when we all go on trips together we sometimes tell about it in writing. It may be what we thought of at the time, or what we imagined on the trip, or it may be what we thought later when we continued to think about the good time we all had together. "Some boys and girls about your age," I told them — "they were really sixth graders, but it won't be long before you are sixth graders yourselves — well, these boys and girls travelled with their teacher to New York City to see the celebrated sky-scrapers. Here is one boy's poem; it is about a building which then was the tallest of them all, The Empire State Building:

THE KING

It grew from a thought
And there it stands,
Tall and graceful,

King of steel and cement
Looking down loftily from the high perch
At its far-flung realm.

There, look above you;
In a heaven of blue mist
Waiting to be praised
Stands the finished skyscraper.

It grew from a thought,
And there it stands!

They were deeply impressed by the poem, so I asked them to repeat with me the last two lines:

It grew from a thought,
And there it stands!

From that time on, those fourth grade children began to compose their own stories in verse, very much as normal children are doing nowadays all over the country.

We passed the idea and the phrase on to other primary school teachers; they reported similar results. Later, at the request of the New York State Department of Education, I prepared a phonograph record to illustrate this type of approach to the teaching of personal writing in the primary grades. The Department used it in a special teaching experimentation in the rural schools of the State. We have had most encouraging reports from those teachers, who say that the children want to hear the record again and again, that it almost instantly stimulates personal writing, and that, best of all, it makes the teacher understand at last what creative writing means.

So, if the next time you find yourself talking to yourself, do not be alarmed or send for a psychiatrist; it may be just poetry.

II

We cherish such devices because one never knows completely how to build up children's trust in their own varying abilities, but the sure way to succeed in this region is to be always trying. However, when we do gather up a small measure of success, we find it almost impossible to explain the way to those who have not had our faith and our adventurous experience.

Abstract books on education, I have found, are rarely helpful here, although I do not mean to disparage them; they have their place. The theme, however, cries out for pictured illustration of the child artist in the mysterious unfolding of his native gifts: the flower of poetry, for example, that lies perfect in this unpremeditated line, "Poetry is like the stars left undiscovered". It is in the quiet voice that announces a personal esthetic discovery, "I am thinking, thinking as hard as I can: *Why have I never noticed the maple trees that bordered the road?*" The quoted illustrations are from Flora Arnstein's *Adventure into Poetry* (Stanford University Press); it brims with the appreciation and the nurturing of children's natural gifts in thinking and feeling when they are "talking to themselves."

Books are useful, of course, but the book leading one to sense the art which makes a child conscious of his unique productive power should borrow from the skill of the novelist rather than from the scholarly report on measurable investigations, excellent as these reports are for their own purposes. As in the good story book, human beings must seem to meet on the printed page and have human contacts; and they must strike the mind of the reader with individual reality. In such books, of which this is one, dialogue flourishes, characters emerge and remain pictured in memory; the reader surrenders to feeling instead of to fact. One lives for the moment in the tale that is told.

III

To build in a child a trust in his own native abilities, I would name as a prime condition that the young learner must have some hours that leave him free to express any thought or feeling no matter how low it sinks in the adult scale of taste. Helen Parkhurst in her book *Exploring the Child's World* (Appleton) gives a picture of just the right relationship of trust and freedom; she permits the most anti-social experiences to be confessed and debated without a drop of prejudice.

Dorothy Baruch is full of helpfulness in all her books but notably so in *Blimps and Such*, published twenty-five years ago, and now, alas, out of print. With all its years it is as modern as this morning's newspaper.

Just for the joy of it let me present from that small volume an illustration of the gift of thinking, of rhythmic phrasing, of unbiased judgment, possessed by very young children. We should know what these abilities are before we essay to build up children's trust in them. Besides, the piece is a shining example of a truth taught us by a child, that racial discrimination is not natural to us at all but has been put upon us later by our elders.

The bit is just one of Dorothy Baruch's "stories", as she called them, which she took down on her yellow tablet, while the little pre-school children played around her and "talked to themselves". The italics are my own; they indicate the way I have read the "story" to hundreds of audiences.

Four year old Nancy sees the Negro water-carrier; she stops to wonder about him as he comes toward her. He is an elderly man and very dark. Dorothy Baruch stands by with her yellow tablet. When the Negro gazes down kindly at what the child has been making in the sand box, she looks up and scans his face for a moment or two and then asks,

> What makes you black?
>
>   (*The Negro's face expresses wonderment, too,*
>   *but he is too wise to answer*)
> Did your face
> Get sunburnt
> Very badly
> And turn black
> That way?
>
>   (*He nods a quick agreement*)
> And your body,
> All over —
> Is it black, too?
>
>   (*He assents with a slow grave gesture*)
> And if I take a too long sun-bath
> Will I turn black?

*(He laughs softly in amused approval. Eagerly
and with delight at the prospect Nancy cries out)*
Like *you!*

(He bows his head before the admiring child.)

Twenty-five years ago such a revelation of the gifted mind
of a child was novel and under suspicion of adult tampering,
but since that time the guides have grown in faith and in
numbers. I can be certain now that thousands of these
would match my ardent enthusiasm for *The Artist in Each
of Us* (Pantheon House, New York). This is Florence Cane's
story of the work of the Art Studio of the Counseling Center
for Gifted Children, New York University. It is limited to
self-expression in the graphic arts but the psychological
implications will be profoundly suggestive to workers in
other creative fields. It presents a persuasive picture of
how young persons as well as mature men and women are
made aware of unsuspected native gifts, dormant potentialities that are possessed, really, by all of us. Nearly 200
illustrations, many of them in full color, accompany and illustrate the warm stories which the participants have made
in the encouraging environment of the Studio. Harvey Zorbaugh, founder and director of the Center, welcomes the
book with a wise and understanding introduction.

Those who have found and recorded the naive art of the
young know that the world is needlessly irritated by the
frank expression of individualism, so they arrange that such
self-revealings shall have the chance to grow and develop
in a favoring and completely controlled environment.

Completely controlled environment, please note. When
children are given the opportunity to create ideas, things,
verse, picture, out of their own judgment, out of their own
imaginings, a discipline of order is self-imposed and accepted
by all without question. Not only is the group "orderly" in
the schoolmaster's meaning of the word, but the members
dig in at self-initiated labor far past the hours of prescribed
study. When the natural and wholesome demands of the
spirit are met, children take on the aspect and calm of mature workers.

CHAPTER XII

The Natives and the Rhymesters

WE HAVE SUGGESTED BEFORE that the native language of little children is often stilled by the adult naive belief that all verse should rhyme. I find it a dangerous subject, so must proceed with care. Older persons flare up when I speak in public on this important phase of the emergence of the creative life. A Western editor flayed me as one opposed to *Mother Goose,* which, of course, I am not, for it is one of my permanent delights.

When the confidential links are made with very little children they may speak out of their heart in their native language. Rarely have I found this speech of theirs to be other than fine. Call it prose or poetry, the classification does not matter at all, it has a rhythmic cadence, a sense for the right word, and an uncanny right placing of that right word for just the emphasis intended; and yet it rarely ever rhymes. To me, and to many others, this language is too worthy to be neglected; we feel that it should be encouraged, brought out, allowed to grow in strength, beauty, and power.

We are beginning now to have records of this untutored speech. Mothers and teachers are recording it; and perhaps our ear is being trained to catch its subtle beauty. Again we must give credit to Hilda and her mother, who preserved for us her native notes in *Poems by a Little Girl* and *Shoes of the Wind.* Those marvelously sure words of Hilda, one remembers, were for years taken down by Mrs. Conkling; so we see before us the casual utterance of a little girl who spoke in her own natural language; but the effect upon us is simply the mysterious reaction that stirs us in the presence of the equally mysterious thing we call art. She hardly ever touches rhyme. In reading Hilda, however, no one thinks to question if it is poetry.

All of her work has authentic beauty, and some of it, written toward her tenth year, has inexplicable child-wisdom and, at times, almost prophetic insight. One of her poems makes such a profound impression that mothers can hardly read it through without tears, for it tells, all unknowingly, to be sure, of the inevitable time when the little girl child will grow up and go away. Some of us have suffered that poignant experience, and lucky are we, following Hilda's beautiful picture, if she comes back to us, with a pine cone in her pocket and the pink sand, as of old, between her fingers, comes back to her own again to tell us of a "golden pheasant's feather," while the mother once more sings the old songs that lull her to contented sleep:

I SHALL COME BACK

I shall be coming back to you
From seas, rivers, sunny meadows, glens that hold secrets:
I shall come back with my hands full
Of light and flowers.
Brooks braided in with sunbeams
Will hang from my fingers.
My heart will be awake. . . .
All my thoughts and joys will go to you.
I shall bring back things I have picked up
Traveling this road or the other,
Things found by the sea or in the pine-wood.
There will be a pine-cone in my pocket,
Grains of pink sand between my fingers.
I shall tell you of a golden pheasant's feather;
I shall tell you of stars like seaweed.
Moons will glitter in my hair. . . .
Will you know me?
I shall come back when sunset has turned away and gone,
And you will untangle the moons
And make me drowsy
And put me to bed.

Another mother takes down the words of her five-year-old daughter, again it is at the sleepy hour, and we have sympathetic understanding of the weariness of a child after a long day of play. We take her in our arms, for the little legs will no longer support the tired body, and the little arms hang drooping at the sides. Out of her own life she brings us images, of the permanent heavens, of the enduring stones, and of the sounds of the earth things at night and the look of the world at morning. She says,

> I'm tired:
> Tired as the lazy stones
> That are always sitting down;
> Most tired as the sky
> That stays up all night and day,
> Whether it's early with spider-vines
> Or late with frogs singing.

This and others of the type are published in Mabel Mountsier's remarkable collection, *Singing Youth.* I have so many similar examples as to make me sure of my ground; there is a beautiful language which children already possess but which we commonly ignore. A youngster has come upon the myth of Pegasus and writes her personal love and understanding:

PEGASUS

> Roaming over valley and dale
> Never was such a winged steed
> As Pegasus the dear of my heart,
> Drinking from the fountains clear
> Then spreading his wings
> For a flight through the fleecy clouds
> And the blue sky
> Like a great white bird.
>
> No master has he, no whip, no spur,
> For he is free.

A boy in the third grade talks soberly of his father, who had come from work so weary one night that he went straight to bed without even waiting for his supper. It seemed to bother the boy greatly. After thinking a long time he said slowly to his teacher:

> I saw a man go walking;
> He walked *far* away;
> When he came home
> He was *so* tired!
> So *tired!*
> To bed went he,
> To bed . . . to bed.

From his Ten Year Group in the City and Country School William Mann Finck gives me:

> I'd like to be up in Nelson's silo
> With the pipe running
> And the damp corn getting down my back
> And floating to my feet.

As a Christmas present Caroline Pratt sends me *The Orator*, for she knew I would prize it. Here is intelligent youth, age thirteen, staring at the grotesquery of man — or is it cunning? — in his absurdest moment, the time of the great elections. The poem has subtile qualities which one may sense by varying the interpretation of the final lines of the stanzas. The first one I read as a simple interrogation; the second, with the suggestion that the orator is a clever, smart rascal who knows exactly what he is about, for it is the mob, including you and me, and not the orator who is "crazy":

THE ORATOR

> He stands aloft the crowd
> And shouts and bites;
> His harsh voice cuts the air
> As he shouts out in defiance.
> The mob nods its head;
> The Orator sweats;
> He's a mess. He must be crazy!
> Is he?
>
> One hour, two hours, his arms wave wildly;
> His eyes glare. . . .
> The mob moves slowly, slowly off.
> The Orator sweats, He's a mess.
> He *must* be crazy!
> *Is* he?

Often our finds in verse are too personal for general circulation; and this brings to us a knowledge of a more or less rare art-form, art for its own sake literally, written solely for the private satisfactions of the creator. One such poem I have before me, dear because of reasons that may not be spoken of here, whose whole meaning can never be clear now but whose strange beauty is altogether real:

I HEAR

I stand alone;
I stand alone, well aware
Of the step, step, step
Of my mind.

I hear —
You cannot make me deaf
To the drum of the treble clef —
I hear my mind.

I prayed and I am praying,
But you shall never know
My mind.

Mary Ann, age eleven, gives us a fine array of summer evening sounds in the country:

COW BELLS

Far, far away, down in the valley
I hear a cow bell jingling.
As it comes nearer, a cow calls for her calf.
A shrill bark fills the air;
Then a low voice calls,
"Come, boss! Come, boss!"

Out of strong feeling will often come words of astonishing effect. A teacher writes me, "My classes were asked by the superintendent to write some Christmas poems or stories for the local paper. The girl who wrote *The Nativity*, which I'm giving you, had recently lost her mother. She was so heartbroken that I had asked her to spend some time with me. One night she waked me and said, 'The only line I can think of for Christmas poetry is "Myrrh for the dead."' I consoled her and begged her to go back to sleep and forget the poetry. The next day she brought these verses to my desk. No one else will guess the emotional power they really express."

They begin in rhyme, impersonal and conventional; then in the last part, which I give here, she turns to her own unrhymed speech and, with remarkable repression of all personal reference, pours forth her grief:

In Bethelem upon the straw
A King is born,
And wise men from the East

Have brought him gifts —
Gold, frankincense, and myrrh —
Gold, for the king;
Incense, for the priest;
And myrrh, for the dead
Myrrh, for the dead!

The Christ Child smiles,
For over Him the shadow of the Cross
Has not yet come.

It is upon this sure gift of a native language that we must work sympathetically if we hope to call forth eventually that superior literary output which here and there we are noting in special groups of children. The cry of "genius" or of "selected children" will no longer do; the possibilities are great among any shy young persons who can talk. But a warning must be given. The native language is used at first for purely personal needs. Hardly any of the illustrations above, with the exception, of course, of Hilda's, is worthy in the sense of conveying to everyone the charged emotions of the author. One must know, in one instance, of the weary father; without the knowledge of the hidden grief, so well concealed in *The Nativity*, a reader might not be so supremely touched. The point is to accept them and know their personal value on the long journey toward mastery of the medium of words.

Here are three quite varying types written in a public-school system, Bronxville, New York, which, from the lowest grade to the very top, has a fine regard for native notes:

GRANDMOTHER

Some old people
Are like potatoes:
Mealy,
And with eyes that do not see.

My grandmother
Is like an apple:
With all the joy
Of the autumn of life.

Grade XII.

RAINY NIGHTS

Rain comes steadily down;
  The streets are all ashine;
A limousine glides past
  Making a whirring, purring
Sound on the wet bricks.
  Two high school girls
With name-besmeared slickers
  Are crossing the street
When a butcher's Ford
  Rattles past
And splashes the girls
  Who giggle uproariously.
                          Grade X.

VESPERS

Slim tapers tipped starlike
In the dusk
Beneath the stained glass window.
Pointing arches —
Dim.

My soul with soft music
Quivering;
My heart groping
In the twilight —
Unquiet.
                          Grade XII.

The discussion here is always of self-expression as a means of growth, and not of poetry; nor even of poets or of literture. To use the delicate tone of rhyme as an unremembered part of the music of words and at the same time to maintain the essential projection of sincere feeling, that — who would doubt it? — is altogether worthy; but mere rhyming will not reach that goal. Nor are we concerned here with attaining. even that end. The business of making professional poets is still another matter — with which this writer has never had the least interest; he is presenting here his objection to the convention of rhyme when it is used with children as a block to the best expression of the spirit.

In the following stanza a young printer celebrates the return of a friend in a passionate outburst that reaches the reader without the loss of a single vibration; I feel quite sure that in his case an attempt to rhyme would have sim-

ply moved him into an artificial region of posing insinceri-
ties:

WHEN YOU CAME

When you came, my friend,
When you came back home,
I was filled with excited joy.
My pulse beat fast. As my press ran on in the shop
I turned on the full power and the machine kept pace with my mind.
All saw and cried,
"Where is the fire, there!
Where is the fire!"
And I yelled out, as a fruit peddler on the street,
"In my heart, you devils!
In my heart!"

II

One lad we deprived of the opportunity to stay with the
freer group because his shortcomings on the mechanistic
side of language made it seem too dangerous for experimentation. He begged us to let him work in the free periods
with the others and offered bits of things that he had done
in private, but we placed him for a large part of the time in
a special class which rigorously kept to the drills and tests
common in most schools. We did not know enough then to
take the risk with him.

At the start, however, I was convinced that he had most
promising latent power in the language arts and that he
already knew how to use it.

We talked much together. I sensed a persistent urge to
write and a determined will to succeed. I felt the pulse of
something living within him that will not be denied. A part
of the proof — it is only a part — I am willing to give here
by presenting a sample of his language skill while in the
ninth grade. It is not offered as anything excellent in itself,
but it will serve, for the benefit of those who are desirous of
knowing what it is we modern educationists are forever
talking about, as one more example of the type of native
language illustrated in this chapter:

TROUBLE ABOVE

No one understands the job that poor old
Saint Peter has.
Yet, we all worry what will happen
When we get there —
If we do.

   . . . .

Apparently some did get there,
Because the other day the crowd
Rushed in from the Heavenly Playground,
With a rustling of silk, and a stench of tobacco,
And swamped poor gray Pete.
They demanded to know
Why that humble, unshaved Carpenter
Had been allowed to enter
When *they* were there.

And Peter, for once, waxed hot,
And swore that all who had complained
Should be thrust out of the gates
And thrown to Hell.
Immediately there was a weeping
And crying for mercy.

However, down they were flung;
All except two,
The unshaved Carpenter — and I
Who hid under the Judgment Table.

Most older persons, I fancy, would miss the significance of the line, "With a rustling of silk, and a stench of tobacco," and every academician among them would condemn "stench" as inappropriate in Heaven. However, that is just the picture, and the odor, of our best society, from the point of view, or, rather, from the point of smell, of a clean small boy who does not smoke.

One of our lads was suddenly stricken with an illness for which there was then but slender hope for cure, but while we were helplessly bereft, he continuously shamed us by bearing his fate with a high heart and even with humor. During those weeks of anxious waiting he gave me large quantities of material. He still lives and holds a high place among the science scholars, but one may understand why I did not publish at the time this jaunty song:

I WONDER

My mind is like a bird, a bird,
Oh, my mind is like a bird
    With a rancey tancey toy!

The world is like a cage, a cage,
Oh, the world is like a cage
    With a rancey tancey toy!

It holds me tight, holds me tight,
Oh, it holds me tight
    With a rancey tancey toy!

But it cannot hold my mind, my mind,
Oh, it cannot hold my mind
    With a rancey tancey toy!

My mind soars through the sunset clouds, sunset clouds,
Oh, my mind soars throught the sunset clouds
    With a rancey tancey toy!

But I am fast to the world, the world,
Oh, I am fast to the world
    With a rancey tancey toy!

If my mind were too, what should I do? should I do?
Oh, if my mind were too, what should I do?
    With a rancey tancey toy!

Science has been his field since anyone can remember. Quietly he has given the most of his life to it and, therefore, it would be the topic of much of his rhyming play with words. Even when his own span was threatened he could jest sportingly of the fossil evidences of the mortality of the greatest:

TYRANNOSAURUS REX

King of the tyrant reptiles, who measured forty-seven feet long from nose to tail, who stood twenty feet high in his bare feet, whose teeth were six inches long, and who was the largest carnivora that ever cursed the earth, speaks:

I was a great grey Dinosaur
My jaws were caked with mud and gore
And I weighed one hundred tons or more.

Over this world I once held sway
And I dressed in no purple mantle gay
But only a pimply hide of grey

The only kind of food I'd seek
Was meat that had rotted for a week
And had a truly lovely reek.

Ah! That was the day, and that the hour!
I ruled the earth with jaw and power
With plenty of rancid flesh to devour.

But the little mammals, quick and fleet,
Whose forms were small, whose flesh was sweet,
Who raced and slithered in the peat,

They mocked at me where'er I came;
They gnawed my toes till I was lame,
And so they put me out of the game.

So my remains repose in pomp
In this museum and never romp
After Iguanodons in the swamp;

While the little mammals come to see
The fossil bones that once were me,
And giggle and point in puny glee.

III

Muriel is now fourteen, but she has the touch of the sure artist in expressing the thought and feeling of her unique personality. Her reading has been wide and varied, but it has only strengthened the marked individual note; throughout her young life she has retained the native unrhymed language, adding grace and range with the years. She fell into the hands of no teacher of ancient prosody, presumably; or, what is more likely, her instinctive good taste and self-regard were so satisfying that no mere master of jingle could win even her attention.

Her work, I like to think, is a promise of what might be the wonder-working possession of many a youth were the surrounding influences of home and school more appreciative of the language forms she has so successfully developed as her own. Of the many and varied expressions of her personality I select for illustration here her *November Days and Nights:*

NOVEMBER DAYS AND NIGHTS

I

The brown, dead leaves '
Are a flock of birds that hover listlessly
Above the city. A flock of swallows
Wheeling and pirouetting
In an antique dance. . . .
A brown, torn garment
On the grey, still city.

II

The thin, black fingers of the ash-tree
Are combing the wind in her bereavement.
The ash-tree is a dark, lone widow
Searching the winds for
Her husband, the Spring.
Searching the winds with tremulous fingers,
And mourning in loneliness.

III

Come back to us, little grey sister,
Grey ghost of the birch-tree,
Come back to us,
Your elderly relations.
We are prim old great-aunts,
We the pine-trees;
And bearded uncles,
We the old oak-trees.
Your little brothers, the maples,
Weep for you.
Come back to us, little grey sister,
Pale little ghost of the birch-tree.

IV

There was frost on my window
This morning. A delicate stencil
Of silvery patterns
Of deep-drooping willows,
And heavy, fantastic ferns
That were scattered over the sill.
An age-honored sign of the Winter,
An infallible omen of Winter.

V

The moon is not a crescent
As in September (it shone above the rose-bush),
Nor a great globe of false sunlight
As in mid-July.
It is only a half-moon,
Half-moon of November,
High over the City,
Waiting for Winter.

VI

The wind is an insolent braggart
That is hushed for an instant
In touching with arrogant lips the dead face
Of his mother, the Earth,
And whispering sadly the old, old promise
Of resurrection.
He has just come from kissing
The white shoulders of mountains,
Yet laughing, and vowing
With a smile on his lips
The same promise of Springtime.
It is strange mockery that he should enter
The dark death-chamber
After revelry such as his.

VII

No pagan gods are dancing in these fields,
But the wraith of Autumn
And the breath of Winter
Have made a rendezvous in the orchard.
The fields
Are barren, and the young acacia-tree
Is numbed and frozen by the laugh of Death.
No pagan gods are dancing in November.

VIII

These things are the heart of Autumn:
The fading of day,
The mourning of all Nature,
A lighted window in the darkness,
And the laughter of heedless children
In the grey stone streets,
After the flowers have withered.

IV

If teachers and mothers did not work so hard to annihilate everything else but rhyme, the more natural and better language might have a chance to develop. To most teachers of young children, to write a poem means to indite a jingle. Without knowing it they step in at the start to block free expression.

In a marvelously liberal school system of the Middle West I sat beside a child who was clearly composing a poem. In that setting it was the natural thing to do, but she had used the word *trees* and therefore was compelled to toss her little thought aside and end her poem with something quite alien about things that freeze. Fancy being forced to write one's most intimate letters in doggerel verse!

In the same building, however, I found a teacher of the upper elementary grades who, by means of an after-school Writing Club, was receiving an outpouring in the native language. We spent an hour or more going over these very private materials. To print any of it here would be to tell only a very small part of the personal story, showing again that the hunger for expression is always a revelation of deep and urgent needs.

A little girl, for instance, who had not quite succeeded in many things she had tried to do — they were secret tries and equally secret failures — had been depressed for a long time. She sought the only peace she could obtain; she gave up trying and flowed with the drift of the world. At that time she had sat for a full hour in silent meditation and then she wrote:

A THOUGHT

I have wandered.
Yet will I no longer wander,
For within my mother's garden
I have found shelter.

This is quite unlike anything else she had written during the year. We went over all of her other work; it was ordinary and inexpressive. Sometimes the spirit seems a prisoner in a deep dungeon calling for help, but no sound is heard, only a shout when a door far below is opened and shut.

CHAPTER XIII

Other Rhymings

THE SPRIGHTLY SURETY WITH which first-grade teachers all over this land gather the new youngsters about them to give a lesson in what they call poetry makes me guess that not instinct, nor originality, nor knowledge of children is the source of those suspiciously standardized "lessons." These fine young teachers are only the retailers, not the manufacturers; one must look to certain training schools for teachers, I suspect, where nimble devices are placed above everything else in the teachers' equipment.

At the risk of hurting the sensitive reader I must give a sample of the results of one of these lessons; it is almost exactly like the output in the hundreds of other cases that I have collected. Such nice, young, healthy, lovely teachers they are who give them to me with a beaming, "I *know* you will love to see what we are doing in poetry with the first grade!" And this is what I see:

POEMS BY THE FIRST GRADE

I had a bat
Who lived in a hat
With a rat
        Henry F.

I have a ball
Who danced on the wall
        Elizabeth R.

A little mouse
Had a tin house
        Louise T.

I had a little hog
He danced on a log

There was an ox
Bumped into a box
        Robert T.

I went to sleep
Said a little sheep
        Stanley S.

I came to a tree
It fell on me.
        Rosy V.

There was a man
He jumped in a pan
        Flora D.

He fell off in a bog
And hit a dog
            Noel S.

I have a car
It goes far
            Joseph G.

I have a cat
Her name is Pat
            Jane T.

There was a potato
He kissed a tomato
            Gladys C.

I had a pig
He ate a fig
And did a jig
            Harold E.

II

Most little children are balked in the use of their best language by the universal insistence upon rhyme, but it is amazing, at times, to see how even this obstruction is circumvented by ingenious childhood. Here are some illustrations of the work of youngsters wherein, in spite of the restriction to their best thinking, they have managed to present a creditable bit. Oftentimes they achieve only a comic effect, but in each instance there was a struggle away from the obvious rhyme-association, a selection and a judgment in the use of a constrained vocabulary.

THE TRUTH

To read, to write, to learn to sew;
But the thing a girl *likes* to do
Is to catch a beau.
            Grade IV.

SLEEP

Sitting on the chair
Swinging my legs so gay:
When I turned around —
It was the next day!
            Age four.

From *Blue Beads and Amber* by the child-author Mary Virginia Harriss.

I WONDER

I wonder what the angels do
Throughout the live-long day.
I wonder why the sky is blue,
And when it rains it's gray.

I wonder where the rain comes from,
 And how a buggy crawls,
And how the great big work-a-men
 Put up the great big walls.
                              Grade IV.

This is packed with the fantastic make-believe and the
eerie scares of ancient All Saints' Eve:

HALLOWE'EN

A laugh, a spark
Bodies in the dark —
  It's Hallowe'en!

A light, a shout,
And more, come out,
  It's Hallowe'en!

A movement in the leaves,
A ghost breathes,
  It's Hallowe'en!

An angel and a divil
Are civil
  It's Hallowe'en!
                              Grade VI.

THE BLACKSMITH

Pound, pound, pound,
Is the blacksmith's work
He sits on a little stool all day
And passes his time
By pounding away.

Pound, pound, pound,
As he soles the horses' hoofs
Taking his time, taking his time,
He goes around to every hoof
Picking it up, putting it down,
Pound, pound, pound, pound.
                              Grade VIII.

I had some carrots
  They grew in the garden;
I pulled them up
  Without asking their pardon.
                              Grade I.

"This one," the children told their teacher, "makes you
feel dizzy."

THE MERRY-GO-ROUND

Very
Merry we go
Around on the merry-go-round,
Up and down
Music we hear
Tunes that cheer
As we go round and round
And round and round.

Grade VIII.

JIMMY

Little Jimmy had a bell,
He went to ring it and he fell.
And then he cried because he fell,
But, *anyhow*, he rang the bell!

Grade III.

THE BEACH

While I was down upon the beach
And waves came up unto my reach,
And the gorgeous sun shone down
And made them seem a sparkling town.

And as I was dreaming still,
The little ships came in until
They filled the harbor wide
And stood, like soldiers, side by side.

Age nine.

Just twelve words, placed exactly as the little girl wished
to have them, but they have astonishing effect:

SOME DAY

Some day
Jane shall
Have, she
Hopes,
Rainbows
For her
Skipping
Ropes.

Age ten.

O MY! HOW IMPORTANT!

Don't interrupt me
　　If you please!
I've a great deal to do;
　　I must sweep the house
　　And wash the clothes
And bake a mutton stew!

Experience has made me suspicious of all rhymed verses done by very young children. Rhyming is not their own language; at best it is an imitation of an adult form of writing; or it is the outcome of an adult drive on the child's fine desire to please the older loved ones. The child who has once found the way to his own rich illimitable store of wonder-thoughts will never even desire to borrow from another.

One of Miss Katharine Barbour's little girls gives us the following astonishingly profound quatrain. In its way it is a perfect thing, and, undoubtedly, it is superior because of the fine use of rhyme.

God keeps a flower garden
Of joys and loves and things like these;
He has a kitchen garden, too,
Of terrible necessities.

STARLAND

Don't you see that little star?
Way up there so far, so far?

Wouldn't you like to be up there
To see the queen with her silver hair,
To see the cats that have no tails,
To see the snakes that carry pails,
To see the rabbits that have no ears,
To see the monster that sheds the tears?
O wouldn't you like to be up there,
To see the queen with her silver hair?
　　　　　　　　　　　Age twelve.

THE KNIGHT OF NOTTINGHAMSHIRE

I heard of a Knight of Nottinghamshire
　　Who lived in days of old,
And he was ever hunting the deer
　　With his wonderful squire so bold

Sometimes he went out with the king
And sometimes he went alone
He loved to go when the moon had a ring
And sleep on a slab of stone.
Grade V.

The following stanza by H. Z., of Westwood, New Jersey, shows a rare gift in the right placing of all the musical elements of verse:

GOD'S WORKSHOP

April! and on the shining hills
The ancient miracle of birth;
Lo! God is forging daffodils
Upon the anvil of the earth.
Grade VII.

III

Even high-school pupils have a difficulty in keeping rhyme in its subordinate place. They use it best, I often think, when they let it strut in premeditated humor, as witness these delightful bits from Miss Beatrice Scott's Creative English class, Montclair, New Jersey:

DRAWING IN CHURCH

I love to draw in church when the sermon's going on
  (Though people frown, for they don't think it's right)
But Mummy doesn't care, if I don't make any noise,
  And snuggle up beside her, very tight.
Once *Mummy* drew a pig with a little twisty tail
  And stand-up ears and a *nawful* funny snout.
We both tried not to laugh, but I got so *streamly* giggly
  That Mummy simply *had* to take me out.

SOMEDAY

I'm not appreciated.
When folks pass, they say
" 'Lo, kid!" in any ordinary way
As if maybe I didn't have fine
Schemes they haven't. And someday mine
Will make them wish they'd said
"Why, *how* d' you *do!*"—when I'm dead.

ONCE I KNEW A LOVELY MAN

Bald men stir me to sympathy:
It is not often that I see
One that I do not sigh
And wipe a salt tear from my eye.

For I will tell you: Once I knew
A lovely man. His eyes were blue
(That is, one was) and on his pate
There grew a hair. But one night late—

"Will you be mine?" he said to me.
I was o'erjoyed, but said, "Let's see,
Tomorrow's Wednesday—I will say
Yes or No on Saturday."

(I really intended to have him, you know,
But it isn't the thing to out and say so.
Admit I was wrong, but, pray, tell me how
I then should know all the things I know now?)

He sighed (It really was a cruel thing,
And I regret; that's why I sing
You this sad song). He took his hat
And, smiling wanly, left my flat.

Straight down the elevator shaft he fell.
("Intoxication," some said) I know well
That, howsoever that may be,
He killed himself because of me.

Bald men stir me to sympathy:
It is not often that I see
One that I do not sigh
And wipe a salt tear from my eye.

My experience teaches me to be particularly suspicious of verse with obvious and banging rhymes. The free rhythms are more likely to be wholly the work of the children. No energetic elders have been putting that into them! And we are more assured if the composing happens orally right before our eyes, as, for instance, these lines, part of a long soliloquy, which were copied down as a boy told slowly, with great pauses in between, of a Make-Believe Land right there back of the work bench in the third grade room:

> There is the High Rock
> Where I talk to the ships;
> And there in the grass
> Is where I sleep,
> Or watch the clouds

Resting or hurrying
In the Big Race
Across the world.

The discussion of rhyme was begun in the previous chapter with a cautious note of fear; it ends with that. Particularly I fear that person with a complex on the subject. He seems to have arrived at a mental stage when he has about ceased taking in the other person's contribution to thinking; and words stir him to madness, not ideas.

That sort of person has often arisen to protest when in sympathetic groups I have tried to draw attention to a neglected value in child language, my sole object, of course, in stirring up so controversial a matter. To my real surprise, I find that *rhyme,* like *liar,* is evidently a fighting word. I wish some even-tempered soul would someday tell me why!

For purposes of record and evidence, therefore, I hereby state that I am not opposed to rhyme, that I believe it to be one of the fine ornaments of verse, that I would not prevent the natural use of it by children, that I rejoice in Carroll, Stevenson, Milne, and others who have given us delightful rhymes for children.

I will even confess that my life-long secret delight is the composing of rhymed light verses some of which have slipped into print and have appeared in anthologies and books of quotation both here and abroad. Several of them have recently bloomed again in the Modern Library edition of David McCord's *What Cheer.* So, your honors, does that acquit me of the charge of being opposed to rhyme?

Not to complicate a simple matter by even more seeming contradictions, space must be given to a kind of natural rhyming which very young children employ when they are undoubtedly expressing themselves in their native language. It is an echo in part, of course, of all that they have heard in reading or being read to.

They bring rhyme in or not as suits them; it rarely interferes with their imaginings because they do not think much about it and do not believe it always essential. It depends upon the effects they wish to make (not that they think too much about that either) and often they mix the rhymed and the unrhymed (as did William Shakespeare) and sometimes they outjingle the best of them.

From out in the Ojai Valley School in California, Nell Curtis writes of one of her eight-year-olds, "He came to me in the morning and said, 'I've got a poem in my mind. When could I have time to write it? I thought of it last night after the lights were out.' It's the realest poem that ever was written," she adds, "because so expressive of the boy."

One sees at once why we are concerned about this sort of performance; not because it is poetry or isn't; frankly we do not care much about the product itself; our interest goes out to the value in growth of personality that comes from genuine self-expression. Here is that "realest poem":

I WISH

I wish I were an engine
A-running on the rails
And every now and then
I would ring my big bell.

I wish I were a steam-shovel
A-tugging at the dirt,
I'd lift heavy loads
Without getting hurt.

No, I don't want to be an engine
A-running on the rails,
No, I don't want to be a steam-shovel
A-tugging at the dirt.
But on the sea
I wish to be
Amongst the rigging
Or down in the hold,
Or look upon the open sea
And know that I am always free. :
And all the time
Down at the bow
The waves would be dashing high
And I'd know that a sailor
Is always full of joy.

Here is one from a seven-year-old who uses rhyme without much sacrifice of thought or feeling. "He handed it to me with a most gleeful smile," says Miss Curtis:

THE SHIP

A ship was a-sailing
  On the sea
  On the sea
A sailor waved
  To me
  To me
I waved back
  In glee
  In glee

As a truce to those who would quarrel over what is or what is not the true expression of the voice of youth, let us end on a high note of agreement with this superb lyric by H.E.M. sent to me in one of the issues of The Evander Childs' *Anthology of Student Verse:*

PRUDENT APRIL

If I can only come safely through April
And keep my eyes detached and cold
And keep my dreams behind my lips
And on my heart a firm, sure hold,

This would be different from other Aprils;
This would be peacefully quiet, and then
I could go softly the rest of the year —
But, oh, my heart is high again!

CHAPTER XIV

Copy Cats

WITHOUT ENTERING TOO MUCH into the subject here I should like to point out what may easily be done to insure a better product from the older and inveterate rhymsters.

I have just finished reading a thousand or more poems written by upper-school boys and girls. All have appeared in school magazines of good repute; but much of it is bad, and much could easily have been made better. I know of one way to make it better, but school poets sometimes do not like to be told about it. It hurts. I am sure of this much, however, that if they can stand the operation they will be on the way to a cure. It may be that some will not write poetry again; which would be unfortunate, for one of the ways of artistic growth is through self-expression, and it is dangerous to stop any healthful, natural activity through pride or fear of pain or any other social terror; but, more than likely, as my experience with young persons constantly proves, these poets — if they can stand the strain — will come upon unknown and unguessed personal powers and will proceed thereafter to exhibit a really astonishing product. Others have done just that.

Keeping always a kindly, bantering tone, I begin by telling them that their work is copied stuff. Their rhymes, for instance, are other people's rhymes. Proof: moon, June; showers, flowers; vain, pain; sky, high; brook, nook; shades, glades; hark, lark; spring, sing — picked out of the first few pages opened. Those ancient rhymes have kept shop at the old stand since grandfather's grandmother wore pinafores. Their presence, to those whose ear has been trained to the finer tones of poetry, is a confession of mediocrity; and unless elevated by superior thinking and feeling they are genuinely painful.

Further, their rhymes are invariably placed upon the spot of greatest emphasis, the end of a completed phrase, giving the monotonous effect of a series of bangs upon the ear. In good poetry the rhyme is not so strenuously emphatic, unless a comic effect is really intended; one is rarely aware of the rhyme at all, its use being that of an important overtone.

If I can get a laugh from them I know then that all is well, so I tell them that their phrases are copied, too. All their streams ripple, all their lakes are silver (so is their moon), and their trees whisper in the gentle — guess what? Breeze? Right! Their rain always beats down or it falls in torrents; their evening shadows are purple; their whippoorwills call tenderly mournful in the solemn night. (My whippoorwill, I tell them bitterly, is a healthy, optimistic idiot screaming, *"You* come here!" to his lady friend up the hill who yells back, "You come *here!"* For hours they keep it up with amorous obstinacy: *"You* come here!" "You come *here!"* *"You* come here!" "You come *here!"* And they just never get anywhere. It's *me* that's mournful. No; *I don't* mean I. I mean ME! About one A.M. I'm shying rocks at their bushes and saying things aloud. Solemn night? Anything *but* a solemn night.)

But to get back to our young poets. His fire shadows dance, his twilights fade, his tall ladies are stately, his little girl's romp, his eyes have a twinkle in them, all his smiles are roguish, and all his laughs are merry.

I do all this because I like these lads and lasses, because I believe in them, and because I know that they are a rare and worthy group. This liking I must be able to convey without words. Nearly all fine prose writers, I tell them, were poets in their youth, but they had to learn much before they were able to take their stand with the best. And one of the foremost things to learn is that one's own good work is never, never, never like anybody else's good work.

The second thing to learn, I tell them, is to stand criticism. And I do not mean mere fault finding; I mean criticism that both points out the evil and shows instantly how to amend.

"Are you prepared for a good blow?" I ask. If I have made the right friendly approach someone is sure to say, "Shoot!"

"Put up your props, then," I say, and go for them somewhat in this wise:

II

You not only copy your rhymes and your phrases and your verse-forms, but you also copy your ideas.

Think of it; I am accusing you of not thinking at all. Prove it? Oh, that is easy! Here is the proof:

When the word spring comes into your mind, as it is bound to be coming soon, you think of the robin hopping on the lawn. That is, you think you think. "The robin is hopping on the lawn," you write excitedly, whether a robin is really hopping on the lawn, whether you have ever seen a robin, whether you have ever seen a lawn.

One would think, from the way you carry on about the robin, that there are no other birds about in the spring. Yet the chickadee, the downy woodpecker, and the European starling are here, I know, for they stay in these parts all winter. The goldfinch is changing his coat from olive to lively gold. This very week four red-winged blackbirds were raising a racket in the snow by my spring; and the bluebird, the cowbird, and the phoebe were busy staking out summer claims. The meadow lark has just arrived and is practicing his first notes, but the song sparrow is already in full song. Without much search in the open wintry scene before me I found the mourning dove and the myrtle warbler, and a junco or two that had not yet gone North.

But none of these are for you! "The robin is hopping on the lawn," you sing, while you gaze soulfully out of your window where six sparrows are fighting on the edge of a tin cup.

Many years ago some real poet sang about a real robin which was really hopping on his real lawn; then the school-book writers put it in the primers. The first thing you read about when you came to school was the exciting story of that fifty-year-old robin, and you came home breathless to tell your mother and sister; and you've been telling it to everybody ever since, until you begin to think you invented it.

For a while, by the way, the bobolink was in style, crowding out the robin, but he didn't last long. I don't know why.

And when the fall comes, you seize pencil to write this original bit of thinking: "All the leaves are falling!"

That's another startling idea you got from somebody else. If you had really thought the matter out for yourself you would have noted that the leaves do not fall in the fall. That is, they do not fall to any appreciable extent while you are looking at them. They come down during storms, when presumably you are indoors, or at night or in the early morning when most of the stiff breezes blow. The really astonishing thing is that the leaves do manage somehow to get to the ground. The whole business is achieved so secretly as almost to make a mystery of it.

And all the leaves do not fall in the fall. Haven't any of you noticed that some oak leaves stay on the tree all winter? And some leaves give up in July; and some keep a grip on their perch until December; and July and December have never been listed in my calendar as fall months.

No; you haven't been thinking at all. Certain words invariably recall bits of information that you have heard from others. The word "fall" suggests that the leaves are falling, and you say it, whether leaves are falling or not. It also suggests that the days are mournful and melancholy; another false fact that you borrowed from the sad-eyed poets of your grandfather's day.

Your prize thought, however, is about winter. One has only to say the word winter and the school poet scribbles on the margin of his history book: "In winter all the trees are bare!"

Of course winter trees are not bare at all. They are beautifully clothed. If you persist in saying that in winter all the trees are bare it means that you have never really looked at winter trees nor seen their astonishing beauty. A live winter tree fills its space in the sky with myriad twigs and shoots hidden from view in the summer; they seem almost to have come out just for the winter to give the tree its appropriate vestments. In winter it is, when the confusion of leaves has gone, that the tree shows its marvelous balance and symmetry; but always, to the seeing eye, it is a picture of strong limbs garmented in lace-like tones of gray; and long before the winter has passed these take on subtle tints of brown and bronze and even green; sometimes, notably with the willows, lighting up the snowscape with a flowery glow of yellow. The artists know winter trees and love to paint them; but rarely do they give them the suggestion of something pitifully stripped and bare.

So much for the outside world. You have not looked at it with the frank curiosity of one wanting to know; rather, you have not looked at all but have taken for truth the cheapest kind of gossip about it. You write of the North Wind and do not know that the North Wind is such a rarity that it might almost be said to be a myth. You got the idea, of course, from an old English source ("The North Wind doth blow and we shall have snow," etc) ; just as you picked from British verse of long ago ideas about larks and nightingales. Copied, every bit of it.

But your real plagiarism is with the world of feeling, the human world of which you are a part. When you write of that you miss the shouting evidence beside your very ears. You think fear is expressed by trembling and excited running about when it is often masked by cool silence. You think weeping is a sign of weakness or defeat. You think that downcast eyes are a confession of guilt. You think cowards are white-faced. You think indignation is an expression of boldness or even of anger, whereas it is often only a revelation of timidity. You think good-natured, laughing, merry chaps are free from worry or depression. You think — but really you do not think at all.

Take a walk, my friends, and look at the world about you. See it as for the first time. Observe your fellows as if you had never before heard of such funny, admirable, odd-looking creatures. And take a most scrutinizing look at your funny, admirable self. Cast out everything you have ever heard about these important subjects; doubt the truth of all you have read about them. Then you may begin to think; and if you once begin really to think you can have the said world at your own funny, admirable feet.

Have I proved that I am interested in you, that I believe in you, that I wish you well? Have I? If you are really beginning to think, you will know.

CHAPTER XV

A Humdrum Lot

IN A LARGE STUDY group of nearly one hundred teachers I could not miss the strong face of an elderly woman who remained for weeks unaffected either by my enthusiastic portrayal of the possibilities of the creative life in education or by the exciting material, "finds," we called them, which were being brought in daily by young teachers. Poetry, paintings, clay figures, models of inventions, stage settings, woodcraft, tincraft, clothcraft, linoleum prints, these and other manifestations of the spirit of youth left my fine old lady calmly and pleasantly cold.

She had an eye, however. It was luminously eloquent and humorous. It talked back at me all the time, forcing me to work twice as hard; often it sent me away with the sensation of having made no more than an interesting fool of myself. I found myself secretly bent upon dislodging that serene calm, but the course had gone on through the winter before even a chance came.

It was not difficult to discover that she had a one-room school in a satisfied village; that she was a genial but perfect autocrat; that the children who sat silently for the five hours of her school day "learned something"; that if they did not, they stayed longer; that in her room the curriculum was next in sanctification to the Constitution of the United States; that she was the leading intellectual light of her village; that the townspeople and the children feared her, respected her, obeyed her, admired her, and, whenever possible, avoided her.

Her powerful spell began to work on me also; but, then, I am easily overawed by powerful women; I also feared, respected, obeyed, admired, and avoided. Yet she teased me with a challenge.

One day she stayed after the others had gone. The engaging smile that mingled with the fine health of her handsome old face was most disarming. I took a long breath and tried not to think of the days long ago when just such superior persons kept me after school.

"You are a most insinuating young man," she said coolly, but with frank friendliness.

"Thanks for the 'young man,' " said I.

"Young is merely relative," she rejoined. "To me you are young. Almost thou persuadest me, young man, to be an educational liberal!"

"Let me show you all the power and the glory of the kingdoms of the world," I begged, playing the Devil to her Paul.

Her bright eye glowed. She loved debate, the active tossing back and forth of idea, but, alas, she confessed to me later, her opponents had never lasted long enough to give her any real fun out of it. She was well aware of the fear she inspired, and made every use of it for her own ends; but she loathed all who ran from her; and she hungered for the companionship of minds of her own staunch virility.

"Of course you would not get the quotation exact," she smiled. "It is 'All the kingdoms of the world and the glory of them.' But then I know that you preach the value of inaccuracy."

"I merely remember that the devil can quote Scripture accurately for his purpose," said I, "so I get no particular exultation out of the classification."

"The devil you say, indeed!"

And so we joked and became very friendly; but she got quickly down to business. "There are no creative geniuses in my school," she said. "I have been watching them for weeks. A humdrum lot of ordinary, natural, everyday children. Therefore I shall have no creative work to offer you as my contribution."

"You control your school?" I asked.

"Assuredly."

"You are the master?"

"That's what I'm hired to be."

"They do pretty much what you want done?"

"Pretty much?" she mocked me. "I have a higher standard than 'pretty much,' young man!"

"Then," I corrected my phrase, "they do what you expect of them?"

"Precisely. If not the first time, then the second time; if not the second time, then the third time; and so on. There is just no escape; so I get my results. I hope I am kind; but I am firm and determined. That takes work, let me tell you. But in the end I get what I am after."

"Orderly, obedient children?"

"Yes."

"Kowing their lessons?"

"Eventually."

"Quiet and respectful?"

"Come visit my classroom!" With pride.

"A humdrum lot of ordinary, everyday children?"

"Yes."

"Without a sign of a creative gift?"

"Without a sign."

I waited and then quoted solemnly, " 'And God said, Let us make man in our own image, after our likeness. So God created man in his own image; in the image of God created he him.' "

She pondered over that, giving me the while a most searching stare of incredulity.

"But you haven't quite succeeded in creating those children after you own image," I continued. "They like you and they believe in you; and, no doubt, they are striving to model their lives upon your conception of what is right; but within them is a disorderly, unquiet protest. That is their creative selves; their individuality, personality, what you will; that is the thing they must live with all their lives, and it is the only thing that will save them and give them place in the battle of the world. You have not entirely succeeded in shaping them in your own image. . . . But they say that even God failed, you know."

After a moment or two she summoned her argument.

The world needs the obedient, the unthinking, the uncreative, the workers.

I agreed. It is inevitable that the great mass will find its low place serving under other minds; the creative persons will rule them and pay them their small wage. A kind of hopeless economic slavery awaits the majority of mankind. I do not know enough to find an answer for all; but I do know a way out for the few who come my way. There is hardly space to move among the mob of servile ones, but there is ample place among the creative leaders. A child who comes my way must be given the chance to step out of that possible future bondage. I summon the individual spirit; I try to give it its chance to grow in strength, although the process is worrisome and fraught with peril. That powerful rebel within us which never really succumbs to circumstance, that creator, who may fashion miracles out of the dust of the earth, that, I often fancy, is the image God created in His own likeness. God, I think, does not fail; it is we who continually miss His meaning.

II

We had other meetings, of great pleasure and profit to both of us. After a while she became conscious of the fact that I was working upon her own creative spirit, summoning it forth to think and feel and act; challenging the undeveloped strength of her own individual personality. She was aware of some of the technique: my faith in her ability to transcend even her own belief in herself; proofs of that ability presented to her, as her active mind brought to the surface this and that extraordinary bit of thinking; a final exposing of an astonishingly well-concealed weakness, a conviction, quite unwarranted, that she was too old to take up new things.

She asked for specific help with her children. I promised to think over the problem and to come with suggestions. I warned her, however, that there was no sure way out applicable to every situation; that none of us knew enough to be dogmatic.

On meeting again I asked her if she ever had anyone in her classes who continued to scribble or draw even after she had called for general attention.

"Not for long!" she said grimly.

"Exactly," I agreed." But they have tried momentarily?"

"Oh, yes." She was always calmly good-humored, even when her words were commanding. "That is one of the bad habits it is my business to eradicate, fooling and trifling, when we have work to do. I teach them to give all their attention to the school job, to concentrate. If I were not on strict guard their silly minds would wander here and there and everywhere. I make it a rule to have all desks cleared, keeping away every temptation to scribble and draw. Yes, there are some who persist for a short time, but — eventually they find I am too strong for them. They soon discover they had better give all that up. Oh, I assure you, young man, there is no nonsense in my room. And the children learn to prefer it my way; they are happier at their school tasks."

"Well, I am asking you to permit a little nonsense."

"Nonsense!" she echoed, intensely pleased with her neat retort.

"You asked me to show you how to discover the gifted creative ones in your class. I am showing you. The next time you observe a child scribbling furtively or drawing, the one, I mean, who keeps it up until you have to summon again for attention to the school tasks, take particular note of that one —"

"Don't you worry, young man!" she came back swiftly; "I will take note! Particular note!"

"You asked me to help you?"

"All right." She grew genial and waved an apology. "Go on with your amusing — nonsense."

"It is from that group," I told her, "that we are discovering our artists and writers. The others have been beaten and have surrendered. As you say, you — and the others of us who fight them — are too strong for them. They give up and find their happiness in doing what they are told to do, that is, somebody else's creative work. But those who continue fighting a guerrilla warfare under your very nose, have too great an urge to create. Eventually they will give up; but they will fight longer and give trouble and be the problem cases in your school."

"All my bad boys are artists, I suppose?" she interrupted.

"Everyone is an artist," I replied. "Whoever creates is an artist; and who does not create? This conversation is an art product. Back of our talk is our secret mind fabricating animated thought that does not even appear in speech. Living things are ever stooping in the dust of the earth and making an image and breathing into it the breath of life; it varies from the servile following of another's will, where it is almost at zero, to the freedom of complete self-expression. Independence is another name for it; the greatest wars have always been fought for it. It is something we must always take care to respect in an individual, or we do inexpressible damage to his best possession. Living things are creative artists every second of time; cash registers and typewriters are not."

"So I am an artist!" she said. "You give me a nice, satisfying thought about myself. In your sense I suppose I am. But I doubt if I had ever thought of giving that credit to anybody else. I grant them to be cash registers. Oh, yes! And sewing machines. And push buttons. And delivery trucks. And phonograph records," her active mind went on. "And mechanical dolls — highly painted, of course!"

"Isn't it, really, the best part of us?" I asked her abruptly as she was caught up in the excitement of her image. "This interplay of mind, the give and take of good talk, it comes out of the best thing we possess."

"Undoubtedly," she agreed. "I am famished at times for good talk. And in my village I don't often get it. Famished! I grow bitter because of my lack and sail into people. I — " She was too proud to tell me more.

"And suppose someone stopped you when you wished most to have it?" I asked, trying to edge around to the topic we had left for the moment. But her eager mind ran swiftly before me and headed off my argument.

"I am always stopped. In the midst of the sermon I would

rise and cry out my objections and agreements. I would say my say in the market place, particularly in our village market place, where they ask the most outrageous prices for inferior stuff. I am always stopped. And a good thing, that, too. I have no desire to be a gesticulating old granny trotting up and down the town streets. Thank the Lord I have learned the antidote, which is control."

"Control, I grant you," I agreed. "We must all learn control. The sign of the best artistry is just that. The creative force must not be permitted to waste itself; it must be directed: slowed up, stopped when necessary, let go to the limit, thinned out, spread wide; but unless the direction comes from the creative artist himself he is nothing more than a machine or an enslaved person. Control is one of the greatest subjects of study; but I do not find it, in my sense, in any curriculum. But that is another and later story. Let us come back to your little rebels."

"They don't remain rebels long, I assure you. I control them."

"Of course you do. And that is why you never find out anything fine in them. That is why you cannot discover a single sign of creative artistry in your group. It is there all the time; but you have stamped it out; or, rather, you have driven it to cover. I am telling you that it is among those scribblers and sketchers that we have found our first able ones."

She tried to interrupt, but I begged her to listen. "The next time one of these little rebels resists you, let him go on with whatever he is doing; and when it is finished, go to him pleasantly and inquire what he is doing. But you had better take a lesson on how to do that. Unless you study this lesson you will simply frighten him off."

"A lesson in what?" she inquired, really puzzled.

"A lesson in how to ask a child a personal question," I answered.

"I think my years in the classroom have taught me how to ask personal questions," she retorted.

"I doubt if you have ever really asked one," I came back. She bristled at that, but I continued, "All our questions in

the classroom are impertinent and highly unsportsmanlike
quizzes to discover and punish the guilty ones who have not
obeyed us. With book in hand we ask questions; but we require their books to be shut. Hardly sporting! We rarely
ask a question whose answer we do not already know. To
show up ignorance is our great game. No wonder that, as a
professional group, we are disliked and caricatured in joke
book and on wayside fences. Now, for years I have rarely
asked a child a question unless I really did not know the
answer myself and believed that he could tell me. The very
tone of such questions is different — more pleasant, more
humanly friendly, than those inquisitions of the ordinary
classroom. So you will have to practice a new art; you must
learn how to inquire, in the tones of an ignorant person who
is really interested in getting knowledge. I doubt if you
could say, 'Do you draw, George? Won't you let me see your
drawing?' I mean, say it without overwhelming George with
a sense of guilt."

"I doubt it myself," she laughed.

"I would suggest practice before a mirror."

"Do you want to discourage me completely?" she asked.
Her really beautiful smile followed, so intelligent and
friendly.

"There!" I cried. "That is just the way to ask a child a
personal question. If you come with that warm sympathy
and that lovely smile no one in the world could resist you!"

III

She went off in fine fettle. Something youthful had come
into her bearing. Of course I had played upon the creative
instincts of her own restricted life; the thought that she,
even at her age, could "make" something out of the child-
material in her keeping, was a kindling of new life within
her. She was off on an untried exploration; and, whatever
the chronological age, it is only the young in spirit who can
have a relish for adventure.

"Caught one at the first attempt!" was her remark on
meeting with me again. "That is, if this is it," she added
dubiously. A rather unclean page of copied cartoons was the

result, rather good memories of this and that national figure among the comics. They were done with a hard lead on the grayish leaves of a blue-lined blankbook. The pencil had slipped through occasionally to make plunging holes.

This is just about the commonest type of drawing urge; I suppose every other boy does it some time or other; and she had brought it in as an astonishing novelty. Here, or something like this, is the beginning of every artist, but if he continues in the copying stage, among the crude flat reproductions of the pirnted page, he may arrive at a dead-end street. To grow, his art must leave this region and begin to collect from his own experience. However, she had captured one of these lads whose private interest was stronger than duty, obligation, or fear.

I showed her that his swift, sure line was an acquirement which he must have learned through many hours of a self-imposed task, but I begged her to give him better materials: a drawing board, some of that nice drawing paper which every school has, a soft pencil, and possibly later a grease pencil.

"A grease pencil?" she inquired. "The man will be having me use a lipstick next!"

"Why not?" I whispered.

"Young man — " she began, but a daredevil light came into her eyes; she flashed a mischievous challenge to me that set us both off into gales of inexplicable laughter.

Finally we got back to our lad. I requested that he be placed at the side of the room — merely so as not to bother her, for she was not used to anything in a class-recitation but dumb attention — and that he be made the class illustrator in a given lesson, say reading. Of course he should have better materials to work with. She said she would attend to that. We have found that the result jumps enormously in value when official recognition is given to it. And this device would serve to drive him away from his beloved newspaper models and throw him in upon himself.

The outcome was rather astonishing to both of us: beautiful dreamy pictures to illustrate *Evangeline*, crude, of course. They went up on the casing above the blackboard, reserved hitherto for perfect spellings and perfect maps and perfect arithmetic papers.

Other artists appeared, naturally, as we predicted they would. A teacher's approval of the right sort is like rain to good ground. These were the ones that had been practicing in secret, too timid (or too intelligent!) to risk bringing their work into that environment. After these came those who had never tried but would serve any popular god.

So began her delightful discovery of servitors of the creative life. A day came when she said, "One of my boys is an expert cabinetmaker. He has a shop of his own in his cellar. And he does the finest kind of dowel work. His father is a barber and has no notion how his son learned to handle wood so well; he says the boy was always interested in tools. He is a good boy in school, and I should never have suspected him. Some of the others told me about him and *I have been down in his cellar admiring*. Beautiful things! Tiny boxes, with drawers fitted like a watch. And he does astonishing lacquer! . . . And he was there all the time, and I didn't know it! That is even more astonishing, for, really, with all my pretence of indifference, I did think I knew my children."

A visiting teacher, an old pupil who therefore knew the lady very well, wrote me the next year:

"She has changed from something admirable but forbidding into a Joyous Light in the Darkness! The heavy solemnity has gone from her classroom. (I know all about that, for I spent some years in it). The old discipline just had to give way. The two things cannot exist side by side. And her room is alive with child-things, not school-things. I know you will understand what I mean. She has some astonishing big pictures in tempera. Gorgeous splashes! She has one of them framed, by one of the boys who does wonderful woodwork, right above her desk. . . . And the community has learned to adore her instead of merely respecting her. And think of the effect of *that* upon her! It has simply taken off a dozen years."

IV

Here is the place to tell a story which I shall carefully keep un-localized. A magazine editor had brought me the verses of a high-school girl to inquire if I thought they could be her own, for he wished to publish them. Their expert maturity was indeed puzzling; but we wrote cautiously to the school, asking for qualifications, as if one were seeking word about an applicant for a job. Of course we said nothing about the verses, but we did inquire about her work in English. All the light we received in reply was, "We think she is interested in painting outside the school but her English is not distinctive."

Later her publications gave her something in the nature of fame, especially in her locality, so that one day she was invited to read some of her work before an audience which the editor had collected. At dinner later I complimented her upon her great power as a reader. "Poets do not usually read well," I told her. "But you have two gifts, you write and you read."

"There is something amusing about this reading," she said, "and about the writing, too. No one knew that I was writing, not even my best chum. I didn't even tell anybody that they were being printed until they found it out. Then I noticed that the school began to take on a pride in what it called its achievement! Of course they had had nothing at all to do with it, but I am very fond of them and I let them. It could do no harm. It was almost comical to see the way some of those teachers would look at me. A kind of 'Behold my work!' look. Then one of them heard of this reading, although I had done my best to keep it dark, and she sent for me. She told me to bring my program of verses.

"Do you know I was stupid enough not to suspect a thing? Of course I brought them. I like her — like her a lot. She has been very helpful to me; I have learned many things from her. But, of course, my verse — that she has never had anything to do with; no one has.

"She asked me to read the first one on my program. That one I did not read today. I can never read it again. After I had finished it she said *she* would now read it. She read it;

in the most eloquent way, and with such world-embracing gestures! She was trying to teach me to read! Horrors!

"I just didn't know what to do, except that I knew that *that* poem was spoiled forever. I just *couldn't* let her go on with the others. She meant well, I know, but . . ." She gave a hopeless gesture. "So I doubled up and clapped my hands to my stomach and moaned. 'I'm sick, I said, 'awful sick!' and grabbed my papers and beat it. I kept in my room until train time. Wasn't that amusing? Her thinking she could read my poetry for me! Of course, she couldn't know anything about my poetry. Nobody else could but me, now, could they?"

I leave with you the picture of the modern intelligent artist-child fleeing from the devastating threat of formal education!

CHAPTER XVI

Roots and Absolutes

AN IMPORTANT GROUP OF the young people whom I knew long ago as children have grown to be men and women. They soon passed me by in the ranking system of the world. One of them outranked me in the Army. Another was one of the chief officers of an educational institution in which I served as simple private. One became an editor and was in position to reject my manuscripts. And one took complete charge of my affairs via a marriage contract in which I was only the party of the second part.

When I bring to mind the clear picture I have of them when they were just likable boys and girls, I ask myself if I could possibly have foreseen then the road they were destined to travel; and the answer is always, "No. I did not have the skill to foresee." Then I ask myself if these young persons had at that time any special abilities that might have given me a clue; and the answer is always, "Yes, but I had not the skill to discover them."

In this vigorous self-examination I should have to admit, further, that not only was I unaware in my early years of teaching of the creative gifts which these boys and girls possessed at the start, and through the use of which they moved upward, overcoming obstacle after obstacle, but that I was part of a group who all unwittingly underrated them, and sometimes blamed them, for having such gifts; and, so great is the power of organized authority that during these years, as some of these citizens have told me recently, they themselves tried to suppress the instinctive powers within them, felt guilty, indeed, in possessing them, and believed us when we assured them that if they followed their own bent they would not only be foolishly wasting their time but that they would regret it in the end.

We were very kind in those early years, remember, and sympathetic; but the proof is now clear that we did not know what we were talking about.

How many children followed our advice and gave up the overwhelming desire to scribble verses, to make funny pictures on the margins of their books, to play baseball during study hours, to construct complicated apparatus of cardboard, wood, and iron, or even to loll about and dream, instead of busying themselves with tasks imposed by us — that we shall never know. But we do know that a few found the so-called evil urge too strong to resist; they persisted, secretly, in living their lives according to the desires of their own hearts; and while at first they "failed" — some having even to give up school because they could not live their own lives and at the same time prepare our long daily lessons — the future has placed them high in their chosen callings.

They "failed" with us, but in reality we were the ones who failed, for we did not recognize their natural genius; or if we did note it, we felt it our duty to censure them for having it.

II

I have in mind one of these, a fourteen-year-old girl, strangely mature for her years, who found no interest that matched her own in our insistence upon studies in cube root, nominative absolutes, the valves of the auricles, the exports of Dutch Guiana, the organization of the superior state courts, Spencerian penmanship, the administration of John Quincy Adams — to name a sample set of actual daily lessons.

She spent her time quietly sketching in a notebook. Interested in drawing she undoubtedly was, but we did not approve her work because she could not become interested in our kind of drawing which centered about the "plan and elevation" of a spool and the perspective of a wooden cube. So she gave up and left us, gave up the only path there then was to high school, normal school, or college, and, without a single word of advice or helpfulness from us — for we knew nothing about her native gifts — put all her hours into her sketchbook.

Her silence is all I remember of her, her silence and her patient and kindly boredom at the long hours in school. When I heard of her again she was being mentioned as one of the young artists who were doing work of promise in portraiture. A little later she came into the news column as the winner of an important traveling art scholarship.

Soon after that we all read with surprise a critique of her work from a recognized authority on such matters. "She has the rare gift," he said, "that is born with the artist and which, to the discerning, is clear even in childhood." Then, finally we came upon her "one-man show," a public exhibition given over entirely to a presentation of her portraits; and all about us we heard of this and that great one who had given high praise to her work.

That gift "which, to the discerning, is clear even in childhood," none of us had had the discernment to see; but the famous William Merritt Chase, so I learned later, had seen it instantly as he watched her early sketches in his large art classes; he it was, not we, who had told her of her exceptional worth, who gave her courage to go on.

She told me one story of him that is pertinent to our theme. He was an uncompromising critic of students' work and wasted no time upon those who had no business in the serious art of painting. Others had received the annihilating rebuke, but for a time he had passed her by in silence. Then one afternoon he stood back of her for a full minute; she waited for the blow; her hands were trembling so violently that she could not continue her work, so dropped them helplessly to her sides.

He began quietly, but she was aware of that method of attack, reserved for the most advanced cases of ineptitude. "Where have you studied art before?" he asked casually.

She strove for breath but managed to say that she had been to no other art school. "Thank God for that," he advised her calmly, as if he were merely giving her instruction. The silence that followed as he scrutinized her painting was the very worst moment of her life, she claimed, more terrible than drowning.

Finally he said, "You have something that none of the others have, something of yourself which you never learned anywhere; which can never be learned anywhere. Now I want you to get away from this place." He arranged that, by the way, in putting all his influence toward securing for her the European traveling scholarship. "The first thing you know," he continued, stirred now into a little excitement, "you will be painting like all the others." He gave a contemptuous sweep of his hand. Then growing really intense he said, *"Worse, you may begin to paint like me!"*

The teachers of painting have always known the dangers of imitation and subservience, the two main practices of formal education. William Chase not only differed from us in his attitude toward education, but he had a quality of teacher-craft of which we knew just nothing: in the crude strivings of a child he could sense the possibilities of future power and distinction.

Perhaps we should not too much blame ourselves for our ignorance of such matters; but inasmuch as we teachers are really professors of childhood, with diplomas reciting our peculiar qualifications in this craft, one might well invite us to know more about our subject and less, perhaps, about our subjects. The life of a gifted child is more important, I fancy, than either cube root or the nominative absolute.

Personally, I am willing to own to a sensation of guilt; not on account of the girl who persisted in her lonely faith in herself, but for the hundreds of others whom I might have helped if I had been more "discerning."

III

I turn now to a boy who was of another type entirely. He had one thing in common with the girl, to be sure, an obvious indifference to our daily tasks; and another, he was equally silent and undisturbing. Not brilliant, but a good boy, I should have described him. If asked if he had any interests outside of school I should probably have said, "I doubt it; he is just a healthy, unaggressive, stolid lad." But I might have added, "Oh, he plays baseball, sometimes to the neglect of a proper preparation of home assignments."

A very young teacher, however, not much more than a boy himself, thought differently. He kept bothering us about the boy's exceptional gift as a baseball player, insisting that it was a special coordination of eye, ear — yes, ear! — muscles, and brain which only the rare great ones had, and that this twelve-year-old lad had it!

I do not recall that any of us attended over carefully to the enthusiasm of this very young teacher. Baseball was not on our daily lesson plans. Young teachers do stir up extraordinary likings for this and that oddity among pupils; but they get over all that after a while. We turned to the real business of life, our cube roots and our nominative absolutes.

A year later the young teacher staged some sort of inter-school baseball game — he was always hanging around with the youngsters after hours instead of training himself in his profession by taking courses at the university; you all know the sort of chap — and he managed adroitly to have one of the great masters of the game drop in to watch the boys at work. Well, in one glance the great master of baseball — I shall name no names, but thousands of fans would recognize him instantly — proclaimed that the thirteen-year-older holding down second base had the rare creative gift of the born player!

"Notice the way he sways," he said, "gently to and fro as he vibrates with the batter. He is therefore always balanced just right. As the batter swings, he senses whether that ball is going to be hit; and as it cracks on the bat his ear tells him where it is going to land. His rhythm is so timed that he has started in advance toward the right spot. And he collects that ball with a motion that carries right into the throw to first, so that no energy is lost. Look at the way he automatically rights himself from the pick-up so that he is braced to make the throw without the needless loss of a second!"

As nearly as I can recall it, that is the gist of the observations of the master player. Five years later that lad played in a world series on the team of the master player — he has a reputation for picking them young — and the boy has since added other world series experience to that.

Now the young teacher who was so persistent in bothering us about the native possibilities in this boy was at that moment exhibiting his own special genius, but I am sure that neither he nor any of us gave that a thought. Problem children and the inadequate social organization that makes them a problem have since been his life study; he is the author of authoritative works on these subjects and he became the chief administrative officer of one of the important national organizations for studying and remedying the social conditions that prevent the fullest child development.

The discerning person who senses the gifted ones is rare, but that should be of great encouragement to the boys and girls who are now facing their mysterious adult future. I do not mean to imply by these incidents that every boy or girl who does not find an interest in his lessons is a predestined success. Nor am I scolding conscientious teachers for trying to instill into their classes some of the rewards of disciplined knowledge. The great truth for both teachers and students to realize is this: A gift exists in each one of us, some sort of gift; but we must find it for ourselves. And we must refuse to be discouraged by the depressing prophecies of some of our elders. There is just a chance that they might not be so "discerning" as they think they are.

CHAPTER XVII

Creative Business

FOR YEARS I HAD been teaching the usual things in the usual way. After an extended experience in both elementary and high-school grades I believed I knew pretty much all there was to know about boys and girls. Good boys and girls, I reasoned, were those who studied the lessons I assigned to be done; bad boys and girls, of course, were the young rascals who did not bother about my lessons at all but went off on their own hook. Well, the good ones got my smiles and my fine marks, and the others got what's what. But eventually I nearly always found myself liking the rascals.

My regeneration was beginning when a certain sinner took my eye one day because he looked so contentedly stupid. Stupid as a cow, I thought as I watched him. His worried father had just been to see me. I had already talked with his worried mother. The boy had failed in most subjects and could give no adequate reason for it. The parents were a much distressed pair, but the boy was seemingly unconcerned.

The mother had asked me, I recall, "Do you think he has lost his wits?" My own thought was that one had first to have wits before losing them. But I did not express this idea to the mother. I had already learned that one does not say such things to mothers.

As I watched him on one particular day when the class was engaged in a writing job, I noted that he had sat without stirring for nearly an hour. Of course I should have called him to task, but I did not; I could think of nothing adequate or useful to say to him. So, "Ox," I said to myself. "Too stupid even to move!"

Still I liked the lad. "Ox," I may have said to myself, but I grinned at him pleasantly when finally he did stir slightly and glanced in my direction. He did not grin back, however, a fact that gave me a creepy feeling; there was not a spark of answering light in his eye; he remained as stolid and lifeless as a fish head.

At the time I thought it merely another evidence of stupidity; but later I learned the cause of it all, and it was far from stupidity. For months that boy had been absorbed with a great idea; it had taken literally all of his mind; for want of a better name I have always called it "Creative Business," for it had to do with buying on an unprecedented scale and selling at a rate so low as to seem silly, but since that time several famous American fortunes have been made in exactly that way.

The idea had spread in his mind until it took up all his thinking time. Lessons dwindled in importance. The idea required a tremendous amount of concentration, for problems came up every day, and the solution of even a part of one of them demanded, sometimes, the hard thinking of several weeks. Often a seemingly unsolved bit would be put aside while other unfinished matters were passed in review; and the mere vacation from the difficult phase would be enough to make the solution easy and simple at the next attempt. In some instances complexities that had remained a tangle for days were cleared up in a flash, as if an outside source, like an inspiration, had sent a distinct message. All this I learned from him many years later.

Now while this highly intellectual process was going on in his brain the boy was outwardly a wooden image. Teachers did most of the talking in that school, fortunately for "creative business," so the classrooms were not at all bad places for the exercise of his type of mind; but these same teachers had a disturbing habit of stopping now and then to stir things up with questions. In the midst of a problem of vast buying that meant negotiating with the copper miners of New Mexico and the toy workers of Bohemia, which included problems of customs, transportation, assembling, and distribution, our lad would be suddenly assailed with such irrelevant questions as, "Who followed Tiglath-Pileser as ruler of Assyria?" or "Perhaps, William, you can give us now the typical case-endings of a third declension i-stem?"

I remember once trying to help him when he was leaning forward and looking straight at me with a startling appearance of interest in what I was doing with that class, "William," I said, "have you ever really written anything with interest, anything outside of a school assignment, a letter or a story or a poem, something that you wanted to do for yourself?"

He continued to stare at me without a tremor of a movement. I repeated the question, but it was only the second laugh of the class that brought him out of the clouds.

He stood up to take his punishment; light went out of his eyes; a stooping dullness crept over him; the whole picture was that of a typical class fool. It took some pedagogical persuasion to keep that merry mob from baiting him.

"I didn't hear the question," he mumbled. As he always repeated the same formula, the class whooped their approval of the lark.

Again I gave him the question, trying by genial tone to put him at ease, "Have you ever written anything, William, because you really wanted to do it yourself? Something that honestly absorbed your interest?"

"Yes, sir," he said stolidly.

"What was it about?" I asked gently.

"Copy of the price of oils, paints, and varnishes in tank-load and hogshead lots," he answered.

Even William joined eventually in the merriment that followed that answer.

He went up in everybody's estimation after that; we all put him down for a humorist, but even there we were wrong. That copy had been done by stealth from the secret memoranda of a corporation that had made its millions through preferential rates both in costs of raw materials and in transportation. A friend, a boy clerk, had permitted Wil-

liam to get it during a lunch period, every minute of which
had been filled with excitement, for discovery would have
meant instant discharge for his friend and possible legal
trouble for William.

Naturally this information was not given to us during the
class session. William sat down without further word, satisfied, it seemed, with his abrupt promotion from class fool
to class funny-man.

II

A few weeks later he told his parents that he had a job.
It was in the basement of one of a nationally known series of
chain stores. When asked what he would get for his services
he returned a characteristic answer that he had not inquired,
but that he thought it couldn't be more than four dollars a
week.

Just everything that boy did seemed to point to a meager
mental equipment.

In school he dreamed but did not study, but in business he
studied and ceased dreaming. His mastery of every operation within his humble field and his terrific drive at the tasks
assigned brought results instantly. The school knows its
scholars and grades them, but business knows its bright
boys, too, and the grading takes the stimulating form of
bigger jobs and more pay in the envelope. From the basement of one of these stores William started up until he was
manager of a string of them.

Let me illustrate this a little further before I give William's answer. The commonest question asked the story
writer is about the originals of his characters. Most of the
readers seem to think that these are careful portraits of
friends and acquaintances with only the names and ad-
dresses changed. Now that would be no fun for the writer;
it would take a deal of trouble to do that sort of job; and I
am quite certain that it would be no fun for his friends and
acquaintances!

The fact is that the writer cannot do so well with persons
he knows intimately; it is the chance acquaintance, the
merely passing stranger often, who gives him his best

material. But even then it is only a hint or a suggestion that he needs, something to stir up the mysterious forces of his creative self; the rest is pure invention.

A word said in the dark may start a complete novel; a gesture or a laugh of a passer-by may be the beginning of a strong story; a newspaper clipping may offer all that is needed for a tale of adventure. The author's pride, remember, is not for the sources of his invention but for the invention itself.

III

Writers and artists themselves, of course, understand all about this and will agree in private that the public doesn't know what it is talking about. Now, William, I maintain, was a creative artist. He knew about the mystery of his mind and he respected it; and he knew exactly what had started him off in the career that brought him ample later rewards.

It was a bit of a conversation he had overheard while waiting with his father to buy a pair of shoes. Two well-dressed men of the clerical type had mentioned several instances of the vast margin of difference between the wholesale price of most commodities of popular usage and the price paid eventually by the consumer; and they had advanced the theory that fortune was awaiting the men who would buy in quantity and dare to sell far below the present market. They gave vivid concrete examples of organizations that had discovered the gold mine which lay hidden in just that procedure.

From that time on, his mind set itself to the problems involved; he read everything that touched on prices and distribution; in imagination he lived the fairy life of one who controlled every step in a given production from raw material to the customer's check, and, naturally, the life of school books became faded and dull.

All the essentials of the plan that he pursued successfully, including employment in the basement of one of the chain stores, were worked out in the dazed-world he inhabited during his last year at school. Nearly all the problems he had confronted in those long hours of vivid thinking were, he has assured me, the problems he met again in actual business; and the solutions of his serious dreaming were practically the roads out that common sense later dictated.

IV

There are two sorts of men in business, salaried persons and creative persons. William belonged to the kind who disdain the routine that leads to a safe if small wage; he was the inventor type who turns old accepted things into strange new things.

He had the fierce absorption of the artist when in the act of creating the new out of the old; and at such times he might easily risk the charge of stupidity, but, in the long run, he becomes the wise man to whom all go for advice, whose very name among his own group is a symbol of superior intelligence.

CHAPTER XVIII

Dumppiddyfetchets

IN THE LATE TEENS there is often a tremendous blocking of native self-expression when the desire to talk of one's personal affairs meets the frustrating fear of exposure.

Mothers wonder what *is* the matter with their young-woman daughters; teachers sometimes report dull indifference to lessons, or stubbornness, or outright displays of irritability. No one seems to be able to guess — and yet we have all gone through it! — that it is simply the natural period of absorption in oneself, and that confession, or at least an outpouring of some sort in talk, is imperative.

What am I worth? What is going to happen to me? What should I do with my life? These are some of the questions which cannot be answered without outside help. Sometimes there may be more depressing questions, dangerously so, such as, Am I no good, as everybody seems to believe? Is there any hope for me at all in this great, selfish stampede to get somewhere in life? What's the use of living anyway?

When this natural and healthy stage is explained to mothers or to teachers they are usually both puzzled and hurt. "Why couldn't she have come to me?" they ask pathetically; or, "My boy surely knows that I would understand and sympathize!"

Mothers and dear friends will not always do. It is not a question of affection or of sympathetic understanding. My own guess is that the young person wants to talk this out and prefers someone he will never see again; it is the talk that is important, and even that he wishes to forget afterward. A friend might easily become an uncomfortable reminder of a moment of weakness.

One of the devices to secure relief is to write to a complete stranger, but it must be someone who has shown a public interest in the affairs of youth, the pastor of a distant church, for instance, or the author of a book.

Here are extracts from two such letters pertinent to this study of manifestations of the creative life: one is from a boy who is depressed because of the possession of an irrepressible native gift; the other is from a girl who finds the traditional course of study not fitted to her creative needs. A reply is presented immediately after each letter.

Only two letters are given here, but they will illustrate the contrasting character of the problems for which no answer is supplied by near-by friendly agencies. A volume could be filled with types of this sincere attempt of older youth to understand themselves in relation to the world in which they find themselves.

While many of such letters fall into easily classified groups, the variety of needs is a continual surprise. They range from the urge of a girl to prepare herself for a man's job, the management of a steamship line (her father is a sea captain), to the desire of a boy to save his parents from a separation toward which he sees all too clearly that they are drifting.

The outstanding fact is that thinking youth is everywhere leading a serious, and sometimes tragic, concealed life with which the machinery of school and home has not prepared itself to deal.

No one seems to believe this. Mothers, teachers, and best friends are particularly insensitive to its existence. They continue to pass summary judgments on clumsy or silent young persons, often exhibiting the crude taste of a public remark. Here is an exact speech, taken down on the spot. It was spoken with friendliness and nice humor, to be sure, but it was ignorantly cruel: "Marie is getting to be such a dear moody Dumppiddyfetchet, always *reading* and never being silly and sociable like the *rest* of us. *Aren't* you, dearie? *Come,* draw your chair up *into* the circle, dearie! Don't hang back and be a Dumppiddyfetchet!"

The general picture I retain from such letters as have

come to me bears no resemblance to a Dumppiddyfetchet. To me these young persons are gay, alert, keen-witted. They toss formalism aside, always an act of intelligence and social assurance; their company gaucherie is completely gone; the hidden creative life steps forth, a marvelously expressive thing. With jest they often own up to their everyday mask; but as they know that no one will believe that they can be capable of thinking, they invariably beg that their identity shall never be disclosed.

Anyone who takes the trouble to acquire the technique of reaching into the secret life of these older youth will find something of great human value. The first step is clear: one must believe in it; one must believe that everyone possesses it, even the seemingly stupid; and particularly one must believe that it is most powerful and worthy among those same inarticulate Dumppiddyfetchets.

II

Robert S., of Illinois, writes:

"I'm always getting sent out of the room. The teacher says I try to be smart, and I say I'm smart without trying, and then we fight; at least he does, for I always laugh and say something that gets him riled and then I park in the principal's office. If he'd only laugh like the others do, he'd be better off, because I like his work and do my best in it and I'd rather stay in the room.

"Sometimes I resolve to keep quiet, but something is always happening and I forget. It just bubbles up, especially when I am feeling good. Maybe you know how it is when you're feeling good.

"I was polite as I could be when I picked up a mistake in addition which he had made on the blackboard and he said, 'I *think*, maybe, I've made an error here.' And I said, '*I know*, maybe, you have!' He was nice about that, although he scared me for a minute. Then I showed him a new way to do the problem and he got sarcastic and said, 'I suppose you'll be a teacher yourself some day.' And I said, 'Oh, maybe, if I can't get a regular job.' Bing! I was trotting off to the office again.

"He's a good sport sometimes, though. He does make mistakes, and one time he said, 'Robert, you're not half bad at math,' and I said, 'You're only quarter bad yourself.' He took that all right. And he laughed when he was giving his favorite do-it-in-your-head problems. He was saying, 'He made eight yards but reversed and went a quarter of the distance back, was tackled and dropped the ball, which went back six yards when he recovered and was then —' 'Fullback,' I said, and everybody laughed and so did he.

"Maybe this is just being smart. I don't know. But one thing I do know and that is that I never have to *try* to be.

"Just the same, I feel rotten most of the time about it."

"Harold's case will interest you. He is a distinguished man now, but I knew him when he was a boy like you.

"Invariably, whenever I talk with the men and women whom I knew as children, I find abundant proof that they have made their successes out of something they always had. And it has these three qualities: it was something they enjoyed, something they did easily, something that many of their elders underrated. Even they themselves thought little of it; so a fourth should be added — they did not know its real worth and suspected that it had none.

"When Harold was a lad of your age he punned and twisted words about in a ridiculous fashion. He was a terrible nuisance. It was impossible to discuss anything seriously in his presence. If a history book belonged to a girl he would call it a *her*-sterry — I am giving his pronunciation — while he would dub his own book a *my*-sterry book. He would say, 'I left my *my*-sterry at home; will you lend me your *your*-sterry and you look off Jack's *his*-terry?' Or, 'If you misspell "misspelling" so that it is "mispelling"' pointing to the word as he had written it, 'would it still be "misspelling"?' Or, to a chap who had grabbed something selfishly, 'You'd get high marks in p-i-g-ography.'

"A long-winded speaker addressed the school one day on 'The Seven Wonders of the World.' The bells rang for dismissal, but he heeded them not. He went on. And on. Teachers stood up, back to the speaker, and glared to keep the restless youngsters quiet and polite. The speaker went on. Finally, he said, 'Now, children, I've told you of the Seven Wonders of the World. What will the eighth wonder be? What little boy or girl will tell me?' Harold's hand went up. 'I wonder when we're goin' to git out,' he said.

"Naturally he was often sitting on the anxious bench in the principal's office. At these times he was a most scared small person. As a rule the principal would take pity upon the frightened youngster and let him off; but there came one afternoon when the boss's heart hardened and he resolved to cure the lad once and for all; and, remember, it was in the days when that meant ten smart whacks from a rattan switch.

" 'What were you sent down here for?' the principal asked swiftly. 'More impertinence, I presume.'

" 'Yes, sir.' The white face looked up, honest and game.

"The principal softened at the frank reply. 'What was it?' he asked more gently.

" 'She said — I'd made her mad at sumpin' — she said, madder an' louder, "What would you say if I sent you down to the principal?" an' ' — grinning and lowering his gaze but still trembling — 'an' I said I'd say — '

" 'Well,' kindly, 'what did you say you'd say?'

" 'I said I'd say, "Well, I'll be switched!" and that made everybody laugh, an' so — she sent me down.'

"The two grinned at each other. Finally the principal said, " 'Well, you will be switched — the very next time I hear of your making remarks like that. You've got to control this funny way of talking back that sets the class laughing and disturbs the teacher or out you go. If you can't work with me you can't work for me. Do you understand what that means?'

"Some blood began to steal back into the boy's face; it had been a narrow escape from a real terror. 'Yes, sir,' he smiled up in grateful friendliness. 'If I don't shut up you'll shut down.'

"Nowadays when certain big executives want a difficult deal put over before a conference or even before a legislature or a Congressional committee, they send Harold in. I presume his plans are no better than any other person's; for the most part he is simply using the ideas of other men in the business; but his gift of repartee and his funny twist of phrase send a warmth through any meeting that simply melts opposition. He has the vote wavering in his favor before he begins to put over the proposal; he has a way of seasoning the most solemn business propositions to make them appetizing. And as an after-dinner speaker he is a rare delight.

"Robert S., of Illinois, you may have a great natural ability, the power to turn the highly artificial thing called language into instant use for attack and defense; back of that is always a special type of active brain; to have humor with it adds enormously to the gift. This sort of thing is rare and men pay high for it.

"Its dangers are obvious. It must never lose its keen edge of healthy and harmelss humor. If it cuts too deep, the world will have none of it. One of my best friends had this gift, but while he rose high, he began to use it with bitterness, and he failed. His friends even began to avoid him, for they were always nervously aware that they might at any time be made the target for one of his astonishing shafts. I recall how he introduced the chief guest at a dinner, a thrifty rich man, one notoriously careful to count his change, who had just returned from Europe: 'The only speaker of the evening,' he said, 'is our honored guest, who will address us on "How I Went to Europe with One Sovereign and One Shirt and Did Not Change Either."

"We all agreed years later that that dinner marked the end of my friend's career.

"Your gift, Robert S., may bring you in hundreds of dollars a performance; and it may thwart you at every turn that leads forward.

"But do not let anyone persuade you that it is not a powerful and rich personal possession."

III

F.V.B., of Massachusetts, writes:

"I have just written you an eight-page letter and torn it up. For your sake I shall be concise and personal.

"I go to school for five and one-half hours each day. Outside I study approximately two. The powers that be at school have told us that in order to pass our College Board examinations we must do extra supervised work of two hours a day. All right! Morning, afternoon and night all filled up. Lovely! But what about the other things?

"In order to go to college, I must give up all else, have no leisure to 'find myself,' and devote my time and faculties to studies, some of which I care nothing about. Is college worth it to me?

"They tell us these are the formative years; the indecisive years; the years in which we must ponder; the years on which so much of our future life depends. And then they make out a curriculum which we must follow and leave us no time in which to explore those branches which promise a career.

"I love to sing, but if I prepare for college, I have no time to study singing. I love and long to cover reams of paper with startling and original thought, but — I have no time!

"In regard to all this — for me — don't you think a special course in one line, even an interesting working position after I am graduated from high school, would be more valuable than college?

"I think I am not lazy. Please understand. I want to follow the course that will profit me the most in character and happiness in the end."

"This letter is hard to answer. The usual return for such frank questions as these is an evasive set of generalizations, for adults are afraid to speak the truth to youth; from the earliest Santa Claus days they have tossed their young a series of safe myths to meet each cry of intelligent hunger. A truthful reply is sure to be misunderstood, they argue; it may even be the means of driving some youth to wrong decisions; it will arouse indignation among certain types of unthinking adults. I propose in my answer to take all those risks.

"Let us get rid of a few uncomfortable facts first. The traditional aim of the college is to make scholars, learned persons. History is there presented with the plan of making one a historian or at least a professor of history. College chemistry is organized to fit one to be a professional chemist.

The object of the course in literature is to equip one with a scholarly knowledge, historical and critical, of the whole range of the literary output. And so on.

"As a student curious of human ways I may wish to grasp the significance of differential calculus. What is it about? I may ask. What does it do? To discover answers to these simple questions I must take the whole course; but the course aims to make me something I have no desire to be, namely, an expert technician, a scholar, and a learned man in the subject. Trigonometry, for instance, has unfolded fascinating things to me concerning the cleverness of the human mind; with it I see how man can measure inaccessible land, can spot the location of a hidden submarine, can guage the distance of faraway stars; but to gather this fascination I had to take a technician's course in trigonometry.

"Another uncomfortable fact is that good scholarship and good teaching do not necessarily go together. Santayana, a scholar and a wise man, once said to me, "There is no necessary relationship between teaching and scholarship; in fact, there is opposition. A sensitive scholar is often hurt by the impertinent demand that he also instruct the immature. Scholars teach mainly because scholarship is not 'endowed'.

"The long fight for the liberalizing of education, which began with the introduction of the kindergarten, has now reached the higher learning. The air is full of the debate on the changing college. In time all our dreams will come true, but, meanwhile, F. B. V. of Massachusetts, you wait for an immediate answer.

"Well, what of you, and the likes of you, who turn to the creative life for your solace and for the final expression of yourself in the community? At the start, as you so clearly see, you face a conflict. The creative life is spun from within; the scholar's life is built of outside materials. You are the artist type, and the artist has never fared comfortably in the schools of scholarship; so, if you are an artist, as I presume you are, college has little to offer, and that little must be won at a great sacrifice. The commonest tale I hear from creative artists of repute is of their bitter struggle against the prejudices of college scholarship.

"To be fair, however, I must admit that if you can live the scholar's life for the four years of college, without too much sense of frustration, you will be able to extract something of great value from it, though you may never be a scholar again. There is no space to enlarge upon this; so I state it dogmatically as a sure truth: even for the artist this temporary life of the scholar may not be wholly waste. No one who sniffs at scholarship because it makes unpleasant demands upon his mental powers is likely to be heard from in the world of art.

"But to you and your sort I say generally: (1) If you must go to the scholar's college, choose one that is friendly to the artist type, and that is open-minded enough to experiment with ways and means for furthering a creative attitude toward life. Better, rather, select a music college or art college, the one that comes closest to your creative gifts. Refuse to follow the crowd to any college, whether it is the social crowd or the athletic crowd. Send for catalogues everywhere. Inquire of those who have been here and there. Search day and night for information concerning colleges which hold the newer faith: that while scholarship may be the proper goal for some, for others the way to wisdom and enlarged living may come through a broad cultivation of spiritual and creative powers. Would there were more of them!"

CHAPTER XIX

Introjection

PRESSURE MOLDS US INTO what we are, and it begins soon after birth. Psychiatrists have given us a handy name for the process by which the social environment puts its eventual stamp upon us. "Introjection" they call it. All of us are the victims of introjection. What we might have been we never can know; the family "introjects" us, and we talk and walk and think like the family, fight for its absurd "political" beliefs, take over its prejudices against this or that "class" or race, bow before its traditional gods; the already "introjected" children of our earliest acquaintance turn swiftly upon us to advance the job, and school and then society complete it.

All this may be as it should be, but it is at least amusing to think that possibly we have never seen a natural "un-introjected" child; and that, if this is true, then parents and teachers, whose business it is to know all about children, cannot possibly know anything about them. One cannot speak intelligently about something one has never seen. "Nonsense," I hear you say; "I was a child myself, and I guess I know something about the animal." But were you ever a child? Perhaps you were merely an introjection.

Some glimpses of the real child, however, have been seen in this our day. It has come about partly because of the slow change in the kind of introjecting environment which the family and the school had hitherto set up around the child. Some of the nagging pressure has been removed, and, naturally, a new kind of child was bound to emerge. And, further, a new kind of parent and teacher has appeared, one who has sought out the real child and has given it a chance.

II

But before I go into that I should like to ask a question of those who think they know children, or rather, of those who believe that the child they see is a natural creature and not the resultant of surrounding and compelling forces. Do you believe that the normal picture of a large group of six-year-olds at play is that of a noisy, darting, selfish, shrill-voiced mob; that they do little reasoning; that their language is on a low plane; that they have little sense of what is really fine or beautiful?

Well, that is the exact picture of the introjected child and not the real child at all. Placed in an environment of hysteria and selfish grabbing and nervous rushing about, he becomes that child which we all know so well; but I could tell you of thoughtful parents and teachers who have made another environment for their children where all the social expectations contradict those listed above.

In such an environment I have seen four- and five-year-old children move with the deliberate pace of older persons; the hum of work has pervaded their group, with nothing of what even a sensitive elder could call noise; the voice tones have been low and the speech calm; there would be no nervous darting about or that nervous fear of the neighbor which leads to grabbing and hoarding of property.

More startling than this is the evidence of quiet, long-planned reasoning, not different in essential character from our own except that it seems more rational and less a clacking of repeated prejudices.

Let me take you to an audience of high school teachers in a small city far from the currents of fresh thinking. A speaker is telling them of the hopeful new vision of a self-reliant and resourceful youth. They listen politely but are not moved. Among the rigid women are a few eager faces. The men have captured the rear seats; they sprawl and look at the floor or face sideways in bored profile; old, most of them, worn but wiry. They hear of the high-school boy or girl who really thinks; studies hard for the love of a far-off and difficult result; speaks a free, warm language; has respect for fine things; turns out a written phrase that is the wonder and the delight of our best men and women. They are still not moved. They know high-school boys and girls. They know how to keep them on the job, how to insure the suppression of mischievous personalities, how to prevent a single exercise in the native language.

I am wondering why these tired and unconvinced souls come to such meetings; then I see one of their number standing at the door with rollbook checking off the late comers. They have been dismissed from school to attend a "teachers' meeting"; they will not get their small pay for the day if they do not bring their reluctant bodies through that door. All day they have been talked to. Three speakers in the morning; two in the afternoon. Horrible!

Relief comes with a thirty-minute play by pupils of the junior high school. They wake up, these stolid women and heavy men. At the conclusion they applaud earnestly. "That was good!" they say, and settle back to endure another speaker.

I watch the play. It is not good. It is very bad. Long memorizations of impossible adult speeches meant to be read silently, perhaps, but never to be delivered as dramatic dialogue. For instance:

A girl, wearing a broad band upon which is printed the legend "INDUSTRY," shouts: "I am the spirit of work. In the many and various occupations of modern civilization" — her face is set in solemn fear; her eyes seem to look terrified within; her whole mind is upon the words, therefore not a shred of personal meaning is given to the shrill, sing-song speech — "of which this city boasts sixty-four per cent. of the skilled employment of the state, Industry, which I and my five attendants" — a sudden jerky wave of the hand to the back of the stage, where six boys and girls stand in scared attention — "represent, will speak to you and show you what we can do. My attendants, come forth!"

They come forth with a sudden and sweaty determination and shout their awful lines, one little fellow beginning, "I am the miner who digs the coal and keeps the wheels of industry moving." Business of picking with an imaginary tool at an imaginary ceiling. "I excavate three kinds of coal, anthracite, which is a hard coal and most prized for the heating of dwellings; bituminous, which is a soft coal and is used for industries! and cannel coal, which is between a hard and a soft coal and is used in hearths and grates." And so on as the five other attendants declaim the faultless facts.

Then the miner says, with a gulp, as one might announce one's immediate suicide, "We will now dance, to show that the best workman is a happy workman."

Oh, incredible and pitiful! Those ungainly children stepped and hopped and turned and humped themselves this way and that to the muffled airs of an off-stage phonograph. The faces were strained and terribly set upon the job. Workmen they indubitably were, but they were not happy. One lad gave the whole thing away by counting with every lunge. To all the world his moving lips proclaimed a steady, "One, two, three, four! One, two, three, four!"

It went on; other groups followed; without humor, without a single grace of healthy childhood. It was some other person's words, some other person's ideas; every gesture and step was controlled; it was a book lesson recited and danced.

The stupendous feat of memory — verbal and bodily — came to a close. The curtain went up unexpectedly, to respond to the applause, and surprised a half-dozen boys and girls on the stage. This was something they had not studied. Startled, they laughed healthily and rushed to get away. Entangled in the side curtains, they called to one another in great glee, tossed the impediment this way and that, and finally found each a way out. That was the single natural thing in the play and it was charming and really beautiful. Their bodies had taken lovely poses, especially the arms as they struggled with the long folds; their delightful faces were charming with mirth; their voices were tripping with fine tones of childhood; their running from one side to the other was full of abrupt rhythms. Undiscovered dramatic treasure!

I talked to the children afterward to see if they had any conception of the stupid artificiality of their enforced performance. They had none. Proud of their work they viewed

themselves as dramatic successes. The teacher coach came
forward wearily to receive congratulations. "We worked
hard," she said. "No one will know how hard we worked."

For weeks that play moved before me: those strained,
scared faces; the shrill, declamatory speeches; the solemn
dances; the boy's lips announcing his "One, two, three,
four." They had no notion of the dramatic power of their
own speech, especially when impromptu; they would not
believe that their own bodies could be naturally beautiful in
movement; they would laugh at the thought that their own
ideas about the world might be even more moving, and certainly more convincingly expressed, than the sweated essay
of that teacher of industrial economics.

They would not believe that children of their own age
had put on plays and operettas written and composed by
themselves — often not written at all but made "on their
feet" when moved by the dramatic stimulus of rehearsal —
dramas which bore no evidence of the stilted language of
adults; that such children had made and given dances fashioned to their own mood; and that every moment of rehearsal and of final performance had been a supreme delight.
They could not believe; for it was a child which neither they
nor their teachers have ever seen. It was a child with a different supervisory environment.

III

Perhaps the most astonishing outcome of these new environments is the skill the children show in using their own
language. All our lives we struggle to express our feeling
and thinking appropriately in words. Without study and
without striving these differently placed children equal us
and sometimes outdo us. Once I showed an old-time English
teacher a group of verses that some children of my acquaintance had tossed off without effort seemingly. He read them
and passed them back. "It's a lie," he said. "I couldn't do
that well myself."

When the child is allowed to appear as artist, a perfection
in the handling of the medium makes us at first disbelieve
that a child could perform so well — like the frank gentle-

man who summed the whole thing up as a lie — until continued experience gives us the essential faith. Words come
forth with astonishing deftness; they place themselves together in a pattern that we have always been accustomed
to call mature. And they rise sometimes to startling heights.

Helen Elizabeth at fourteen has a portfolio of manuscript which her mother has shown me; the contents seem
astonishing until one realizes that her home environment
has been just the traveled and literary sort that would
make creative writing a natural outcome. She writes:

> Give me a man with a pie-bald mind
> And a brindled love for roaming
> And we will travel with the wind
> And never think of homing.

That man "with a pie-bald mind and brindled love for
roaming" has been roving through my own pie-bald mind
for the many months since I first read it. In granting the
liberty of life to these young persons they repay by the most
startling novelties. View, for example, her fearsome picture
out of elf-land; the Queen's child pages have made a brave
attempt to gather the lilies which Her Majesty has commanded but, daunted, they retreat to the safe shore, as one
may readily understand after a threat like this:

SELFISHNESS

> These are *my* lilies! You cannot go
> Out to get them. I keep them so —
>
> My golden mermaids will invite you!
> My bigly blackish snakes will bite you!
> My own quicksands will pull you down!
> And I will laugh to see you drown!
> Great bass bull-frogs will lullaby,
> Soft pollywogs will slither by
> Where your bodies lie!
>
> You big sillies,
> Go tell the Queen these are *my* lilies !

To show the wide range of their imaginative activity I
could give you sonnet or ballad or song from Helen Elizabeth's varied store, but will restrict myself to :

HIS EXCELLENCY'S MAKER OF PERIWIGS

Jane would walk (full-skirted disdain)
Down the cobbles of Hollyhock Lane.

Once she met the bespeckled man
With plebeian look of an artisan;

And though his buckled feet danced jigs
He made His Excellency's periwigs.

"And do you know," Jane winked her eye.
"The color of the sunset sky?"

"For that, my dear, a thousand figs!
For all I see are periwigs."

Miriam's mother has shown me another sheaf — again it is fourteen — one poem of which has given me a figure to stalk benignly beside all the great ladies and great gentlemen of the world. It is:

THE QUEEN'S MASTER OF MAKE-UP

The Queen appears in all her loveliness
In the heavy perfumed court;
She is enveloped in the mist
Of Royalty that rounds the corners
Of the world and hides the ugliness:
A Queen's eyes must see only Beauty.

"The Master of Make-up!" says the page,
And entering the Queen's boudoir
Followed by pages bearing great caskets —
The Master of Make-up.
Before him he sees a woman;
An hour later he leaves a Queen.

The Master of Make-up sees the Queen,
The superb creation of his art,
Lady of blue-green mist garments
In the *lourdeur* of the court.

The Master of Make-up
Knows a peasant woman
Who wears the mask
And garments of a Queen,
But he is loyal, and is silent.

Again to show the multifarious character of their young minds I give you from Miriam's manuscripts a different picture and a different feeling:

AT SUNSET THEY CALLED ME

I look after you as you disappear in the darkness;
It is too late to try and follow.

I remember you when we walked together across the fields;
You walked quicker than I and waited every little while for me to
    catch up.
You often stopped to pick a flower,
But you soon tired of it and would toss it carelessly aside.

There were others who tried to amuse me with childish unrealities;
You told me things I could not quite understand.
Still, I thought about all you said, and sensed your meaning.
You said beauty was related to mind
As twilight to the harshly impersonal lucidity of day.
You said lives were trivial, ephemeral,
But life was real.

Recently you have talked little and kept alone.
Often I have seen you sitting beside the pond at night
Staring at the luminous water.
I have come close to you and called your name;
You have rarely heard me.
But once you turned suddenly and said,
"When you, too, are old, the moon's reflection will seem lovelier
    than the moon."

This morning you did not speak to me at all.
You touched my cheek—I could feel your hand trembling —
And kissed me. Then, clenching your hands, you walked out of
    the house.

They say you sat motionless in the meadow all day,
And at sunset you rose and started to walk westward.
Then they called me.

I am here now, but all I can see is a dim shape far off.
I look after you as you move into the misty shadows.

They slip into unheard-of language, these unfettered ones,
which delights us because of its charming surprise, as witness this highly philosophical effort of a four-year-old:

EVERYTHING IS SOMETHING ELSE

O the towel and the bath,
And the bath and the soap,
And the soap was the fat,
And the fat was the pig,
And the pig was the bran,
And the bran makes sausages,
And man eats the sausages,
And God gets man.

The last illustration is taken from *Singing Youth*, Mabel Montsier's storehouse of children's verse. The early Perse *Playbooks*, of which *Home Work and Hobbyhorse* and *The Play Way* have been published in America, and all the publications of The City and Country School, New York City, are valuable for research students in this field: *Before Books*, a year's record of four-year-olds; *Adventuring with Twelve Year Olds; Experimental Practice*, a record of seven-year-olds, and *Eight Year Old Merchants*. Harriet M. Johnson's *Children in the Nursery School* is crowded with new information about the early years of the very young child.

Although published several years ago these and other books that exhibit the creative work of free children have a curious timeless quality, as have three recent reports from those who have entered wholly welcomed into the secret regions of child life and have affected that life for ever-lasting good. They are Helen Parkhurst's *Exploring the Child's World* and Florence Cane's *The Artist in Each of Us*, previously noted here, and Gladys Andrews' *Creative Movement for Children (Prentice-Hall)*. Dr. Andrews' volume is beautifully illustrated by most attractive photographs. It shows how one can use creative rhythmic movements to help boys and girls develop their desires for self-expression through art, music, language, science, all the school subjects; and it will still be effective and up-to-date fifty years from now.

And just this morning comes an old friend, the latest issue of *Poems by Camp Fire Girls*, delightfully individual and refreshing, edited by Ted Malone.

CHAPTER XX

One Food of the Spirit

READING, INCLUDING THE DRAMATIZATION that goes with reading, silent or openly played, is one of the important foods of the creative life. It is rich in vitamins, the right sort is; those who have been deprived of its energizing units, either through lack or because of a repugnant school diet, may suffer later dangers in abbreviated lives.

If reading be the food of more abundant living, then we should do something about it, we mothers, fathers, and teachers. For myself I have a method for bringing the non-reading child, and the non-reading adult, for that matter, into a participation of my interest in the written word, but I touch it here with hesitation, for it is just not possible, without grave misunderstanding, to translate into printed phrases what is really a performance, a reaction of spirit upon spirit.

With misgiving, then, I say that in tempting others to try the creative world of reading I do not hesitate to dramatize whatever I present to them. If I cannot so dramatize it I cannot read it to anybody. We must "be" the thing we read before we can appreciate it or have others appreciate our reading of it. If it is sad, we must be sad; if it is gay, we must be gay; and if it loves, we must love, too; and if it lilts and springs about and dances and sings (and here I know I shall be misunderstood as a unique fool, which I hasten to say I do succeed in not being) we must lilt and spring about and dance and sing. We must do all these things in our hearts and so become one with the written word; and if some of it escapes to a suggestion of visible and audible acting (I pray you do not let all of it so escape!), then our spirit takes on new power, becomes clairvoyant, and sees and speaks with the hosts of the invisible.

A higher appreciation of art always follows dramatization, whether it be of literature or of history or geography. When those little Western children stood in a semicircle, hand holding hand, and thought of themselves as the great Sierras which look down benignly upon their native California and forever, night and day through the ages, protect their land from blight and storm and the desert drought; and when they swayed gently and sang a recitative of the protecting might of the hills, I am sure that their imaginations were so touched that all their days they will feel the nearness of those mountains which they have once been themselves, and they will be the better for it. And those other children who sang and danced in the imaginary valley, who called joyously to their friends, the mountains, and named themselves orange blossom, apple blossom, down-o'-the-peach, wheat field, vineyard, these, too, grew in everlasting appreciation of their wonderful land.

All great literature is dramatic. That is what makes it literature. Just because literature is itself dramatic — a play in which the reader is always the actor — it needs less theatric props and make-up than do the other branches of learning. I have seen dramatizations which simply swamp the poem under consideration and often make a caricature of it. In literature dramatization is only a device to make the appreciation more easy; its object is to bring the listening spirit out, to make it less self-conscious by making it a silent performer, to have it sway with the right vibration. For that reason the reader should often be the sole company of players. But woeful memories! I have heard just such a reader, in classroom, in the nursery, and on the radio, when every character was simply miscast!

To get the creative spirit vibrating properly — in tune, as it were — is the object of dramatization in reading, whether that be done by the teacher or parent acting a part, or by the children living over the reading in a play of their own making. Now the children, as a rule, give us no trouble. Their creative spirit is easily accessible. It requires only a touch to bring it out. It is so easy to set the little chaps in tune with a fine art. The older person has only to beckon into the land of make-believe.

As we grow older that beckoning gesture becomes an increasingly difficult thing to make. The struggle of existence hardens us, puts the grim lines about our eyes, sets our mouths, brings out the worst in us and congeals the better. Unless we watch, and perhaps pray, the creative spirit dies within us, or retreats so far into the recesses of our being that it may come out as seldom as the ground hog, and, like him, looking only for trouble, flying, indeed, at the sight of its own shadow. But these are just the times when the art of the reader becomes superlatively the art of the actor, of assuming an alien part. And this is my faith, that if we put on the appearance of life and cheer and interest in things, our own hidden spirit may be enticed to come forth again.

Indeed we may thus teach it to grow and arise at our bidding. We may bring our will to fight age. "On my soul!" we may confidently cry, "I shall not let my light die out! I will not! I shall pretend, assume, put on gaiety when I feel least inclined to gaiety; I shall of a truth act well my part! At heart, at least, I will never grow old!" Literature summons the eternal youth in us to be eternal. It is a constant challenge to Old Time.

With even more hesitation I add, again from purely personal experience, that the reader is helped if he believes still more fervently that life as well as literature is dramatic. To me every day is a drama, a sort of tragi-comedy, filled with incident, alive with surprising dialogue, and charged with the drollest fun. Often it is shadowed by sadness, but more often it trips fantastically; and always there is the romance which may end happily, or, more happily still, not end at all! I play all parts, from high priest to clown.

Many may reasonably feel that these thoughts on bringing youth into the communion of the saints are not personally applicable; but it is never too late to be young.

II

When a mother wrote asking for a private consultation on a very serious matter concerning her twelve-year-old boy I was prepared for many intimate disclosures, but not for her nervous and almost tearful ejaculation, "My son reads nothing but the Motor Boat Boys, one after another, and then begins the series all over again. What *is* to be done about it?"

My answer did not please her at all. "Nothing need be done about it," I assured her. "It is a normal, healthy sign. Be thankful that he reads at all."

"But we are a literary family!" she cried, annoyed at my light attitude. "We read the best books. He is surrounded by — everything; but he just will not look at anything but the Motor Boat Boys, and we've tried both punishment and money to make him stop."

She represented a common worry of literary mothers, who do not seem to understand that taste is a matter of normal growth, that it has its juvenile stage as well as its adult stage, and that, like all growth, it cannot be uprooted or transplanted at will without danger. Literary mothers and teachers generally are disturbed when children read books appropriate to their growth-stage; so they introduce penalties or rewards to cure what they believe to be an evil.

At the beginning of the consultation, therefore, I proceeded to break down the false fears of this worried mother, and I could do so with assurance because for some years a group of us had been studying the growth in reading taste in a considerable number of children in all school grades from the first to the end of the senior high school. At that moment I had before me a plot of the reading-for-pleasure of the oldest group. It was most satisfactory from any standard that one might raise; and I had records of the reading of these same children when they were twelve-year-olds. I could show the mother how the girls had gone through their *Campfire Girls' Larks and Pranks* and the boys their *Boy Scouts in the Philippines* to emerge five years later with an unaffected delight in George Meredith's *The Egoist* and George Bernard Shaw's *Caesar and Cleopatra*.

It was easy, I recall, to bring assuring proof to this literary mother; and she has since found justification for our faith in her own lad. He came out of the Motor Boat Series at the proper season, and one day she dropped in to tell us gleefully how the boy had been holding forth rather vehemently in the home circle for three books which they had not yet got around to: Flecker's *Hassan*, Stephen's *Crock of Gold*, and Maurios's *Ariel*, literary enough, each of them, to suit the most ambitious of mothers. "He seemed just a little annoyed," she smiled, "at our failure to get the books immediately and make up our lack, and a little impatient, too, I think!"

"Ah-ha!" said I, and she grinned at me guiltily.

III

In our study of the reading tastes of children we took at various times a random selection of the favorite books of each young person. The simplest device for getting a cross section of the taste of a group is to secure the titles of the last few books read and the book now being read. Of course one must have worked up a right attitude toward such private confessions so that there is total absence of posing and no fear of the authorities. We were always at an advantage here because for years we had had no compulsory reading and had welcomed the worst penny dreadful with the same studied indifference as that of a limited edition on handmade paper.

The objective of our experiment was to discover what would really be read by healthy children if given complete liberty of choice *in a book environment of the most tempting sort which we deliberately placed in their way.* Please note that we were not interested in what unassisted children would happen to like.

Almost invariably in such surveys the seventh-grade children were found enthusiastic for juveniles, or for books of adventure by standard authors, or for books about children's affairs; and gradually from grade to grade the interest swung toward writers of distinction. To take one such list that I have before me, fifty-six per cent. of the seventh-grade titles are juveniles, divided equally between a literary group like *Bob, Son of Battle* and *Treasure Island* and non-literary types such as *The Rover Boys* and *Campfire Girls*. In the ninth grade the juveniles drop to twenty-eight per cent.; in the eleventh grade to two per cent.; and in the twelfth grade there is none at all.

So with standard authors and contemporary books of distinction. About one third of the seventh-grade list might have this high classification, mainly because standard authors like Dumas, Kipling, Marryat, Dickens, Cooper, and Doyle have contributed enormously to easy-reading adventure; but this classification accounts for sixty-five per cent. of the ninth-grade reading-for-pleasure; and in the twelfth grade the voluntary reading is almost wholly on a good mature basis, over ninety per cent.

This rapidly taken general view of the book-likings of the whole group gave us other interesting information. We learned, for instance, that for the seventh grade the "mode," or type of book attracting the most readers, was among the non-literary juveniles; for the ninth and tenth grades, among standard authors before Kipling; for the eleventh grade, among standard authors from Kipling on (Kipling, Conrad, Masefield, Shaw, Barrie, Synge, Stevenson, Moody, Frost, for example); and in the twelfth grade it rested among contemporary writers of consequence.

IV

We did something more, however, than watch children grow; we made a conscious effort to increase strength, endurance, and control of impulses. To spend five years in discovering that children do become older in time would not be much of a final announcement. That would be the Bo Peep Theory of children's reading. If you let them alone I should not be willing to guarantee that they will *all* come home with their literary tails wagging behind them. They might, at that! Certainly I prefer the Bo Peep Theory to the Old Woman Theory, devised by a lady, you remember, who was stupidly satisfied when she had spanked them all soundly and had sent them to bed.

In our work with children we achieved our best results from a persistent use of the Slow Mandy Theory, my own contribution to Mother Goose — as suggested by the following text:

> Slow Miss Mandy,
>   Her babies weren't fat,
> But they always wanted
>   What they couldn't get at;
> On the very top shelf
>   She put the cream in a crock,
> And she left the ladder handy
>   And the key in the lock.

The Slow Mandy Theory is worthy of a book, but all that I may do here is to make dogmatic statements about it as learned in a five-year experimentation; although in the volatile and unpredictable material called youth, I have learned to discount dogmatism.

Perhaps that is the first dogmatic statement to make: Never be dogmatic and never be superior. To sneer at taste is caddish at its best; and certainly it is futile. Taste is taste and should be respected at whatever level found.

Second, taste grows through the stages of saturation and surfeit. When all the Motor Boat Series have been read the fourth time the lad finds himself naturally ready for a slightly better grade of material.

Third, that material should be at hand at just that precise moment. Without a good library and a gifted librarian, none other than Anne T. Eaton, our advance would have slowed up seriously.

Fourth, the material that is to lift the Motor-boatist through the locks into the next level need not be really good in the adult or literary sense. Of course the Old Woman would cast it out the window as trash; but that is because she conceives taste as a leap from the ground floor to the roof (I always picture her pitching her children to bed into the top of that prodigious boot. She lived, you see, before the day of steps). A study of children's tastes will someday show us an inclined plane through many stages of inferior material up to that high literary standard over which teachers have customarily grown so frigidly ecstatic.

Fifth, an atmosphere of enticing suggestion must be set up, preferably by the children themselves. An honest enthusiasm from a child will easily convince another child of the worth of trying a book, while the most engaging smile of mother or teacher, accompanied by that lulling voice of pumped-up delight associated so often with bitter medicine, is as transparent to discerning youth as advertisements of fire sales.

Sixth, teachers, mothers, governesses, and elder sisters must cultivate honesty. In the matter of reading we are all afraid of disclosing our real likes; so we advocate the world's best literature when in our hearts we know that, for us at least, it is often the world's worst. We fear that if we tell the truth — so we rationalize — our influence with youth will be gone. Well, that should not worry us, for, to speak only of esthetics, that influence went long ago; and it will not come back until we elders cease playing safe on the matter of our personal tastes, for youth has ever been a foe to hypocrisy and pretense.

V

A large part of the Slow Mandy Theory, one sees, has to do with the discriminating withdrawal of some adult standards that do not correspond with child standards. Youth is the sole judge of what it likes. Another large part has to do with our own honesty in recording personal reactions to reading. Youth finds honesty in this matter easy enough and needs no lessons in it, but for adults it is a stiff course with failure almost certain.

Posing is so ingrained in us that few — let us be fair to ourselves — are even aware of practicing it. So the Slow Mandy Theory should not begin with children at all but with classes of adults. The subject for the first year should be a struggle to answer the question, "Now, honestly, what do I really read myself for pleasure and delight?" It will take the whole year, and there will be a lot of liars uncaught at the end.

The course should be compulsory for teachers, principals, superintendents of schools, textbook writers, publishers,

makers of courses of study, college entrance examiners —
oh, don't let us omit the college entrance examiners — and,
finally, governesses, elder sisters, and literary mothers.

CHAPTER XXI

Putting the Screws on 'em

As THIS STORY OF the creative life is a friendly challenge to the schools, one must face the conditions that actually exist in the highly mechanized organizations of so many public and private educational institutions. Personally I am most encouraged by the general outlook. I have just returned from a journey, made at the invitation of groups all over the country, during which time I came into personal relations with nearly twenty thousand persons. Their cordial welcome to the belief in the fruits of the spirit satisfies me amply as to the trend of education. And one year William Bogan brought me before three thousand of his Chicago teachers; they came from long distances after a day's work in the classroom, and their outspoken interest and their intelligent laughter I remember and prize as proof of the right sort of educational preferences.

Young teachers and artist teachers of experience, however, continue to tell me a different story of school conditions wherein the creative life has simply no chance for existence. Some of these are so worried over what they wrongly conceive to be their own failure that, again as with children, I must play psychiatrist to remove the great evil of depression.

To them I say, "Under the conditions you can do very little. No mere classroom teacher could do anything. Not only are the administrators of your school against free life but the community also; and even the pupils would oppose it. Cheer up and be thankful that in a small measure you may reach a few of your children. The problem in your case is not a classroom affair at all but a social problem that involves the whole of your little world. One might as well invite a savage tribe to remove the ring from their respective noses!"

Every part of a great country like ours does not advance with the same stride. Among certain groups of our population one hears the screaming of irate mothers, observes the wild shaking of children, the fierce smashes of mother hand to child face, brutality, really, which the children seem to accept as a useful and necessary part of living. School authorities in those neighborhoods would have difficulty in getting results from the children by more humane methods: certainly at first the children would not respect them if they should try. Of course, Angelo Patri obtained both respect and acquiescence; but, alas, Angelo Patris are not plentiful.

Here is a picture that is presented to me by a colleague in the University; he has permitted me to copy the letter which has just come to him from one of his teacher-students:

"You may recall the writer as a member of your class in Methods in Geography at Blank last year," she writes. "I am in a very unusual situation, a mouse in a huge cheese which has fibers so tough that it seems I cannot gnaw my way out. I need and crave your help.

"I have taken a position at Blank School, in a 100% foreign section. The homes of the children are for the most part very unhappy, with a sprinkling of happier ones. There are knocks and kicks, cursings, dirt, some vermin and other unhappy mixtures in the families. Perhaps you know the type in Blank?

"My 'job' is Geography, thirty-minute periods, ten periods a day in fifth and sixth grades. Promotions are made every three months. Specifically grade 5C is to 'cover' the Northeastern Section of the U. S. with stress on State Geography. Grade 5B is to cover North Central, Southern Plateau and Pacific States. Grades 5A and 6C, mixed, have South America and Europe; while 6B and 6C are to take Europe and Asia, all in three months. And they are expected to 'pass' an examination. I have one set of books for eight classes, Mc-Murry and Parkins, and only one.

"The child's interpretation is limited. We cannot call upon his experience except from his play on his own street. Very few read anything at all, and when they do it is the 'Tabloid paper.' They are up-to-date on murders and crime. As you may guess, it requires a big person to handle the situation.

"When I went there they tried me in a hundred ways — marbles, spitballs, rubber balls by the dozen. They laughed and talked and fought and disobeyed right and left. They did not respond to 'please' any more than a cow would. I was a pin in a heap of dirt.

"Little tots of nine are mixed in with huge fellows with I.Q.'s of sixty and less. There was not a thing I could tell them or show them that would interest them *all* at the same time. Even when they were not malicious they did not want anything I had. Finally with a huge stick brandished in the air I got attention. It is now five hundred per cent. better but so far from what I want. With forty-five in a class, of ages from nine to fifteen, it seems to me a stupendous task.

"You may know what I am up against when I tell you that a Miss Blank was there for years. She is now practically insane at the age of thirty-eight, in a sanitarium. The teacher who came after her resigned after six weeks. Men have a worse time than women, they tell me.

"Now, what do you think is the trouble? Is our system all wrong? What is the need of the child? Is it just lawlessness on his part, or rebellion against the lack of receiving what he needs? My principal is a kind man, sympathetic and human to a high degree. He wants smaller classes and opportunity classes for the defective or slow. We cannot have them. I feel as if I *must* succeed and help him. If I go he says he cannot get any one as good as I to come here. But I am not satisfied. The defiance, the bad habits, the inattention, the restlessness of the ones who cause the trouble make one's life miserable.

"How am I to find what the child needs? When found, how shall I meet them? I can't even get simple materials. I asked for labels from cans. They eat the same things every day — tomatoes, ripe olives, beans — I have about twenty so far.

"Assuming that the fault lies in me *alone* (I have never met rebellion in Geography work before), that I am inefficient, not big enough for the work, can you give me any suggestions as to what to do? I shall be willing to pay money for it and give you the glory.

"As it stands now, I am making little progress, tho far from giving up. When I get on the right track I shall steam up. By the way, yesterday I taught the Mississippi flood to all classes. *I* did all the talking and the map drawing. They merely listened. But they *did* listen. Is that teaching Geography? I got attention, but at night my throat ached. Then the old question, 'What shall I do now?'

"I know you are a busy man. I thought of writing you because I know you are so human; and you, if any one, can help me. Can you spare me some time?"

For anyone who has ever faced a classroom of children, that is a heart-rending picture. One's pity goes out to the brave young woman who is sticking it out, but one knows that the real trouble does not lie with her but with that whole community. Of course the school organization does not fit either individual or community needs. It would be a long story to tell what should be done, but many a reader knows without being told.

The commonest answer to a bad social condition is to outdo the community in the fierce disciplining of its children. "They're a bad lot," one principal told me, "so we put the screws on 'em, and then they are not so bad." Long experience with the screws had turned him, I noted, into the type which in the Army we call "hard-boiled."

A young teacher of experience in just such schools writes: "Education as it exists in most schools is cruel. I cannot see one redeeming feature about it. Thank goodness, the children do not seem to realize the extent of our cruelty until they themselves are grown and circumstances have forced them to take their places in the equally awful adult tyranny.

"There seems to me to be nothing in this world so wonderful or so beautiful as a child, and how we abuse them! Beautiful little bodies, aching to stretch their tiny growing muscles, and forced to control those instincts, upon the exercises of which their future health may depend.

"It's wrong, of course, but what is a poor teacher to do, with the standards the way they are? She is forced by everything about her to keep up the maddening effort to force those restless, inquisitive, adorable little hands to stay tightly folded, or they will get into what our school calls mischief. She says, 'Pencils down! Hands folded!' a hundred times a day, until they become meaningless sounds, until she finds herself saying one when she means the other, and hasn't strength enough left to smile at the joke on herself.

"What else is there to do? Caldwell Cook thinks that children can learn without sitting still, and he is undoubtedly right." She is referring to her reading of Caldwell Cook's book, *The Play Way*. "But the teacher realizes that that very common and really vulgar individual who inhabits the office down the hall, may walk by at any time and glance in through the glass window of the door to see that everything is in 'perfect order'.

"You really cannot fight against her. She is so firmly rooted in the practical methods of a discipline that admits of nothing but uncompromising rigidity and silence."

Whenever I read this letter to groups of teachers there is always a shout of recognition; and I am assured on all sides that the notion of child control as pictured is a common one.

Anyone taking over such an institution would have a hard time making a change to the newer ways. Perhaps nothing can be done with the children of the upper half of such a school. One must wait until they get out. The transition stage, if one were courageous enough to make an about face in the school procedures, would be long, and the results, in the meantime, would be so unsatisfactory as to lead, in all probability, to a community protest. It takes about five years to make the readjustment from the old to the new; no wonder, then, that the established disciplinarian is not eager to risk his reputation, and possibly his job, for the ultimate good of that community's children. Especially as he is not at all likely to receive any public gratitude for his pains.

Nevertheless, every forward looking superintendent of

schools knows that his first business is to go out into his
community and win it to an acceptance of the new ideas in
education. That is a criterion for judging the worth of any
public school administrator. Communities (including boards
of education) notoriously lag behind the best professional
thinking; they must be continuously urged to step forward.

This is a job easily shirked, and it is a hard one and a dangerous one. My acquaintance among superintendents of
schools is largely drawn from those who risk their professional lives daily in the difficult business of educating the
adult citizenry to understand what is best for their children. In some instances the risk involves their own personal
safety and that of their families. Unknown to the public at
large a serious war is being fought by courageous men who
have gone, like missionaries, into backward communities for
the fine social purpose of raising the general standard
of public education.

One autumn I stood beside one of these superintendents
in the main thoroughfare of a mining town while a crowd of
sullen men milled around him menacingly. An enlightened
Board of Education had selected him as a fearless and intelligent administrator — which he is, every cubic inch of
him — to bring into that community the advantages of a
modern school system; but local hotheads had started an
aggressive battle before he had had a chance even to get
acquainted.

At their instigation a strike had been called among the
pupils, who had been encouraged to parade the streets with
insulting banners. He had managed to get the children back
into the schools, but a series of underground slanders, some
of them most vicious and damning, had inflamed the opposition once more. They had petitioned the Board of Education to dismiss him and, at the moment of my arrival, were
awaiting the decision. There was no doubt in anybody's
mind that the Board would stand by the superintendent
unanimously, so the open threats made to his face that
he would be shot some night as he drove home were, in that
locality, not to be taken as mere gesture.

The superintendent moved all day from man to man in

that crowd. Often he offered a cigar as a genial truce to debate; always he smiled and listened, was courteous and tolerant. While the Board was meeting in solemn session in one of the buildings near us he worked with the leaders of the opposition.

"Just tell me one thing you have against me, North," he said to one tall miner. (Of course I don't remember any actual names.) The miner shifted about awkwardly, while the mob craned forward; here was an encounter unexpected, but the superintendent had deliberately sought it. The superintendent proffered a cigar, while he bit off the end of one for himself. The miner hesitated, then took the cigar and bit into it. That American offer-and-take was good sign language for permission to open negotiations.

"All right!" the tall miner accepted the dare. "I'll tell you!" Then followed a harrowing tale of alleged misconduct while he was Superintendent of Schools of Albany. The crowd surrounded them but kept a slight distance off and watched solemnly.

As the miner grew more and more denunciatory in his recital the superintendent slowly lowered his head and studied the ground; it was to the crowd a satisfactory picture of guilt apprehended by righteousness. But when the long story was done the superintendent raised his head and disclosed a face alive with suppressed mirth. "Would it make any difference to you, North," he said, "if I told you I never was in Albany in my life?" The genial laugh that followed shook even North's confidence.

The crowd observed that North was discomfited. They saw him chew at his cigar, while he was muttering, "Well, that's what they say," and puff away vigorously, excellent American sign language, all of it, for defeat.

"It's all right, North" the superintendent said kindly as he left him, "you and I can stand that kind of talk about us and laugh it off, but we can't spend all our time on that sort of thing, for we've got those children in the schools to take care of. And that's a big job all by itself! So long, North!"

To another opponent he said, "George, that's something any foolish old woman can say in ten seconds, but it would take me three weeks to gather all the proof together and make you sure that it is all a vicious lie. Anybody can say things like that. Give me time and I'll prove every one of these accusations to be a dirty falsehood. Look at the story about my being a slacker during the war; and kept going for weeks by the American Legion, too! That's the prize one! And when they found out that there wasn't a man in the county who had gone into the war earlier, left later, or seen more fighting service, *didn't* they look foolish!"

George asked, "But why didn't you tell them you'd been in the fightin', when they was raisin' all the fuss over it?"

The superintendent squared off and looked every inch a fighting man. "If any man comes straight up to me he'll hear the truth from me. I'm not going to rush around wherever I hear there's a meeting and answer accusations that have never been put to me personally. I let the American Legion rave until one of them came straight up and asked me my war record. I told him. Just the same as you, George, he wanted to know why I hadn't denied this and that. And I told him why, and he shook hands and said, 'By gad, you're right.' And I am right. After all," a complete dropping of the belligerent tone, "this isn't my fight. What does it matter what they call me? We've got those children to take care of. That's the real fight, and it will take a lot of pulling together to win. Give me time, George, and I'll win that fight, too. Be a sport, George, and give me half a chance."

An ugly group lunged up; we were told that they were striking miners from a near-by district. One of them said, "We know your car and we know the road you take nights. We'll get you." The superintendent smiled, with disarming lack of malice, and said quietly, "All right, boys. After this I'll always drive slow!" They were none the less ugly as they moved awkwardly away, but they did seem puzzled.

The ostensible cause of the latest outburst was credited to the new superintendent's order modifying an old rule that had required the immediate whipping of children for certain school offenses. The real cause, of course, was the objection to any sort of progress.

That night, when we knew that the local paper was carrying a headline, an eight-column bold-face "screamer," announcing the refusal of the Board of Education to dismiss the superintendent, and that, therefore, it was now a question how far the individual campaign in the streets that day had affected the issue, we sat together in the living room of his home and talked the whole thing out.

His brave wife told me that she had been called up in the night to receive telephone messages from men who threatened to put out the eyes of her children and let them find their way home if she and her husband did not leave town.

But she said, "This is a fight for all the children, and the majority of the people are with us. The others are really good people; they will come around after a while. The Board of Education has begged us to stay. If we leave now, they say, they will never be able to get another good man to accept a place here. My husband and I have talked it out, and we have decided to stick."

The latest news from the front is that he has won over an important group of those who were opposing him and that lately the pupils, former strikers, cheered him as he entered one of the buildings. Improvements that he had thought must wait many months have been adopted with a really surprising acquiescence. As his comprehensive plan placed health first, he has quietly reduced the importance of the athletic "teams," substituting games for all. A trained physical education man has been permitted to replace the "winning coach." Recently he has persuaded a public-spirited citizen to present an ample athletic field to the schools. He moves swiftly, but he has worked openly with his community all the time, and it is already responding hopefully to his professional touch and keeping pace with him.

That unselfish fight for social betterment is a picture that should give courage to educators over the land, for it exalts our profession, as all acts of heroism do for the special group it represents; and Heaven knows that the profession of public education is in need of just such sacrifices to redeem it from the constant charge of selfish sloth and insensitiveness.

Here is another letter and another picture. Such communications as these have come to me unsolicited; they represent a huge correspondence with forward-looking teachers in the grades who know the right but are not permitted always to perform their best service:

"Let me describe our primary school assembly period. First, the classes filing in, thirty or forty tiny imps in each, some tramping loudly, some sauntering casually; the teacher, a stern-faced, tight lipped woman at the head of each line, clapping her hands, 'Left! Right! Left! Right!

"The children scramble into their seats, noisily stowing away their books. The teacher shouts at them to sit up and fold their hands.

"Silence comes and complete immobility. To turn their heads ever so little, or to raise their hands to brush away a few hairs, is to call for a sharp individual scolding before everybody or, possibly, a rushing pounce and a severe shaking. Poor darlings. It is agony to want to scratch one's nose and not be able to do it.

"When everything is absolutely still, one of the teachers ascends the platform, a chord is played on the piano, and these little tots stand and salute their flag. Then they are harried into a strict listening to a passage from the Bible, which I am sure the teacher herself does not understand or she would never read it the way she does.

"How the children stand it I don't know. The teachers group around the sides of the room and gossip, although no one else dare speak to a neighbor, while one teacher, who is master of ceremonies for the week, raves and rants and preserves perfect order among the children, who sing a lot of songs they hate and wouldn't think of singing if they didn't have to.

"To laugh is a crime. I saw a teacher in the assembly period give a child a terrible shaking while informing the little one on the subject of good manners, thus: 'Have (shake) you (shake) no (shake, shake, shake) manners at all?! (shake and slam)

"Only teachers, one of them informed the children, have the right to laugh.

"O John Dewey, what is a poor teacher to do when she is set down in an environment like that!"

It seems incredible that such an environment for children really exists in these days. Why, that is exactly the sort of prison I suffered in, a half century and more ago. I recall those scarecrow teachers, strong, sinewy, dominant; and an even stronger and sinewier one in the office behind the glass partitions where beatings, it seemed, went on all day. Scandal broke loose and claimed that one of the teachers had been caught sitting on the lap of the married grocer man who, it was alleged, was kissing her; but not a boy in the school would believe that tale!

With all the preachment and all the successful practice of a more humane way of schooling little children, is it possible that these outrageous and really iniquitous institutions still take revenues from the State? Edward Yeomans, a business man who took time off to visit schools in order to find out what was actually going on behind the scenes, reported this same sort of ignorant tyranny as hopelessly common. It is like coming upon a big merchant who has not given up haggling with his customers over prices; or of finding a physician who still sets himself up as an accomplished cupper and leecher. Evidently the work of the preacher and the satirist must still go on.

A great obstruction to forward movements in child education comes from men who raise the cry of "soft pedagogy" against all the refinements which patient professional research is developing. We say men, note, for this is almost wholly an exhibition of the male psychology of dominance. "Soft pedagogy," of course, is an unfair use of an *ad hominem* analogy, as any student of logic knows; but it works, as such catch phrases always do, upon the uninformed and upon the professionally obtuse. It is strangely like the cry raised years ago against anesthetic surgery, some echoes of which one still hears in remote rural districts, where, by the way, it takes on that same male aspect of hardness, justifying itself and its ways with women and children by arguing, for instance, that the removal of the hand wash-tub and the sixteen-hour day from family life would be the softening and the consequent demoralization of civilization. "Blood and iron!" was their male cry then as it is now when they seek to impose their small tyrannies upon the young. Then as now they seem to believe in being hard without purpose, in multiplying difficulties and in constructing artificial hardships, in obstructing youth for the sake solely of obstructing youth — as if there was some singular virtue in being disagreeable! One wonders why they permit a roof over their houses or springs under the front seat, why they continue to suffer the advantages of central heating and sanitary plumbing.

Natural and appropriate drudgery, of course, is one of the saving ingredients in healthy life; in its right functioning place it is a thing to welcome and rejoice in, like any other fine restricting rule of a game; if life could be constructed so as to be free from toil and trouble, which fortunately cannot be accomplished, we should then go out of our way to invent some. *Hardship, difficulty, wearying struggle, these are the very meat of the new education when properly understood in the light of the larger purposes of self-discipline and self-mastery.*

But such larger purposes do not seem to interest those other hardy souls. Any fine thing that a child has been led to choose with a strong and healthy interest, that they would abolish, the free choice being the criterion of its wickedness. Although a parent or teacher may have worked for months to achieve the great moment of right choosing, the victory becomes at that very moment "soft pedagogy."

Well, the Sermon on the Mount is "soft pedagogy"; and the sinking of the *Lusitania* was not.

II

I spend so much of my time in joyful consultation upon common problems with the liberal group that often I forget, until my University students remind me, that the old discipline of torture still lingers balefully to obstruct every forward movement for which we stand. Sometimes, however, I drop into one of the highly mechanistic schools and ask to see the best "reciter." And often I take down the whole pro-

ceeding. It makes amusing reading among the adherents of
the other school of thought where that type of recitation
just does not exist at all; where it is considered, for the educational outcomes which the newer group believe to be important in child life, indeed quite useless and time wasting.

In one instance, where a good friend was the governing
officer, I was met with the response, "Sure, I'll show you a
'reciter'; and she is a good one too, the best in the business,
I'll tell the world." There was pride in his step as he showed
me into her room.

A lovely young person smiled healthily in the front of that
class. I could not conceal the effect upon me. My friend,
the principal, was watching me for just that result. He
whispered, "Didn't I tell you she was a knock-out!" Beautiful and intelligently alert, was my thought; and one glance
at that class of ordinary city boys, grubby and clumsily
clothed, showed me that they were her ardent and groveling
slaves.

She had already held a written quizz as the preliminary to
an oral recitation on five pages of history. Occasionally she
glanced at her wrist watch, for she was working on a schedule that demanded a certain position among the five pages
at every minute of the time allotted for the oral work. But
she was cool; watchful but cool; one knew that she would
calmly drive the lesson through on schedule time. And she
was altogether lovely.

The recitation began as the papers came up the aisles, the
collection done by a series of appointed assistants, itself a
piece of efficient, quiet machinery. All books closed at a nod
from her head; at another nod, and a most disturbing smile,
all books went silently beneath desks. (Naturally I have not
used the real names of her pupils.)

"Who was the undoubted leader among the Republicans,
McCann?" she asked. Her voice was easy and really charming. The gentle smile played upon McCann, who seemed
dazzled by it for the moment, but he managed to say, "Adams."

"McCarthy?" she said dolefully. McCann slid into his
seat, crumpled and defeated. McCarthy rose and guessed,

"Hamilton?" It was such an obvious guess that she smiled broadly at him and said, "McClure?"

McClure was now sure of the answer, for only Jefferson was left; so he said "Jefferson," and was rewarded by, "Right!"

The whole class seemed to withdraw from tension at her exultant "Right!"

Then she began again. "Who was the real leader among the Federalists, McLaughlin?"

"Adams," said McLaughlin.

"Again!" she said, which all knew meant that someone was stupid, for there was a general movement and a slight laugh, which she suppressed by a mere raised eyebrow. Who was the real leader among the Federalists, Manley?"

Manley suggested, "Jefferson."

"Mann?" she said.

Mann suggested, "Adams."

"Steady!" she admonished. "We're talking about Federalists this time, Manners?"

I noticed that no one had a second chance, and that almost secretly she was jotting down a record in a tiny book that she was able to conceal in her hand. Also I felt grateful that she didn't call on me, for I did not know a single answer to any of her questions!

Manners rose and announced his disgust with all the other lunkheads, and incidentally his loyalty to the lovely teacher, by drawling a sarcastic, "Hamilton."

"Right!" She looked at Manners with such complaisant indulgence as to make one assured that Manners was amply repaid. Like a good sport Manners returned the warm look with equal steadiness while the blood mounted among the short hairs at the back of his neck, and every mother's son of them would have given a silver dollar to exchange places with him. This, one is confident, was one of Manners' great moments in history.

Reluctantly she glanced at her wrist watch and asked, "Why wasn't Hamilton chosen to lead his party for the Presidency? He was too _____ Manuel?"

"Popular," cried Manuel, certain of being right and already seeing himself the recipient of one of those laurel wreath glances.

"March?" she went on, turning from him coldly.

Silence.

"Marcus B.?"

No response.

"Marcus L.?"

Ditto.

"Marcus S.?"

"Unpopular."

"Right! Adams won by how many votes, Marigold?"

"Sixty-eight."

"Marks?"

"One hundred and sixty-eight."

"Marsh?"

Timidly inquiring, "One hundred and fifty-eight?"

She gathered up speed and frightened them by her indignation. "Marks?" she asked, and "Mathison?" "Mattold?" "Mayer?" in rapid succession. Then she stopped satisfied before a pale little Russian lad. She let the class see her confidence while she waited for a second or two. The little boy smiled back with equal confidence. It was a compelling stage picture. Then she said slowly, "Mazurkrewitz? repeating softly, "Adams won by how many votes?"

"Three," said Mazurkrewitz quietly.

This was good for a great laugh. The prize boy had blundered. They laughed on. She let them, but she sent a luminous smile to the little Russian boy. The laugh died down into puzzled quietness.

"Right!" she said, and looked them all over good-humoredly as a pack of pleasant idiots. "The vote was 71 for Adams and 68 for Jefferson, so Adams won by three votes. Ears up, everybody!"

The laugh rose again. The joke was on them! Someone waggled hands to ears, so that the suggestion of donkey, which she had so deftly tossed to them, might be emphasized. The tense moment had left them sprawling in comfortable attitudes.

She straightened herself just a trifle and said quietly,

"Position!" Instantly that detachment came to attention, legs in, bodies stiff, eyes front.

"The most obnoxious laws," she resumed, "of this administration were — Metcalf?"

Metcalf began with a rush on a part of the lesson that he had committed with care, "The breach with France, 1796-1799. The new President had barely assumed office when news arrived — "

"Meehan?" she broke in, and shattered Metcalf's dream of victory. She turned to the discomfited Metcalf long enough to whisper a smiling, "Ears! The *obnoxious* laws, I said."

Meehan did not know. Meinz did not know. Melby did not know. Melcher merely stood up and sat down again. Merwin did not move. Metzitziski said, "The Alien and Sedition Acts, 1798," and received a grateful, "Right!"

She asked, "What were these laws, briefly?" She asked Miller, A., Miller, B., Miller, D., who merely said, "These laws were_____," But when she came to Miner in the front row she found him frowning and staring ahead with thoughts of his own. "Asleep!" she suggested to the rest of the class, which brought Miner to with a jump. "What were the Alien and Sedition laws?" she was sport enough to repeat, but Miner shook his head. "Minnis?" she turned with evident relief in getting over a hard part of the roll.

Minnis went off at high speed in what everyone will recognize as a perfect recitation: "The Alien Ack authorized the Pres'dent t' order any aliens he shall judge dang'rous to the peace an' safety o' the 'nited States to depart outta the terr't'ry o' the 'Nited States. The S'dition Ack make it a crime f'r any person to unlawf'lly c'bine with an intent t' 'pose any measure o' the gument or t' impede the' operations of any law, or t' imitate any gumment official."

"Right! *Intimidate* not *imitate*. . . . Right! Wasn't that right, Miner? . . . Still asleep!"

A joyous moment while Miner came out of his daydream, discovered himself the subject of one of her jokes, frowned, but melted into smiles as she continued to give him her friendly regard.

A quick snap of the wrist watch. "Position!" Swiftly she darted ahead. A hand waved, attempting to get recognition, but she was sailing through the matters of the Virginia and Kentucky Resolutions, with her eye on the wrist watch. Monroe, Montgomery, Moody, Mooney, Moran, and Moore gave some or little assistance, but the hand, still propped up, begged for permission. Morgan, B., Morgan, C., Morrison, and Mostino had been put through the ordeal before she turned to the chap who really wanted to say something.

"You've had your turn," she told him, but he swung his arm pleadingly, so she said, "Well, be quick; we must cover the ground."

"Them Alien and Sedition Laws," he drove in breathlessly, "my father says that they're just like what we're having today when the State elects Socialists and the government won't let 'em take their places in the legislature, and puts 'em out and won't let people speak when they think the government ain't doing what's right, and my father says——"

"That will do," she stopped all that. "We haven't time to go into that now." Followed her battery of prepared questions, step by step with the textbook, until each member of that class had had two turns, and all of the failures had had an extra chance to redeem themselves in a review.

That review was a magnificent piece of recitation teaching. Suddenly she increased her speed, darting question after question, exactly the same ones as she had used more deliberately at first, until that mass of seeming failures had turned into seeming successes.

Miner, however, could not be enticed from his absorbing dream. She awakened him again and again, but even her skill could not convince him of the importance of the ancient party quarrels of Adams, Hamilton, Jefferson *et al.* He was the only failure announced at the end of the period.

He seemed like a healthy intelligent boy; my whole interest went out to him and to the fierce thinking that had held him aloof from even the spell of that charming young woman.

Hands were raised occasionally, but she dominated with a compelling eye that would permit no interruptions.

She still had a smiling minute to go while she was reading the names of those who had made A, B, and C grades and the single failure, Miner. "The next assignment," she announced, but I was surprised that no one moved to take note until I heard her say, "the next five pages."

A far-off bell rang in the school. "Attention!" She added, "Ears!" for the few that had not snapped into it. "Rise! ... Turn! ... March!" As an Army man I thought that they held an excellent file, but this officer was not satisfied. "Mooney, out!" she announced. "Moran, out! Morgan, B., out!"

These three dropped into seats and faced her with happy grins. Lucky they to have this longer view of her. With a kind of playful adoration she looked at them and commanded softly, "Attention! ... Rise! ... Turn! ... March!" the which movements they performed with military precision amid catlike silence.

The bells in the upper hall were ringing as the last lad stepped through the door. Five pages, everybody quizzed, lessons announced for the next period, all out on the split second; and no interruptions from merely excited youngsters who had got up an outside interest in the subject of the lesson.

III

"Didn't I tell you!" said my friend, the principal. "Isn't she a wonder!"

"Yes," I agreed.

"She's the most popular teacher in this school," said he.

"She'd have no difficulty being popular with me," said I.

We conversed upon other matters in the office; there did not seem to be the least hope in discussing with him the relation of the recitation to the creative life, or to any kind of life.

While the principal talked on, extolling the marvelous control of that popular and lovely teacher, I was thinking of youth I knew whose hours had not been altogether subjected to the strong will of another, and who, therefore, had found a voice of their own.

As I reflect now upon that history recitation, the words of another schoolboy pace through my mind. Roy Helton, his teacher, had permitted the boy to build up out of himself a store of astonishing things, beyond words to tell; he had reached carefully into the quiet center of life within him and was made wise. At about the age of those lads, and like them, no doubt, with a history lesson to learn for the morrow, W. K. F. had written the verses that follow. One should know that he had spent his earlier years in England, so the lark and the wild hawthorne were part of his natural experiences.

WISDOM

Ask me of blood, I who have been to the wars,
Ask me the way the meadow looks in the spring,
Ask me to conjure up the mystical stars
And the white moon glimmering;

Wild bees tasting the honey of sweet wild clover,
Murmur of tall grass that is ready to mow,
The gay lark's song, and hawthorne bursting over
The hills like a drift of snow;

Beautiful ships beating home from far places,
Shattering opalescence of pounding seas,
Abasing beauty and sadness of women's faces;
Ask me of these.

When beauty leaps to the heart like a great cry
Not to be stilled today or ever after,
The voices of dead men out of history
Are only an echo of laughter.

CHAPTER XXII

The Conservation of Youth Power

IN ALL DISCUSSIONS OF education one should be convinced at the start that we know next to nothing about youth. It is most important that we should be sure first that we know next to nothing about youth, if we are ever to do anything about it; for progress in the matter is stopped at the outset by the universal assumption of perfect knowledge.

What we have indubitably gone through we have somehow forgotten. Forgotten? I doubt if we ever really knew, for as young persons we were not aware of the law of our own life, and as elders we have taken over the conventional prejudices of elders.

Our memory is false memory, for it gives us almost nothing but conventional adult pictures: it remembers youth as something pitiable, stupid, weak, and often contemptible, and in each age of civilization this adult false memory has nourished a traditional enmity to youth, a matter which I shall leave the Freudians to explain.

"Crabbed age and youth," goes the old song, "cannot live together." They cannot. It is the oldest of wars, and, like all wars, its basis lies in a stupid but profound misunderstanding.

In fact, youth, as youth, does not know enough to comprehend itself. And it does not want to know; it has been trained to desire the things of maturity, its ideal is to be manly, womanly, to grow up. It stretches itself, adopts the swagger and trick of age, seeks passionately to get out of the guilty role of childhood; it denies itself, disclaims its own worth, and the reason is to be found in the overwhelming social pressure brought against childhood and in favor of adulthood. Formal education is this pressure organized, but the world at large is almost as formidable.

We underestimate childhood and make most of our jokes at its expense: its will is obstinacy, its indignation is bad temper, its artistry is idling, its poetry is silliness, its enthusiasm is noise, even its passion is only puppy love. We have an evil name for all of its natural characteristics; we praise it only when it apes our own. No wonder, then, that youth does not rise to its own defense but agrees with its adversary quickly.

Youth, of course, is quite able to give a good account of itself if it had an unprejudiced hearing, but we do not offer it much of a chance. The first truthful word, and all the immediate social forces are in arms, the charge being anything from disrespect to vulgarity. Repartee is resented as "talking back," or, if cleverer than our own, as impertinence. Questions whose promptings are in the best spirit of scientific inquiry are either not answered or they are parried with evasions or, from the point of view of youth, with lies. So with questions whose fine urge is the search for economic truth, religious truth, moral truth, for explanations of our mysterious and perilous physical and mental make-up.

As a rule adults have a petrifying influence upon the young. I have often watched this powerful psychic benumbing; I have seen groups of children change in a flash from highly intelligent artists into clumsy stupids, owing to the mere presence of an alien adult. And the adult is often a fine fellow, smilingly unaware of the world that has vanished with his entrance into it; so when one of these fine fellows talks knowingly of youth and the ways of youth I think of Josiah Royce's favorite classroom metaphor, "It is like an arc light roaming about the world seeking its own shadow."

Teachers, alas, have often this stiffening and denaturing effect, and I am not even thinking of the arrogant ones, but of those bright, tolerant, and able persons who perform successfully, and often with student approval, the prescribed schoolroom and textbook routine. They illuminate, but, for that reason perhaps, they never see the shadow.

No, even these, professors of childhood as they are, would not do. For an adult to enter the region of youth as I am conceiving it here requires a special quality of silence and self-effacement; he must be like William Beebe in his diving suit under the tropical seas, a creature without disturbing vibrations. If one is really desirous of observing and noting the phenomena of youth I doubt if advice of any sort can be given directly, as a superior to an inferior, I mean; and I am sure that admonition, chiding, or punishing has never a chance, nor satire, nor adult smartness at children's expense (usually done in public with withering effect)—that would be as if William Beebe should throw a harpoon into his tranquil fish world.

Some of us have been in that child-world, often only partially in it, wholly in it only at rare intervals, and when we have succeeded it is because we have practiced the slow and self-effacing methods of deep-sea observation. And if our recorded data are at all worthy it is because we have learned to move with incredible slowness; and because we have not once carried a harpoon.

II

Youth power is undoubtedly lost in the language arts by what might be called the harpooning theory of instruction. For years I have sought intimacy with children who have been publicly labeled "poor in English." As a lot they are invariably convinced of their inability, the unanimity of teachers being impressive if the scores in the coldly scientific and impersonal "composition scales" were not sufficient. With natural self-respect, therefore, they expose their written or their spoken product as seldom as possible in the presence of a so-called English teacher.

"Oh, I am no good at English," is a common expression that juts out in familiar conversation, a sign of inward worry, sometimes a pathetic attempt to ward off an interest which, to their way of thinking, could lead to no good result.

"Well," I would often remark, "I am not too good at English myself." And somehow I am able to convince them.

"I am not a perfect speller," I would tell them truthfully; and my first writing is always clumsy; it takes many writings before I can say simple things so that anyone else may understand my meaning."

That interests them, but when I tell of my own school days — so like their own — and of my own difficulty in my youth in writing the kind of English that my teachers demanded, well, that makes me almost one of them. They swim fearlessly about my diving suit, display their mottled colors, blow their natural bubbles, wave their marvelously graceful fins.

When they write for me, these who are "poor in English," I do not "correct" their papers. I figure that they have had enough of that ritual in the past, and obviously it has not led to grace. Instead, I look for the idea, thought, picture, feeling, argument which they are seeking to convey, and whatever it is, I try to admire it. And usually I can admire it, for, a strange thing at which I have never ceased to wonder, the "poor in English" have often the most alluring things to say. As a rule they are unconventional in their thinking, and often they have a natural gift of invention and an instinctive feeling for art values. Perhaps it is because their earliest teachers, in their proselytizing zeal for conformity, tried to kill that originality with "corrections"; and so these unique youths had learned to scuttle out of sight, losing all chance of training. Or it might be that this loss of training was their real gain! Blessed are the poor in English, I am often constrained to say, for they shall see with their own eyes.

So I learned to look with care into badly written scrawls for that untutored gift of transferring thought, feeling, and image into right words. My earliest discovery, the case that gave me a clue to the principle involved, was found in a well-nigh illiterate welter covering many pages.

A strong feeling had impelled the writer to continue on and on, forgetful for the moment of his deficiencies. Out of it came, as I read, the crude shadow of a stark story; it took me to the French vine country, to a wayside shrine where peasants stopped to bend the knee, cross themselves, water their horses, and gossip; I saw leering, and cringing, and flippant superstition, gross humors of men and beasts; I saw the muck of a swampish pool, the battered figure of the Virgin; and a moment later, through the eyes of a stranger coming back after years to the homeland, I saw his boyhood image of the Pool of Peace at the foot of the Hill of the Lady of Mercy.

With the enthusiastic reception of the idea in his story— there was no word at that time of its bad form — his illiteracy cleared. Without instruction it vanished. It just left him; it was like the miraculous cleansing of conversion. A little later the author appeared in a magazine of literary distinction. Since then he has found his way into magazines generally; he is the author of a striking novel; he has contributed verse to one of the memorable collections in the modern movement; he has achieved high ranking as an international correspondent. But most of his juvenile life had been in school before a teacher noted his native power.

I am reminded in this connection of the boys among my friends who have left college because they could find no instructor interested in what they had to say but only in how they said it. Form, the clothing of the idea, good manners in words, these represented seemingly the sole interest of their teachers. But that attitude gives a statuesque immovability to the college instructor; form is a thing that one may note without being moved. "You couldn't move them," one lad remarked, "though you presented them with *The Scarlet Letter*. They don't read to be moved. They are on the Sacred Blunder Hunt."

Another boy said, "I handed in five stories and got a total of ten corrections, three of spelling, one of paragraphing, and six of punctuation. Just proof-reading. I didn't go there to get proof-reading, so I left." Three of these stories I have seen later in print; it is difficult to understand how some human approval could have been avoided. That boy has now three books to his credit, and a fourth is on the presses!

Among the prose of pupils which was printed in our school magazine, commendation comes generously for two stories written by young persons who were so conscious of their faulty English that it well-nigh drove them inarticulate. At first in my presence they grew coldly numb. My plan was to require nothing and to wait. Think again of William Beebe floating quietly — stiller than still as the Germans have it — on his bit of undersea coral. Of two accomplishments that were the eventual outcome, one took two months of waiting, the other took six. As they watched the contented effort of others about them, their fears must have lessened and their suppressed hopes and self-belief must have gradually increased, for not once did they see the menacing hand rise, nor even the shadow of a harpoon.

III

And what of the fluent ones? Seemingly they have no bar to the fullest expression of native power? Well, they have, powerful bars, but they are not usually aware of them. In the conventional exercises that adult authority permits they perform satisfactorily and often with the distinction of high grades, honor marks, and oher symbols of excellence in conformity. Set long in this groove they soon give over any native power that might really distinguish them from their fellows — and your artist is always so distinguished, his style being his own and like no other mortal creature; indeed, if they continue long to express the common approved pattern they might even come to dislike the invitation to summon from within that rare and nonconforming artist-self.

And then one must set no limits to the kind of thing they would express. This means that we, the elder guides, must prepare ourselves for shocks. Youth has a gift of satire and caricature; he might begin by satirizing or caricaturing — us! His notion of dignity, of respect, of humor, of reverence even, does not correspond invariably with our notion. But if we would bring out and strengthen the best powers that he has we must not stop him here; nor need we presume that he lacks dignity, respect, humor, or reverence even; On the other hand, we must be most careful to treat decently his attempts to show us what to him is worthy of attachment, worthy of his loyalty and his serious attention. It is a platitude that in the realm of his most solemn worships we have made youth the sport of our cruelest jests and even of our superior scorn. To laugh it out of him, to shame it out of him, are our justifying phrases, along with that fast obsolescing phrase, to beat it out of him.

It is a question of the conflict of standards, you see; and I am proposing that in the matter of art expression youth should be permitted to have its own. But first we should open our minds to discover what those standards really are. In my own judgment we shall not find him lacking in the instinct for beauty and for truth; indeed, his power in these age-old fundamentals is often superior to our own.

If permitted, then, he will express himself on many matters from which his elders have commonly debarred him, on love, death,

> Moon, stars, and sun,
> kingdoms, galleons, caravans,
> with hell and god and the four archangels.

and, if permitted, he will not continue to take our point of view but will venture on his own. To keep to subjects that we select as "proper" — such as "How I spent My Vacation," or "The Poetry of Matthew Arnold" — and to treat such subjects in the manner that we prescribe, that is the way of imitation, but it is never the way of the artist; it is the way to suppress the powers of youth, not to conserve them. For youth has much to say on "moon, stars, and sun, kingdoms, galleons, caravans," and even on "hell and god and the four archangels"; and having said it he will never be the same youth again; he who once has led can never again be comfortable as the subservient follower, maxims to the contrary notwithstanding. Once the deep vein of originality has been made accessible — and in every normal youth is an untouched El-Dorado — the exchange to the poverty of obedient imitation will never be made willingly.

Struck by the unanswerable anguish of the death of a beloved child a young girl writes:

CLOCKMAKER'S SONG

Bits of rubies and bits of steel
Intricate brotherhood of spring and wheel
Ticking away on my mantel shelf,
Clocks that are ornate or pretty or plain,
Ugly, unusual, ugly again,
Each one is mine, for I made it myself.

I oil it and dust it and love it and mind it,
And I never, never forget to wind it.

Another Clockmaker, quite close by,
Has a mantel shelf reaching from sky to sky.
He can make a clock in an ecstasy
Of wild unbridled artistry
And set it down among clocks that are plain
Where it never enters His head again.

And it ticks itself still on His mantel shelf,
For no clock is able to wind itself.

My mantel shelf measures five feet or more
And His is boundless from shore to shore,
But I make my clocks just as carefully,
And each has the same loving care from me —

And in this, perhaps, I am greater than He.

She could not have written so independently, with such calm dignity, unless she had been permitted over many years to express her wise feelings without even the suggestion of the fear of rebuke. We have reason for our assurance that the reverence and understanding which have come to her with the years are all the more lasting and secure because her moment of despair was thus so bravely and honestly faced.

Nor could the following casual contribution to a history lesson (it was Daniel C. Knowlton's class) have been possible unless the classroom environment and the school environment had been for a long period of time friendly to this boy's own sense of cleverness, to his own judgment, and to his own taste:

FOUR EDENS

A Medieval Legend

Saint Peter who in weariness did lean
    Against the seventh wall of chrysolite,
Aroused himself, for yonder could be seen
    Four Medieval men come into sight.

The foremost one, a Lord of high degree,
  Sedately strode him toward the pearly gate
As if this Paradise would only be
  An acquisition to his vast estate.

The second came, a bishop most benign,
  Who, waddling in his velvet finery,
Bore ample proof that partridge broiled with wine
  Was part of conscientious piety.

The third, a serf, whose fate had been to plod,
  On seeing Heaven's ramparts in the sky
Cried out in fear, "There must be serfs of God
  To hoist the lumps of amethyst so high!"

The fourth, a monk, who followed last of all,
  Approached with halting steps, for he was sad
To see that Paradise must have a wall. . . .
  Yes, even as the monastery had!

Saint Peter tipped his halo with respect,
  "Good tidings and a welcome, Sirs," said he,
"What part of Paradise will you select,
  In which to while away Eternity?"

"I sicken of my castle," said the Lord.
  "Give me the simple cottage of a serf,
"And let me dwell with nature," he implored,
  "To reap a frugal living from the turf!"

"My pomp is only fraud," the Bishop said,
  "So let me live a monkish life alone.
"I would forgo my scented feather bed
  "To sleep upon the monastery stone."

The serf, revolting in his feudal yoke,
  Declared, "Good Peter, pray bequeath me this;"
And fingered at the Lord's brocaded cloak;
  "And give me castles on a precipice!"

"The stark privations of my narrow creed,"
  The monk avowed, "are much to my distaste.
"Oh, could I but afford the Bishop's greed,
  And let a partridge swell my sagging waist!"

                *   *   *

As each request was promptly granted then,
  We find ourselves incapable to tell
If these four Medieval gentlemen
  Consigned themselves to Heaven or to Hell.

There are possibilities of shock in each of these contributions, but I happen to know that the adult friends of the two youths, teachers and parents, had agreed long ago to lower their shock exponent measurably, both as a matter of expediency as well as a matter of wisdom.

It is not, I hasten to add, that we adults should not be shocked by youth. The real point is, however, that it is only by permitting youth to err in taste that, under guidance, a healthy taste is arrived at; and it is only by gaining confidence in what powers he has that youth may grow in power. We think it better to have even the worst side of youth exposed to us, who are professionally trained in guidance, than to have it concealed from us and thereby develop into a possible social evil.

We might here put to vote a specific illustration of a debatable matter of taste. Should we or should we not receive the following parody with welcoming laughter? One set of adults shook their heads when another set of adults voted to print it; here, you see, is division among the elders, but youth received the ditty with a unanimous shout of acclaim.

One needs to know only that the school had suffered an epidemic of fudge parties, wherein each hostess had fabricated her own experimental brand. From a convalescent couch, therefore, a young girl wrote:

O ! OH ! O !

O bowl, I cannot hold thee close enough!
  Thy smooth white porcelain rim,
  Thy contents somewhat grim,
And I, this summer day, that ache and sag
And all but cry with anguish, a limp rag,
  Bowl, bowl, I cannot get thee close enough!

Long have I known that something had gone wrong,
  But never knew I this!
  Here such upheaval is
As retcheth me apart — Lord, I do fear
Thou'st made good fudge too plentiful this year!
  My soul is all but out of me ... let fall
  No clattering thing ... prithee, let no friend call!

Equally diverting examples could be given of other attitudes that normally are repressed by the standards of mature dignity and good taste: celebrations of sincere self-love; of love for others, sometimes brotherly and sometimes not; of philosophical probings disturbing to the orthodox. Among these one is sure to find pictures of villains done with

ironic pretense of sympathy — the irony and the pretense
usually are missed by literal elders — as witness:

ANCHORITE

Time is elusive;
I do not waste it
toiling to aid and serve
a thankless universe

But, as a heedless Nero
oblivious to all,
I play my squeaky fiddle
in a burning world.

Or this, from a very nice young girl whom one never
would suspect to look at her, of letting her fancy flirt with
the idea — and with more than the idea! — of a temporary
lapse from constancy:

COUNTER ATTRACTION

My bonny lies over the ocean!
My bonny lies over the sea!

I'm sick of long-distance emotion,
So — meet me at Huyler's at three.

Our disagreement with the older system of education is
mainly concerned with the dominating position of its unthinking routinists; but we all know that under a teacher of
educational vision, a teacher who comprehends the ultimate
individual and social implications of his subject, formal education has often been thrillingly alive and powerfully effective in awakening right desire, stirring at those times the
very roots of the creative life. To have come within the
influence of such persons, rare, alas, though they be, was to
become in some sense forever scientist or historian, mathematician, philosopher, artist, or litterateur. Not the subject
matter, nor the logical arrangement in course of study or in
textbook, performed these subtile transformations, for
other teachers used the same materials without the same
resultant effects; the constant factor was always the teacher
of insight and vision who used his subject, not as an end in
itself, but as a means toward those larger ends which he
alone was wise enough to comprehend.

Here is my tribute to those exceptional teachers for what they gave us beyond scholarly guidance, for what personal contact with them wrought everlastingly in us: Albert Henry Smythe, George Palmer, William James, Hugo Munsterberg, Charles T. Copeland, Josiah Royce, George Santayana, and later in graduate courses, Felix E. Schelling, George Stuart Fullerton, Cornelius Weygandt, Clarence Griffin Child, and William Romaine Newbold.

The conservation of youth power is one of the platforms of the new school program; it awaits only the coming in larger force of the new type of administrator who will give approval to the new type of teacher with her new type of classroom technique. These differently adjusted persons will not arrive in plenteous numbers, however, until we cease choosing teachers entirely from the good scholar class; nor so long as we insist that the only test of good administration is ability to do research.

Though we will have none but Masters of Arts in our first grades, that will not guarantee possession of the art of caring for the life-roots of your six-year-old child and mine. A superintendent is not necessarily preparing himself for the highest professional achievement, although we force him to quit his job and give the most productive years of his life to, say, a fact-finding thesis in which he computes, for the x and z groups in ten selected urban elementary classes, the varying co-efficients of correlation among such disparate data as loose buttons, I.Q., and the lower quartile media of tests in the nine table.

If that last exercise seems too learned, incredible, and preposterous as a requirement of qualification for a public school administrator, I could exhibit genuine ones which, to use the language of Alice, are learneder, incredibler, and preposterouser.

CHAPTER XXIII

All God's Chillun

MY CHOICE OF CHAPTER title was "All God's Chillun Got Wings" until I remembered that all God's chillun are not permitted to use them. I visit many schools which, in spite of a modern cheerfulness and a seeming acquiescence of pupils, are to me places where the wings of God's children are gradually and painlessly removed. High marks are given to them who know least about flying; future advancement is open only to those who keep their feet always on the ground. When the creative spirit strives here and there to flutter, it becomes an activity that must be practiced in stealth, rarely with full approval of the authorities.

The creative spirit is something more than a product in print, clay, canvas: it is dancing, rhythmic living, a laugh, a flash of the mind, strength of control, swiftness of action, an unwritten poem, a song without words; it is life adding its invisible living cells to more and abundant lfe. But these products, picture, poem, clay figure, which we show in our public exhibits, will serve, however inadequate they are for us, for our eager interest is rarely on the product; we use them to tempt the unbeliever to loiter a moment at the shrine of the true gods. Our argument may not move him, but the grace of our service may win him into the faith.

To the unbeliever, then, I address myself when I would tell of the creative spirit and its varied manifestations; and also, of course, to those who believe but would have their faith strengthened.

The creative impulse is more easily observed in young children, but the housewife who bakes unerringly without book or recipe knows it; the carpenter fashioning a cupboard to his own notion of shape and line, the office man given free sway in the phrasing of a sales advertisement, the lawyer playing upon the mood of judge and jury, these practice it without knowing it; my true love's letter is the perfect product of instinctive artistry; all our adult ways of interacting one with another, in short, call on the creative spirit, and our life is artistic or dull in proportion to our creative gifts.

But adults are in the main wingless; convention, tribal taboos, mechanistic living, long years of schooling, something has stilled the spirit within or walled it securely. It is to children we must go to see the creative spirit at its best; and only to those children who are in some measure uncoerced.

Outwardly it is harmony; a unity of eye, hand, bodily muscles, mind; a concentration upon the object of desire that sets the world aside. It is frequently balked by the need of special information or of special skill; these are the obstructions that it must surely overcome or the heart's desire is not achieved and the spirit dies; there, too, are the strategic places where the wise teacher is at hand with just the right assistance. But of that later; the outward picture concerns us now. Not only is there harmony of mind and body, but there is the closest connection between the thing conceived as worthy to be done and the media necessary — brush, paint, language, wood, metal, clay, musical instruments, blocks, script, tool, machine.

It flourishes, of course, in what we call play, but mindful of our religious inheritances, in which play has been conceived as touched with evil, I hasten to note concrete illustrations of play that has taken on all the characteristics of work: a butterfly collection occupying five steady years which brought technical knowledge of family and species, of habitat, environment, breeding, and culture, a correspondence with other collectors and with foreign sales agents, and an ability to present orally to an assembly of several hundred children and adults the serious business of preparing such a collection and to lead the discussion that followed with the skill of experience; a study of biological specimens that led an elementary school boy first to museums and then to summer school (Wood's Hole) until all unwittingly the avocation put him so far outside the role of pupil that an ornithologist and later a marine biologist claimed that they must talk to the lad as a colleague and defer to him in his special scientific field; an elementary school boy who constructed photostatic apparatus and motion-picture cameras from lard cans found on the village refuse pile, and from odds and ends picked up at rummage sales; a young artist who built herself a five-thousand-dollar studio through a persistently applied scheme of savings, earning, and commercial borrowings.

Illustration of such activity is at hand in every classroom including the college classroom, if one has the skill to look for it. *The right kind of scholarship is always creative artistry.*

The common ingredient in each case, that which makes it different from formal instruction, is that the "urge to do" is self-engendered; it seeks its own way to fulfilment; it is not stopped by time, space, apparatus, or by teachers or school administrators, although because of the last two it may often conceal every outward trace of interest in the thing that occupies the main tracts of the mind, in this regard behaving like a conquered people in the presence of the ruling race.

It may even at these times assume a cautious stupidity; for neither to the unsympathetic nor to the arrogant and unfeeling will it confess an interest in the inner dream. Under unfriendly questioning it may even deny, and thus, through clumsiness and inexpertness, get into the coil of adult morality.

II

When the creative spirit is at work, not only are body and mind cooperating with instinctive harmony to secure the desired result, but the language art is functioning at a high degree of excellence. A child may speak haltingly in classroom recitation, or in a school "composition" may write with despairing inadequacy, who, in the midst of a bit of self-initiated artistry, the making of a toy motor boat, a radio set, a cartoon, or a play, will talk with the effectiveness of an inspired expert. In his own language and idiom, of course, and provided you do not bring with you the flavor of the impossible linguistic standards of adult perfection.

You may ask questions then, if you are not of the forbidding sort; and if you have an ear for right rhythmic speech you may have cause to marvel at the language sense that these youngsters really have; and you may wonder why we as teachers do not take advantage of the gifts that children have in this line instead of damming — both spellings apply here — their utterance through our insistence on the use of an alien tongue.

The claim is made that the work we love to do does not teach persistence, but who can equal the persistence of children when engaged in creative work? Ask the mothers and fathers who have tried to keep up with the demands of their offspring for continuous attention to a loved story or game! And the work which they set for themselves is not stopped by the ending of the day; it carries over, day after day, until the accomplished end is reached.

The astonishing paintings by second-grade children which decorate Katharine Keelor's room were not done at a sitting. Day by day they grew. She has just told me the history of one remarkable water color of an autumn orchard, how the house and the trees and the far-off hills came slowly to their present places in the picture, and then one morning a shy voice confided, "I was thinking about it last night in bed, so I put some apples on the tree as well as on the ground, for, of course, they all wouldn't have fallen off, would they? And the red apples are so pretty I wanted more of them."

A teacher has just dropped in to tell me of a remarkable speech delivered from a most unexpected source at a recent Lincoln Day assembly. "It was done with such ease and masterfulness," he said, "with the modesty of a trained speaker, and yet it was the boy's first serious public appearance. We found out that he had been at work for weeks in various libraries. He had concentrated on a bibliography that no teacher would have had the heart to give anyone as an assignemnt, even in the old days; and no one knew he was at it! He saturated himself with material like an expert research student, and then calmly talked out of full knowledge. The school is so thrilled by it that they are thinking of naming him for the most responsible position in the vote of the pupils, chairman of the Student Council, a most coveted office, I tell you, and never held but by the all-around best man in the place!"

"And no one knew he was at it!" That is a quality that must not be missed, in which regard these young artists are one with the older artist. The same artist-shyness is here, the same fear of spoiling the picture through the wrong word from outside; even suggestions, the artist knows, are dangerous until the work is finished.

And flattery can knock one out of the humor — shatter the inspiration — as well as dispraise, or stupid misunderstanding, or nagging (parents and teachers, elder sisters and governesses, please take notice!), or that unfeeling looking-over-the-shoulder which has dished many a promising canvas. Artists and children hide from onlookers until enough of the work is done to insure a possible completion (that's why they should have their own rooms, studios, workshops). They perform cheerfully enough among their own kind; so in some schools the artistic work is done out of hours, and teachers never hear of it; but in the schools that respect the creative life, one senses that the artist has been protected from the cold eye of the outsider.

"I'm painting that red barn," I heard a Woodstock celebrity once say to a group of gushing ignorants, "but if you ask me what I am painting I shall have to go fishing for a week." He was bitter with a sense of outrage at their unfeeling impertinence in hovering over him, but all they said was, "Isn't he just *screamingly* funny! And don't you *love* it! It *is* the barn you're painting, is'nt it? I'm just *crazy* about it!" And as he folded up his work he remarked hopelessly, "I'm off! Fishing it is!"

But at the right moment they want praise like any other artist. Or, rather, they want what the artist-student calls a "crit." "Oh," cried one of Miss Keelor's little boys, "you didn't hang mine up!" It was a moment of real torture. Miss Keelor brought the painting out slowly (while, no doubt, she thought hard) and looked at it again. "I didn't think it had enough in it," she explained, but not with an air of really knowing. "So much space here," she mused, and then looked at the pictures of the others. He looked, too, and understood. "I could do some more!" He caught the idea eagerly, explaining spiritedly new thoughts that began to come to him with a rush. And away he went, satisfied with the judgment.

And at other times, just like real artists, they are dismayed at praise. You hang their pictures; they are grieved. "It is not good enough," they say in real distress and go sturdily to work to make a better one to take its place.

III

This, then, is the torrential force that comes unbidden out of the mysterious recesses of personality and fashions things out of wood, color, fabric, clay, sound, and words; the thing that dances, sings, leads a dozen dramatic reincarnations; the thing that drives a small child into profound research or sets him digging into a difficulty with the energy of a dog at a woodchuck hole; whose ways are sure, whose outcome is beauty.

Not that I would say that the conscious end is beauty. Children seem to be driven by an inner necessity of putting forth something; that it shall turn out to be beautiful is not their concern. Their impulse at its best is to place something in the outside world that is already (or almost ready) in their inside world of perceiving, thinking, feeling; they measure their success or failure by the final resemblance of the thing done to the thing imagined.

In their best moments they seem to know exactly what to do: the muscles ripple in perfect harmony to the right touch, line, blow; in painting, the brush is swung fearlessly and surely, in pottery the punches and patches are thumbed without hesitation. In this regard they are in tune again with the professional artist. Experience has loosened his fears; he trusts his instinct for level, balance, the swift adjustings of his medium and his materials to satisfy those flashing demands from within.

One needs to emphasize here that the modern discovery of the child as artist — a very ancient bit of knowledge, of course — is coincident with the realization of the beauty of primitive art generally. The child is a genuine primitive. He needs little or no instruction, but he must have materials, and his surroundings must be such as to call his effort worthy; he is susceptible to condemnation and will give up all his precious art and lose one of the most gracious of nature's gifts — for, alas, it may be easily lost — if his overlords command. The art of the uncivilized tribes, ancient and modern, is just that untutored art of our own children. And it is fitting, now that we are treasuring every trace of the craft of the primitive peoples, the native art in Africa, Mexico, Egypt, the South Seas, it is fitting that our educational leaders should be rediscovering with joy and understanding the work of our own young "natives."

The undeniable result, however, is beauty; and fortunately we do not in these days need to justify it. Here and there, to be sure, its utility is questioned; but the sense of its importance in American life is growing at such bounds that we no longer worry over the eventual result. Some further argument is necessary, however, to meet the demands of those ascetics, often in power in education, who still have faith in information, in assigned tasks, in "the discipline of artificial difficulty" and other fading theories of the way of life.

Those of us who have watched young life grow from dependent insecurity to independent power through the opportunities for the cultivation of the spirit which the newer schools afford, are assured that something ever so much more important than a beautiful product is the result of the new freedom in education. Personality develops with the springing certainty of a dry seed dropped into moist earth. Character emerges; and with it knowledge, a kind of wisdom, so sure in its judgments as to make us listen and attend rather than command and instruct. Taste is never, as with us, a hypocrisy. Confidence comes into the spirit and thrives there, for fear and bewilderment—the acknowledged tools of the older education — never yet begot faith in oneself. New hungers arise, new desires, new satisfactions, and these are the very food of education.

The cultivation of the creative spirit makes for great artists, giant scholars, and thinkers; it is the recipe for distinction.

The story of the leaders of the race is the story of those who cultivated the creative spirit in spite of the schools. Why is it, I wonder, that we have never taken that lesson to heart? The masters of men have been superior to formal education, or they have cleverly turned it to their own uses. But these are the strong of will who have fought their way to the right to be free. The mass has not been strong of will: a little fluttering of the wings, and then an acceptance — that is their story.

The newer education is learning the uses of the mysterious forces of the spirit through which one may literally educate oneself for all the important needs of living. It is like the heartbeat: no one has found the source of its power but no one doubts that the source is within us. The creative spirit is another heart; it will keep us alive if we give it a chance to beat for us; it may be stilled, but there is then no more life.

When we meet, those of us who have dealt with children on this side of their nature, we talk a different jargon from the professional pedagogue because our classrooms are set to another rhythm than that of our more military brothers; nor do we speak so despairingly of the work of school children; rather we ply one another with this and that astonishing product of their effort. Information we do not prize so much—"the world is so full of a number of things!"—nor the "skills" that one will supposedly need at maturity (mostly very bad guesses, as any textbook thirty years old will abundantly testify); nor are we much attracted by the prevailing drill psychology ("Force them to do it a certain number of times and they will contine to do it joyfully for life") which we are apt to classify flippantly with the claim of the New England catechism as a formula for insuring the pious life. In this connection I am reminded of the illiterate Kentucky mountaineers in the Army whom we insisted upon teaching to shoot from the shoulder; with the gun at the hip these lads could pick the whiskers off a bouncing rabbit!

We dispute in the most friendly and heated manner when we meet, for we are very much concerned that no mistakes shall be made in a matter so vital to human kind. One group, for instance, believes so much in "growth theory" that it will hardly permit any instruction at all. It banks all upon Nature. With these "naturalists" some of us have delightful disputes. Nature is wonderful, as all the poets tell us, but we, some of us, don't trust her altogether. She is a powerful jinn to summon, and also a lusty, sly wench. We must make Nature work for us, that is our contention; but, of course, we should know what help and what interference we may expect of her.

Because of having written a book on the poetry of youth I am in constant receipt of sheaves of poetry from all parts of the country. "See what my children have done without any instruction whatever!" is the tenor of the accompanying letters. My pity goes out to the children; so obviously have they needed someone to be by to point out the way. Not to tell them what to say! Heaven and Poesy forbid! But they never should have been allowed, I say as I read, to continue to write in the style of yesteryear, and even in the style of the year before yesteryear; and their copyings, their hackneyed phrasing, and their silly platitudes should have been gently made known to them — an art of teaching required here that is nothing but the highest.

If growth under pleasantly free surroundings were all of the new education, then my occupation is gone; for I conceive of my professional skill as something imperatively needed to keep that growth nourished.

Notably is this true of drawing, painting, and color work generally. Children do very good work, and they do very bad work. If no one is by to suggest to them the difference they may never grow in taste, in discriminating art judgment. Nature, the jade, may or may not help them. They may even turn away from the sure voice of the instinctive creative spirit within them to copy the work of others or, worse, to copy themselves.

The teacher must know enough to entice them into the right road. And just any teacher will not do; scholarship here is a smoky flare, and the diploma, Master of Pedagogy, is not exactly enlightening. Children, for example, are often too satisfied; then they need an immdeiate experience with a better performance than they have hitherto known. Nothing so surly disgusts one with poor work as a goodish experience with something better.

But it must not be too much better. (At this point the standardized teacher presents the "classics" in literature and in the fine arts, with the usual classic result.) The newer type of teacher, herself always more artist than teacher, knows the better, really knows it for what it does to one; and she knows how to place it in the child's life so that—most important!—it may be wholly acceptable.

Further, children are balked by difficulties in the handling of materials, how to make an effective linoleum block, for instance, or what to do with color that changes when brought into contact with other colors; they want to know the uses of crayon, charcoal, grease pencil, India ink, fixatives, the mechanics of enlarging illustrations for the printer, and so on endlessly. It is the new business of the teacher to provoke children into wanting to know about these and other varying matters, and then to provide materials and such help as is asked for.

Growth is not enough, nor is environment enough, unless, as I believe it should be, the teacher is considered an essential part of the environment. Richer results may be expected of children than the standardized schoolmaster has hitherto considered possible; richer results may be expected from those even who are leading the way in the experimental schools; and that richness will come no faster, I suspect, than the coming in greater numbers of the gifted artist-teacher.

Something Greek is coming back to education; for the beauty and the power of the Hellenes were always a result of self-cultivation in taste, never a slavery to information; they danced, sang, talked endlessly, turned the body and mind to its best rhythms, and through these intangibles they probed the limits of human understanding; but they

did not know that the earth is a globe, nor would they have
been concerned to discover that the chief city of Madagas-
car is Antananarivo.

Information and knowledge are always of secondary importance in education and are so conceived by the best
minds. It is the pedant and not the true scholar who has
elevated them to ends-in-themselves. The leaders in education understand this distinction, and they know that it is
pertinent to higher as well as to elementary training. In an
address before the Chamber of Commerce of the State of
New York, President Lowell of Harvard University once
said:

"The cultivation of the mind by the colleges is an attempt
to train the imagination to grasp things that cannot be felt
or perceived by the material senses. It is not merely to give
knowledge.

*"The real thing we want is not knowledge but resource-
fulness.* The art which creates things both great and small
is not the capacity for solving problems. That may seem a
curious statement, but the real art of life consists in finding
out what is the question to be solved, and the person who can
find out what the problem is to be solved is the man who
really makes the contributions to life.

*"It is comparatively easy to train anyone to solve prob-
lems* when they are stated; but the man who can see a new
problem and state it is the man who makes the real advance,
and that is true in everything. You all know perfectly well
that *the man you want in your business is the man who will
perceive something that needs to be done and has not been
done;* and then the question of finding out how to do it is
comparatively simple."

IV

We talk of these and other matters when we meet professionally, but we consider it no particular justification
of our work that the "free children" surpass the controlled
children not only in an enlarged and gifted personality but
in the customary school branches. Superintendent Wash-
burne of the Winnetka Schools has the proof, if anyone is
interested. We note the fact, to be sure, because of its in-

fluence upon parents and upon the powers that control educational organization and administration. We may win our argument by way of the results in the standardized tests — and we do not despise winning our argument — but our main interest lies not there but in the sure knowledge we possess of the effect of our sort of education upon the mind and spirit of youth.

When interest is properly motivated the acquisition of fruitful knowledge cannot be denied. I have watched primary school children carry on research in book and in museum that could be dignified by the name of science, requiring an amassing of data, judgment in selection of material, and a functional use of that material in cooperative groups, while the outcomes were thrilling in lasting information about the present and the past of the world we live in. I am acquainted with Latin classes whose students really know Latin, an accomplishment acquired by the steadiest kind of "digging," but it irritates some folks when they discover that a skilful school organization has succeeded in motivating that study in terms of intense interest.

We are all familiar with the college laggards who turn into incontrovertible "grinds" when they at last find their life work in law school, medical or engineering school. In certain large machine and electric corporations many of my young friends are giving their nights and days ungrudgingly to the lowest, dirtiest, and poorest paid tasks; they stick to their jobs willingly and without shirking because they intelligently conceive that that is the only way to a mastery of the complex informations and skills of that industry; and they are motivated further by comprehending the eventual outcomes in future managerial and sales functions.

The spirit that drove Edison and his kind to a life-long endeavor in intelligently motivated toil is our spirit; it does not balk at sensible difficulties nor is it eventually uninformed.

The greatest success of the creative approach is that it has put the tools of knowledge into the eager hands of youth. Reversing the situation of the fact-driver of the old school —one cannot think of the old driver without his whip—

our position as teacher has often been one of worry lest our stimulation should carry a youth to a continuation of school tasks beyond his physical limit of endurance. When groups have begun a genuinely self-motivated drive it has seriously been our problem to stop them for the imperative needs of outdoor play; and often we have been in secret conference with parents to devise counteracting motivation to keep a lad from working into the hours that should be given to rest and sleep.

And it is simply inexperience or bad thinking that quarrel with us, as some of the older pedagogues do, on the charge that we are neglecting the acquisition of the world's heritage of useful knowledge. No single person can be the repository of all the knowledges of civilization. From the time of Plato's pilot the facts that keep the world together have been distributed among many special groups. It must be so in the naure of things. The folly of formal education has always been its attempt to crowd everything into the curriculum.

CHAPTER XXIV

Newer Types of Learning

WE ARE FAMILIAR ENOUGH with the general picture of traditional school learning with its fixed curriculum, its single textbook, its lessons mapped out for all to learn and recite upon at the same hour, its material limited to specially selected information about the outside world past and present—and mostly past—but having little relationship to any experience of daily living. Here I have no word to say about this age-old instrument of education. It worked amazingly well for the scholar type, and it has important uses still.

My interest here is in the newer types of learning, previously neglected by formal public school education, namely, experience-learning, research-learning, sharing-learning and creative learning.

Experience-learning is the kind that comes to us by being present ourselves at a place where things are done, the kind that appears when we see and hear with our own eyes and ears; when we do something ourselves instead of just listening or reading; when we come to judgment on the spot without needing a book or a teacher to assist us.

Studying the guide book to Mexico could be wholly traditional learning; travelling in Mexico would give us the richer results of experience-learning. Children may study civics from a book; but those who, with preparation and professional guidance, explore their own community, these acquire experiential-learning that is something greater and more influential for civic betterment. In such explorations children see for the first time what they have lived with intimately but failed to see, and they see them in the larger relationships of social living; further, they become critical for the first time; their questons become insistently more intelligent—a sign of mental growth which is the very first aim of education, and eventually they become even wiser than their mature neighbors whose dulled minds have never been taught either to see or to question.

And, best of all, guided experience-learning leads almost directly into effective behavior patterns. Knowledge without a good behavior outcome is apt to remain sterile. Usually children who make guided trips and excursions want to do something about it.

Sometimes the resultant activity of an experience takes the form of construction, sometimes of discussion and further experiencing, and often it sends eager youngsters off to books and magazines. So research-learning begins.

Research-learning, however, is a natural outcome of any school activity which is based upon a genuine desire to accomplish something either as a group effort or as an individual matter. Whenever knowledge is needed the first thought is to go to books. So the library, and the "library corner," looms large as a friendly helper.

A child goes to books, for example, to find out how the early Spanish explorers really dressed; or how Indians look today; or the way city water is purified and brought from the faraway mountains; or how men can breathe locked up under water in a submarine.

As with mature persons research does not always bring the desired result. After fruitless wearisome reading, one fifth-grade group brought back the answer that they could not discover, and that probably nobody could ever discover, how the Pilgrim fathers really talked to one another. The only documents we have, they concluded, record an impossible poetic speech, or a stiff written speech. So, for their little play, they had to invent a colloquial language which was at once friendly and jolly but which would still preserve the quiet dignity which we seemingly must associate with revered persons of the past.

As different from traditional learnnig, experience-learning and research-learning cover a much larger area of knowledge: from the study of sanitation, for example, it may range all the way from Roman sewers to the latest typhoid epidemic; from ancient ceremonies of burial of man and animal to the thrilling stories of modern microbe hunters.

And all this vast search for learning is brought into everyone's experience by the process of what we call sharing. Sharing of this sort is a powerful form of learning, because all the members learn eventually what each child or each group has been investigating separately. *The magic catalyst of eager desire and feeling-of-worthwhileness make that learning stick.* We have proof on proof now that those who are freed from enough of the regimented type of learning to permit, under professional guidance, a sharing of the rugged labors of experimental and research-learning, learn more, retain longer, and learn more profitably. In test they far surpass other children in the so-called fundamentals and even in the academic studies, not omitting Latin, modern languages, mathematics, and the sciences. The report of the Wrightstone tests tells this story for both elementary and high school levels.

Another kind of learning comes from simple self-expression. We call it creative learning; it is an indirect, and often unnoticed, accompaniment of all self-absorbing work.

Creative work is the unique individual outcome of what we do with hand or mind, whether it be the writing of a letter to a friend, the composing of verse, the planning of a party, the attempt to draw or paint, a decision uninfluenced by group opinion, absurd and even fantastic imaginings, thoughts about life and its people. Creative work may be known by its signal mark of originality; the genuine creative product is always an expression of one's own inimitable individuailty. Maybe you talk and laugh like your age-group; if you were more creative you would talk and laugh like yourself. You, the real creative you, has no duplicate in the wide world.

Except for the predestinate artist — one whom neither heat nor cold or gloom of night, nor rejection slips from publishers, nor sneers of critics, can stay from the steady expression of his appointed creative impulse—the ordinary person, like you or me, rarely moves forward unassisted to further and superior creative adventures.

II

You may, however, continue to write a good letter — a native gift with nearly everybody — but, without professional help, you may not write a better, and a better one. We know something now about how to make that letter a better letter. Let me indicate to you some of the simpler steps; it will help us later to understand how adults in teaching may move forward in creative learning. The headings are acceptance, approvals, criticism, indirect teaching of principles, and, finally, that miracle of artistic superiority which you might call something approaching the work of genius.

Acceptance. We receive each crude product of creative effort, asking only if it is individual and sincerely meant. That procedure removes fear and sets up hope of success; and it stimulates marvelously the urge to create anew.

Approvals. We find something to like in each effort. This is not just flattery, and it is not indiscriminate. One must approve only the original element, not the imitation of things read and heard or observed in the work of others. And such approvals must vary in intensity and always must be given sparingly. Instruction, meaning correction, has no discouraging place at this stage.

Criticism. When mutual trust has been set up, criticism may nearly always be profitable if it is associated with strong general approval; but there are two better places for criticism, the "low moment" — Florence Cane's discovery — when one is discouraged because of lack of technique, and the "cold moment", long after the effort when all interest is being turned into a new creative venture. We can stand a strong dosage of criticism in the cold moments without once blighting the growing creative impulse. The old work does not seem to be our own really. That which is now emerging, however, is another matter. It absorbs all our affectionate interest; to criticize then is not to help but possibly to destroy.

Indirect teaching. The best teaching in the creative arts is so indirect as not to be noticed. We usually make no reference to principles of composition and design until the perfect illustration of their perfect use appears in the work of the learner. Then when a small group has gathered around, we point it out, exult over it, and give a name to it. "See how good you are!" is the effect of our reception. And we are almost sure to say something like this: "There, you have made the perfect spondee those two long notes, placed exactly where they should appear, at the end of a phrase. And you never had heard of a spondee, had you? Well, all the good rules in the books, about harmony, balance, suspense, dissonance, design, and the like, were made by persons who observed what we human beings naturally do well. We don't need to teach them to anybody. We just wait until someone illustrates a well established rule, as you have just done now. But it's a good thing to know what it is, for sometime you may want to produce this effect again, and then you'll remember the spondee and use it deliberately. That's what good craftmanship is, the result of instinct, experience, and applied knowledge."

We do not need to wait until we get to college, when it is almost too late, to learn about the principles of any genuinely human art. We guarantee to find most of them, done with instinctive skill, among very small children. A girl of five observes spring for possibly the first time; she has also in her mind a picture of her first remembered winter. Quietly she looks at the new grass and the leafless trees and says slowly, "Rocky old earth has a new green coat." Without a wasted word she presents the dissonance of grand heavy words, like *rocky* and *earth* coupled with the equally discordant word *old* and contrasts these with the bright slowly measured phrase, *new green coat*. She not only observes the principles of dissonance, contrast, rhythm, climax, and condensation — these eight words are packed together expertly — but she has employed a device ancient in our English speech but which has just never been noted or named by the textbook writers, the "three long notes" to decorate a diminuendo close "new green coat". The grammarians have listed the spondee, the two long notes at closing, because the Romans had named it before them; but they missed the other types of ending. And that, I suspect, is because they got their learning about language from books and not from living speech.

Some day the book rhetoricians will discover, what children already know, namely, the four long notes, the five and the six. They are used to produce strong effects of climax. When Shakespeare wanted to speak impressively of the great dread, death, he used a line of ten long notes: "Or what strong hand can hold his swift foot back."

Now we come to *the miracle*. I have named this among the five teaching steps in summoning native creative power. When lines of trusted communication have been set up by a general acceptance of all sincere attempts of pure self-expression, when, through approvals of the more genuine material, criticism is natural and undisturbing, and when indirect teaching is having its stimulating effect, then suddenly the fresh original phrase appears and the strong line.

The illustration is from writing, although the same phenomenon appears in all the arts. A student painter ceases suddenly to imitate other painters; a student composer abruptly strikes measures all his own; a child develops the cool, unprejudiced judgment of the scientist; another puts aside the history books and interprets events like a true historian. That sudden birth of high accomplishment is what we call the miracle.

We can recite the steps forward to complete self-realization up to the point of the emergence of that unique product, individual artistry, but no one understands completely why or how the miracle appears. All that we know is that, in the kind of set-up presented in this book, one day the individual speaks out in his own unique voice; and further, that *the contagion from one may carry a whole group on into superior self-expression*. After that the progress is always forward and always on the heights.

III

Now to apply all this to adults and particularly to teachers. If teachers would move with the times, they must themselves experience the new learnings but, it must be admitted in their defense that they are blocked from going forward by the fact that all their examinations and all their promotions are still based upon traditional learning. It is what they know that is examined, not what they can do. They must be able to recite "the seven cardinal principles of secondary education", but no one will ever inquire if they make any use of them.

In spite of the inadequate measure of examinations, however, the example has been set for a break away from imprisonment in limited curricular studies. The good book psychologist, for example, is turning away from books to the clinical exploration of human behavior; the alert younger teachers are declining to spend the best years of their lives with "Evangeline" to the exclusion of vast new literature created since 1900. Teacher and pupil alike have gone adventuring in the new fields of advanced science — in P. S. 208, Brooklyn, New York, a group of elementary children are working with their teacher on the new sulfa drugs; teacher and youth alike are coming to new and unheard of conclusions about future world planning; they are re-examining and rewriting history and economics; they are together revolutionizing our concept of education — see "The Eight-Year Study" in which thirty high schools participated; and they are soberly investigating the new meanings and the new possibilities of that which we have always contentedly called democracy.

These new ways of learning, which both children and their teachers are now practicing, do not imply a neglect of the traditional learning, but simply that traditional learning is given a less monopolistic place in education. I am simply reporting an obvious trend in American education. These newer learnings are conspicuous and very much alive in public schools throughout the whole country, in elementary as well as in high schools, experiential-learning, research-learning, sharing-learning, and creative learning. Children nowadays do learn from textbooks (traditional) but they also learn from seeing, examining, questioning (experiential); in addition, they learn by getting together all the published data on the topic they are studying (research); they report their findings to the class (sharing); and they learn by making things with their hands and by using their native imagination, invention, and artistry in self-expression (creative).

The older form of learning stressed information and mental skills, and we still use it for that purpose; the newer forms stress individuality, its growth in strength and power. One set is interested in things to be learned; the other is interested in what is happening to the learner. There should never have been any clash between them because both are good procedures. Let us never forget that fact.

Many other new kinds of learning flourish in the elementary grades, tactual learning, for example, the kind that comes through the feel of things and from improved dexterity in manipulation. It is illustrated beautifully and convincingly in a pamphlet published by *Childhood Education* called *Children Can Make It*. Skilled teachers have brought the material together under the editorial assistance of A. Adele Rudolph. More about this in the next chapter. Although I have worked largely in literature and the arts I recognize here the same creative outcomes in "making things": the rapid assumption of maturer attitudes by the children; the emergence of self-initiated ideas, the final product which is not so importantly a thing made as it is a personality enlarged and better equipped for new ventures.

The emphasis in this chapter is upon activities that arouse strong and lasting interests. The moral effect of a deep interest in any socially beneficial activity cannot be over emphasized. Good interests shut out and obliterate the temptations of socially bad interests. The battle of youthful delinquency is in part a fight between the strong absorption in decent activities, which the school and the home should sacrifice much to develop, and the easy allure of other youth over whom the school and the home have long ago lost control.

CHAPTER XXV

Creative Hands

THE SURE EDUCATIONAL FOUNDATION for "making things", illustrated so convincingly in the *Childhood Education* pamphlet, demands a fuller treatment here.

Making things is an important and necessary phase of elementary education. Furthermore, it is a natural for children. It arouses and stimulates immediate and enlarging interests. The whole child pours into the effort. He surrenders completely to the task before him. We rarely capture this sustained cooperation of all the children in any other kind of learning project.

The willing surrender of the child to our tempting program of making things—if that were all, we could not count our effort as wholly satisfactory. Professionally we note that, in making things, important abilities are exercised: to imagine, to feel, to summon the inventive mind to invent, to discover new means for the overcoming of obstacles, and, finally, to achieve under helpful guidance a finished form pleasing to the child.

> *This is elementary practice in what is man's chief accomplishment: the prolonged control of mind and body in the making of something that is considered worthy of his peer group.*

The greater the variety of materials with which the child has experience, the greater, we note, is his confidence of his ability to express his ideas. Children have two languages, the one they use and the more adult vocabulary which they understand but do not normally employ. However, as we talk with them about the work that absorbs their complete attention, they find quickly the need for using a more mature speech. They would come to that stage in time, but making things, under competent and friendly guidance, speeds up their language growth. They will use our words now as they explain or inquire; a strong necessity has driven them; so they move naturally into a swift acceptance of more mature language standards.

Maturity of bearing also comes to the worker. The things that we have to offer may have been around him all the time. We are helping him really to see them, to understand them, and to learn to use them. That is our job, of course; our reward comes, not entirely from the new skills of manipulation that appear, but from the gradual transformation of child-like and even childish behavior into something finer — the control of thoughtless impulses and the quiet persistence that works steadily toward a well-conceived goal.

In every school activity, there are things to make. The children read about their Colonial ancestors, for example, and were impressed by the grim importance of candles. The members of the family had to make them, for there was no other practical light for them at night. To get the real feel of this ancient necessity — put into their minds deftly by the teacher, of course — the children studied how to make candles. Then they made them. It was a long hard job. Later in a darkened room with their own handmade candles lighted before them, the children lived imaginatively a winter's night in the wild new country.

The need for making tambourines, rattles, and tom-toms for a forthcoming pageant may lead to experiences with sound. This in turn might expand into writing original songs, or to research in cultures of other peoples who used similar instruments, or perhaps to the construction of xylophones and stringed instruments.

Masks of their very own making, more attractive and more exciting than those sold in the stores, help in celebrating Halloween. Another group might make water wheels and windmills, and, in so doing, recapture something of the experience that man has had in using natural forces to supplement his own limited capabilities. Thus they gain glimpses of the part that power has played in the history of man.

So children today practice some of the "new" kinds of learning — experience-learning, research-learning, sharing-learning, learning through imagination and invention and experimentation. This is creative education.

Although I have worked largely in the area of the language and visual arts, I recognize here the same creative outcomes in making things: the rapid assumption of mature attitudes; the strong absorbing interest; the emergence of self-initiated ideas, ideas which beget fresher and superior ideas; the final product which is not so much a thing made as it is *a personality enlarged and better equipped for new ventures.*

Wherever this kind of schoolroom procedure is reported, as it is so fully in the *Childhood Education* pamphlet, it is evident that the teachers' main contribution, naturally never mentioned at all, is their own spirited selves. These adult workers are fundamentally creative persons.

No superior outcome is possible in this field without the creative teacher. She it is whose subtle directing keeps the whole activity going. She shows her admiration for high achievement but honestly and without flattery. She will be patient with the slow worker but she will not give her approval to work that is shoddy. Quite often she will withhold assistance to a child in difficulty, who, she senses, is persisting rewardingly in the right direction. She is sure that being sensitive he will come through successfully. Her mature use of language, her taste, her confidence in the worth of her work, her genuine interest, all the elements, indeed, that make her an influencing personality — these are at work on the children all the time, although they may never be aware of it.

CHAPTER XXVI

Youth Calls to Youth

CHILDREN'S VERSIFICATION HAS BEEN used in this book largely for convenience. Their prose bulks too large for illustrative purposes, although all that has been said here about the creative impulses is equally applicable to their creative work in prose.

The stories and familar essays in *Lincoln Verse, Story, and Essay,* a Columbia Teachers College publication, were all voluntary contributions to the school magazine. Not one was ever a classroom assignment. In the progress toward their final form they were, to be sure, subject to many an informal sharing with a teacher, and often became topics for group discussion; but they were never the result of tasks imposed. The object of the publication in book form was to show how a school magazine may be used to bring out latent ability and to guide it to creditable achievement; and for the stimulating power such naive contributions would have upon others of the same age. Youth calls to youth with an inspiriting influence which we elders can never hope to match.

The limited book was so swiftly absorbed by teachers in other schools that we were led to make inquiries as to its use. The almost unanimous answer was that it had become the most thumbed book in the classroom; that pupils had gone to it, every type of pupil, the literary and the inarticulate ones, with an almost greedy interest; and that rereadings did not seem to diminish that interest.

Many teachers and parents told us that it had awakened inspiration among boys and girls who had not hitherto found themselves; that nearly always after a reading would come an attempt at personal composition. We asked particularly if the results seemed imitative. Hardly ever, was the usual response. Evidently the creative life itself had been touched, whose vibrations are always unique.

We believe there is a point here for teachers and parents who are interested in stimulating in the young the impulse for creative writing. Books written by adults, even the best of them, do not seem to have the powerful suggestive power to the creative life of youth that the good work of their actual youthful contemporaries has. "These pieces of writing," they seem to say to themselves, "were done by boys and girls just like me; written because they wanted to write; done the way they wanted to do them. I have things of my own I want to write about. In my own way, too. They must have had fun doing it, Why shouldn't I?"

Provoking the creative impulse to bestir itself by being brought into contact with the superior work of young creative writers is undoubtedly of great importance, but the greater dangers of disappointment must be faced in all frankness. We admit that it is quite possible for any boy or girl to duplicate the simple originality of the stories and essays in our collection but without some guidance it might not be possible at all. Let me give what help I can here by showing how in prose composition we restricted the output in some instances and how we drew the work out in others.

Our first prose compositions were largely imitations of the work of adults, to all of which we refused to warm. The early imaginative prose was spurious, founded upon no promptings of the creative life; its source was, indeed, quite often outside of any life at all in the "latest fiction." We reserved our excitement for their use of the only life they really knew something about; and again we trotted out our favorite criterion that their best work would be like nobody else's best work because it would be founded upon their individual interpretation of the world about them and within them; that, therefore, it would be "something that never happened in the world before."

After a deal of waiting this had the fine result of driving the youngsters into a reflection upon their personal experiences. A considerable portion of our own energy at this period was spent with individuals in making them believe that the everyday happenings of their own lives were alive, dramatic even, interesting to others and worthy of serious portrayal. I told them endless stories out of my own everyday life, just to show them how one could extract the moving thing out of seemingly trivial events. "Something is always happening to you," they would say, often with the suggestion that I was adept at the long bow. "Something always is," would be my retort; and then I would show them by a concrete instance how I had taught myself to watch for that "something".

They had no trouble in seeing the point in the old newspaper yarn about the young reporter, returning from his "cover" of a fashionable wedding, who had announced to his editor, "No story. The groom didn't show up."

Those who had had other experiences than that of mere school life were, of course, strongly invited to make use of them. Some had been abroad, for instance; one had lived for a year in Constantinople; one was in the Army with her parents; another had spent a long period on an Arizona ranch; another had visited the Pueblo Indians at Santo Domingo; one had had a year at a boarding school. Our scenes, then, were those we knew something about; our characters were those we had really met and understood; our opinions and points of view grew out of a personal contact with living.

All those prose compositions are marked, therefore, with the stamp of assurance. One leans timidly upon no outside authority when one quotes from experience. Casually and surely the young fisherman speaks of lafayettes and pilot fish in schools of hundreds, of the great shoal of blue fish snapping at the fleeing menhaden, of metal squids, gunwhale, and tiller, the beach guard at the sculls. The army youngster writes unerringly of the C.O., the bronze discharge button, the guard house, the bugle salute to the colors. The shriveled life of Miss Meachim, guide and protector of alien boarding-school girls, is almost sickening in its authenticity. That boy's accurate notetaking on the careless indolence of a school-scheduled class-meeting comes out of life. The horse in a Southwest corral, the Pueblos dancing in the sand storm, the younger brothers bedeviling

the older sister and her girl friends, these are characteriza-
tions that may not be doubted.

No one can write until he knows what he is writing about.
Really knows, not as information merely but as something
lived until it has become a part of him. Each individual has
a region, small or large, upon which he may speak with
authority; and by judicious cultivation this region may be
enormously enlarged. Each person, in other words, has a
story to tell; and, most fortunate for teachers if they could
only be made aware of it, it is the only story which the world
is really eager to hear. To discover that purple land is the
finest help a teacher of the written word may give to youth.
The test of having found it is always in the outcomes: solid
ground, real persons moving inevitably right, comment
touched with authoritative knowledge, a mature assurance
in the telling.

One must know, further, that some of our contributions
did not spring full-armed from the head of their creator.
Several of them were at the start but single paragraphs.
That is where the watchful guide comes in. He should have
a keen scent for the big thing concealed in a few pictured
sentences.

One of the best stories in that collection began with a
paragraph or two which rest now in its very middle! In
that instance I went back eagerly for more. "What happened before this?" When I had obtained what happened
before this I went back, with even more eagerness, to ask,
"But what happened afterward?" And when I had found out
what happened afterward I was able to say: Do you know,
you've got the beginnings of a good story here! But at this
spot you sum up a great scene in a sentence. Isn't there
more, really, than just that?" A voluble recital of the details of the great scene followed. "Quick!" I cried. "Write
it down, just the way you told it, conversation and all, before it gets cold. That is rich! Alive! Scribble it on any old
paper, and we'll insert it in the final good copy." Several
other "great scenes" were magnified in exactly the same
way. We pinned them together, or pasted bits here and
there; it was a "mess," as the author insisted joyfully, before we had that fair copy finally rolled out into its wonder-

ful length. "Phew!" the author cried, after a two-days' typing, "I didn't know I'd written so much!"

This process takes a tremendous amount of time, but I prize it as the best method in my repertoire for enticing the creative spirit to do its utmost and for teaching the youthful possessor how to make it work for him. But note, that at no time does the guide suggest what should be written; he merely asks for pictured and dramatic expandings of abstract statements or of those summaries of experiences which the amateur is prone to give as a substitute for experience itself.

And, of course, some of their stories never "happened" at all. We treat pure imaginative writing in precisely the same way as other prose.

II

Here, I see, I must give away another from my bag of tricks, but I hesitate, for two reasons; first, it might not be so effective with youngsters if they should see how it works, and, second, the disclosure always makes some nice lady teacher very angry indeed. I never do know why, but often they scold me when I talk about it, or they sit stiff at a meeting and walk out in a huff. All of which is disturbing to a sensitive soul whose main aim in life is to please women and children. But duty is paramount; the soul, as always, must suffer.

You have waylaid a youngster in the hall, let us say, with the news that he *has* something, a big story, in the few limp paragraphs you thrust at him. You question swiftly about "what went on before" and "what went on afterward"; and he catches the contagion and begins to stir. Now, if you are a good fisher of men you will recognize that disturbance known as the "stir"; but you must wait until you are sure of it. When you are certain that that lad or lass will not rest night or day, other lessons or no other lessons, until the volcano inside has been relieved by a flow of hot words, then — you say this in an excited undertone of the utmost intimacy: "Don't bother for a minute about spelling, capitals, or commas and semicolons. Get that stuff out and down on paper while it is still hot! Scribble! Say everything, whether

it belongs or not. Don't stop to think even. We'll fix all
that up afterwards. I've got a couple of castors full of
commas and semicolons. We'll sprinkle 'em all over it —
after it is good and done. Like a broiled steak! Don't you
bother about any of that; I'm good enough at it for both of
us — professional pepperer and salter, that's me! Away
with you and — scribble!"

And later you do salt and pepper it for him right before
his excited nose. As you edit it for commas and semicolons
and quotations marks you show him why you do it. Show
him, remember. Not send him off to fight it out with a cold
textbook, hardly any of which is written with an understanding of the sublime ignorance of children. Show him.
Not scold him, nag him, intimidate him. Show him.

Even the showing, however, is not done unless the creative activity has still gripped his whole being. If he has
cooled completely, you drop that phase until you catch him
stirring again. The point is one of labor-saving simply.
Once caught in the excitement of creative writing he can
be cured of the whole business in the sixth part of a jiffy.

Do not miss the point, however. To cast out the fear of
inadequacy by poking fun at the mechanistic side of writing
by thus belittling it seriously, for your tone must show that
personally you don't give a thrippenny darn for all the commas in pie-dom (and you don't), that is almost to put the
Demon of Inhibition completely out of business. The insistence upon "Scribble!" does the rest for him. Aaron at
the rock is nothing to the flow that this simple psychiatric
trick will do for fluency among the seemingly dumb.

(Now for a pack of indignant letters from perfectly respectable ladies and gentelemen which will announce that I
have taken the last prop from a tottering civilization! Well,
it *was* a good little civilization while it lasted.)

III

Having gone thus far in exposing myself as a person of
low standards — for the purposes of salvation I have often
dropped to the level of publicans and sinners — I may as
well confess further: deliberately I plant in likely souls a
faith in the possibilities of creative ability even when they

give no outward evidence of having any. Many may conceive this procedure to be immoral; that it works, miraculously almost, is my simple utilitarian defence.

In effect I tell them, not all of it, of course, at any one time: "You have something to say. Perhaps you don't believe that. But, nevertheless, you do have something to say. Everybody has. It may be so deep inside of you that it is below consciousness. Waiting to be brought up. Perhaps you have had glimpses of it at times but have thought it worthless. On the contrary, it is one of your most valuable possessions. The world always pays a high price for it, because it is rare; so few persons are able to discover it within themselves, or, having discovered it, so few are able, or have the courage, to bring it boldly forth.

"Perhaps you have thought it just silliness, those thoughts and imaginings that roam about deep inside of you. It is not silliness. On the contrary, it may be the very height of sense. Perhaps you have been ashamed of it. On the contrary, it may be something to be proud of.

"You have something to say. Something of your very own. Try to say it. Don't be ashamed of any real thought or feeling you have. Don't undervalue it. Don't let the fear of what others may think of it prevent you from saying it. Perhaps not aloud, but to yourself. You have something to say, something that no one else in the world has ever said in just your way of saying it.

"When people talk around you, don't you often have your own private views? Too terrible sometimes even to think? That may be the something you have to say, or a part of it. Haven't you imagined yourself in all sorts of absurd situations? That may be it, or a part of it.

"The thing you have to say is bigger than you. No matter how much you bring forth, there is always more. It can continue to emerge all your life, and just as much will remain unsaid. Only a part comes out at a time. But you must get that part out of you. It will not be the best part, but it must come first. Once get it started and more and more will follow. And it will be better and better; or, more like it, better and worse, then better and worse and better. It has terrible ups and downs, but the long trend is always up.

"You have something to say, something important, but the thing itself is not half so important to you as what the saying will be to you. If you can teach yourself to find that unique and valuable possession inside of you and succeed in getting some of it out of you, you yourself will grow astonishingly in personal power. So search for it early. Get it started in order that you may begin to grow.

"You have something to say. Find out what it is. That is the beginning. Once really started, it will carry you through life; for you will be doing for yourself all that education can ever do for anybody, encouraging that deeper and powerful self to rise within you and take possession.

"What you have to say, of course, may be in other media than words, in sketch or in design, for example, in music composition or in interpretative playing of music, in the dance, in walk, bearing, in tone of voice, in laughter, in acceptable social behavior, in dramatic portrayal, in reading aloud, in craftsmanship generally. Express yourself and learn to take the consequences and to learn through that experience; it is the proved recipe for personality growth."

IV

The general method in prose composition, one sees, is writing and revision many times repeated, but there is no attempt to cure every error or to straighten out every sprawling sentence. Far from that! The standards set are not at all those of a textbook; the criterion is simply that of the effect upon the interested reader. The perfection of aim of the ordinary book of rhetoric would absolutely spoil the tang and pull of the artistry before us. The beauty of imperfection! Those books know nothing of that; and their disciples know even less. It is the difference between naturally good-mannered children and children without manners who are perfect in etiquette. But the figure fails, as all attempt to make clear fails before those who have never sensed the difference between corrct manners and good manners, between correct English and good English.

Once, as a boy in England, I saw a scullery maid poring solemnly over a book whose label was, "Ten Thousand Aspirates Properly Pronounced, for Maids, Butlers and Higher Servants of Her Majesty's Possessions Who Desire to Associate on Terms of Intimacy with Persons of the Better Sort." Ten thousand of them! There are that many imperfections of English in the books. What price industry? Mainly the loss of creative ability.

Our instruction has not always been apparent as such, therefore. As fellow writing persons we have met to discuss values and effects in our chosen art. We are often tolerant, therefore, where teachers have been notoriously severe, for, as writers, we know something of the stages through which a story, essay, or poem must usually pass before it reaches a presentable form. There is first the idea, which at the start may not be at all clear; then the attempts to put it on paper, crude and bungling, often illegible; then, likely as not, the complete emergence of the end before the beginning, or of the middle without either beginning or end; then the cutting down or the enlarging of parts to fit proportionately a whole that may not even have been conceived at the start.

Teachers, unless they write themselves, are often unaware of this side of creative writing; therefore they are likely to demand finished products at the first draft, or they may divert all the energies of the artist toward those excellent matters, script, spelling, punctuation, margins, clean paper, and the like. Or they may have too clear an idea, learned solely from textbooks, as to how imaginative writing should be done, producing patterns that all must follow. Perhaps it is for these reasons that successful writers speak so seldom of their courses in English!

Instruction, we think, must not quarrel with the supporting scaffolding, mistaking it for an obstruction; nor must it have a fixed and single notion how such structure should be raised. I trust that in no place in this book, written with sympathetic understanding of the enormous difficulties that beset the path of the teacher, have I intimated that there is only one way of salvation; and I should feel that it had failed if, in my excited optimism, I should have given anywhere the impression that my own way is perfect or infallible or at any point incontestable.

V

To turn now from the narrower discussion of classroom technique to the larger considerations of this book, the problem of releasing the powerful and valuable energies of youth, for the purposes, under guidance, of self-education, one must be willing to admit that freedom as well as repression has its dangers. Rugg and Shumaker in *The Child-Centered School* (World Book Company) made long ago a searching criticism of modern schools based upon a sympathetic understanding of their aims and of their necessary shortcomings. The story is not complete unless one comprehends this criticism. We parents and teachers who side with the larger freedom do not often voice it aloud, for the enemy of young life is still powerful, and we are not in the fight to strengthen *him;* but to one another we willingly pay tribute to our opponent. In his long experience he has perfected much that we may not discard without peril; the difference is that, while we may use his things, we refuse ever to follow him in worshipping them.

Further, this book surveys child life from a special and limited viewpoint; it makes no attempt to tell the whole story of education, nor to deny that there are other and equally valuable viewpoints. It aims simply to add new knowledge to what we have already so laboriously gathered in our long experience with the fascinating mystery of spiritual growth.

CHAPTER XXVII

Each of Us Has a Gift

MANY YEARS AGO, WHEN I was not much more than a boy myself, I took charge of my first class of children in the upper grades of a city grammar school. The faces before me were stolid and expressionless; for them it was a new experience, male teachers being then a novelty in an elementary school room.

To relieve their tension at meeting a new teacher, I jested with them about my own ignorance. They laughed, but not too loud. I asked them what I was supposed to teach them, and they named some of the subjects. "Oh, yes, and physiology," one small girl piped up.

"What's that?" I asked.

Laughter, but pleasant and friendly. "It's about the bones," she reported rapidly, "and the blood and the intestines and the stomach —"

"Ugh!" I interrupted. That amused them immensely. I pondered. "Physiology? I don't believe I could even spell the word." Then they did laugh, a roar and a scream of laughter.

An elderly teacher thrust her head into the room. "Any trouble?" she asked.

"Why, no," I replied.

"I heard a laugh," she snapped; "and laughter is not permitted in the classrooms of this school." She closed the door abruptly and went off.

Their suppressed souls burst forth in hilarious glee. And when finally we wiped the joyful tears from our eyes and settled down, that group and I were on a most friendly relationship.

We had more laughter before that getting acquainted session was over, but came a lull when their faces lost some of the healthy hue of youth. I sensed worriment, and invited them to tell me about it. Two things stood out, concern over the monthly grade for "conduct" and the possible failure to pass the year-end examinations. Some spoke of unbelievably harsh treatment at home when the conduct mark was less than "Good". I was indignant; immediately I assured them that in my class there would not be any conduct mark less than "Good." It worked! A load had been lifted from their little lives and they repaid by being always really "Good."

As to the examinations, I promised that I would take sole responsibility there, but in my own way. Recitations were held later, never with the object of uncovering a culprit, but in order to discover what they needed to learn better. It was nearly all strict *memoriter* work in those days, exact memorization of large portions of the United States Constitution, the difficult and absurd matter of learning how many minims in a fluid drachm or how many square yards there were in four perches. The curriculum included cube root, the special peculiarities of the isosceles triangle — including its correct spelling — and that matter of the famous square on the hypothenuse; and we had to know book definitions of nominative absolute, positives, metonymy, synecdoche, syntax, prosody and the like.

Keeping my promise, I saw to it that eventually they knew these and other matters equally remote from the experience of their daily living. How we drilled over such phrases as "The electors shall meet in their respective" — *not* respected! — "States", and over that real stumper, "One of whom at least shall not be an inhabitant of the same State with themselves." We knew that no other but that eighteenth-century phrasing would be accepted by the examiners.

When the last group was leaving me on that first session, I remarked, "What a good time we had together!" They agreed unanimously. One lad spoke out, "Do you know why we laughed so loud at first? It was because you laughed. We never saw a teacher laugh before." I pondered over the matter and finally said, "Well, now that I think of it, I never did either." That was a long while ago, of course.

As I had found no place for "detentions after school" those boys and girls hovered over my desk when class was dismissed for the day, and talked and talked of their real interests. I need not state that this had nothing to do with school tasks. They poured themselves out in a chatter that was outright, interruptive, but to me wholly captivating. Strange psychological data I was gathering about motives, aims, and child values. Laughter predominated always. Day after day the children would linger until the janitor's dust drove them home. I was thrilled by what I was learning. They held nothing back, as if, like the psychiatrist's couch this was at last the hungered place for pent up thought and feeling. However they disclosed little that was like my own youth. Perhaps, I thought, no one remembers his own younger days; the pictures he retains are shaped by desire and unconsciously invented by pride.

With that first laugh they gave me their faith and their friendship. I paid them back by sticking at it until they all had the right answers for that far off final examination. Other schools permitted only their top scholars to take the high school tests. We sent all of ours up and all of them passed.

In these after-school meetings I came upon a treasure of unsuspected gifts. There was a boy who had invented quick ways of adding. He could total up a column of figures as fast as one could write them on the blackboard. Here, too, I came upon a boy with absolute pitch. With his back to the piano he could name any note struck on the instrument; and he said he had to allow for the fact that the piano was a half note out of pitch. A young girl took quiet possession of our social activities and built up among us a fine sense of belonging. At the time I simply accepted the results of her contagious, cordial spirit; years later I observed her gifted skill with larger social and civic units.

This intimate relationship, I know now, turned up the raw material of a new educational psychology. I have worked with it consciously in teaching, from these elementary beginnings, through high school to graduate students in a university. The material accompanies but is distinctively different from any subject taught.

Let me list a few of these human phenomena that are always there: the native friendliness that can be enticed out of hiding by a laugh; awkwardness based on unfounded feelings of insecurity; absorption in self-confessed trivialities (which may not be trivialities at all) ; the derision of adults that obliterates crude but decent self-expression; the yearning for respect among even the so-called reprobates; the mature conclusions of youth that are often more worthy than the conventional adult acceptances; simple productions that often have a touch of high art; adult contacts that assure the child of his own potential worth; the quiet word of commendation, even in trivial matters, that stirs up new loyalties and strengthens self-faith; regulative ideas which, if deftly planted, will grow in power for good; the importance of good humor and honest tolerance in all social relationships.

Of cousre, the list is really endless, for always we are understanding better and better how the mind and spirit work (which is psychology) and how they can be influenced and directed worthily (which is education). We now know, for example, that vibrations of friendliness or unfriendliness go forth constantly from eyes, voice tone, body and spirit. Without a word being spoken these may close all communications or kindle hope and willingness in another. This has nothing to do with one's learning but solely with what sort of person one really is.

And of the thousands of other situations that belong properly to the field of educational psychology we dare not omit, first, a stirring up of a strong interest in right doing that may direct youth away from a dangerous beginning interest in wrong doing; second, the leader's gift of estimating the value of the first crude expressions of creative power, and the procedures that encourage the further development of such power; and, third, the slow introduction of better material in literature, music, and the arts, that develops an unconscious gradual acceptance and therefore, the possession eventually of higher taste.

Although I have done the prescribed courses in psychology, have listened to the lectures and have read the books, and officially I have held the post of psychologist, I found little in my studies that even touched an understanding of the throbbing, vital forces, the very essence of psychology, that I had taught myself to apprehend and use in living day by day with children, youth, and adults. My own books, from *Creative Youth* to *The Creative Adult* are simply the record of the outcomes and accomplishments in this comparatively unexplored psychological field.

Too many teachers, alas — and this includes many professors — seem never to travel far from the books they have studied, but that is only where the instruments of learning are polished and got ready for personal adventure. The peculiar mark of the creative teacher — as different from all other businesses of man — is not his learning alone but his ability to transform others by the contagion of his own peculiar creative powers. If he can only repeat the studied work of another but is unable out of all that to create something of his very own, his teaching will be of minor importance.

Good teaching is not solely the business of instructing; it is also the art of influencing another. Primarily, it is the job of uncovering and enlarging native gifts of insight, feeling, and thinking.

II

Though few children are geniuses, all children, I early discovered, possess gifts which may become later their special distinction. A thousand talents await recognition! In the able ones who have a decent, sporting job; in those with special interests beyond school demands, like entomology or stamp collecting; in those with a flair for decoration or design; in the natural housekeeper. The young inventor may be so absorbed in his work that he neglects important studies; the skillful user of tools may need adult appreciation to protect him from the snobbishness of the book learners, including teachers.

Someone should stand by in the early years to watch for and foster these natural endowments. It is not enough to discern a native gift; it must be enticed out again and again. It needs exercise in an atmosphere of approval. Above all it must be protected against the annihilating effect of social condemnation. The fair-minded boy may be called "softie" by his mates; the low-voiced girl may be accused of posing for adult favors. The budding scholar may be discouraged by the epithet "bookworm" and the young humorist may be suppressed as a troublemaker. All too often adults encourage only a limited range of traits, those commonly believed to be essential for success, to the detriment of the whole vast range of gifts which children possess.

Often it is the seemingly unimportant gift which is most useful in life. The ability to communicate confidence may at times serve a doctor better than his medical skill; a passionate love of justice, discouraged as forwardness in a child, may one day contribute more to a lawyer's success than the ability to prepare a brief.

This discovery opened for me a way into the secret hopes and delights of childhood, so with like-minded teachers, I helped a few years later to found a private school which specialized in discovering and encouraging hidden abilities. We watched the children in their recess periods — not for the bad traits, which we noted, but for the good traits that show up best in free play.

To see a small boy, probably a new boy, crying softly beside the iron gate, to see a girl of ten dart away from her fellow players, kneel beside the child, dry his tears and stay with him to bring him in smiling when recess was over, that is to know something about character, feeling, behavior in the far-away future; and it reveals much to be done by the wise guide now.

A fifth-grade boy who was uncommunicative in class had therefore been labeled stupid by his teacher. Quite by accident I was able to watch him as the catcher in a sandlot ball game where his vocabulary was profuse, strident and annihilating. He kept his team together and won the game by continuous invective behind the plate. I asked him to write me an account of that game, but insisted that he do it in his own colorful language. I showed him exactly what I meant by seriously quoting him in the tight spots of the game.

Here was a naturally fluent lad who had been driven into silence by unsympathetic correction. Now I convinced him that his rough way of telling a story had merit. After a year or two his lapses into tough speech were eliminated. Later that "stupid" boy had no difficulty with college entrance examinations. Approval is a powerful stimulant to the forces of self-education.

So, when parents ask how they can go about discovering unsuspected gifts in their children, I say, by cool observation. Minimize the attempts to make children what they eventually ought to be, and take up the practical business of seeing what they really are now. Set aside the reproving eye and the authoritative command, and substitute impersonal observation, as if these were some other person's children.

The author of some distinguished books writes me that I was an important influence in his boyhood. All that I did that I now remember was to accept from him a daily outpouring of his writings. *His intense desire to produce seemed to me an important gift.* That is why I rarely stopped his early effusions with a disturbing word of instruction. There would be time enough for that later. What he needed at the moment was encouragement.

The best time for watching children is when they are off guard: on picnics, at out-door games, during visits to places of public interest, at young people's parties, in the informal hours of home life. Here the often overlooked gifts are exposed: wholehearted sharing, grit to contest against odds, natural leadership, care for the younger and the weak, cheerfulness, an interest in planning.

For these reasons parents should be as concerned in having their children become members of the Scouts, the Campfire Girls, the 4-H Clubs, and the like, as in their getting high grades in school. The important thing is to expose children to a multiplicity of activities and interests, so that their inherent gifts will have as many chances as possible to show themselves.

Besides the discovery and encouragement of an aptitude, it goes without saying that opportunities for its exercise should be made convenient. The wise parent will see that the raw materials are at hand. Parents who take a childish interest to heart will go out of their way (and even stop the car) to aid a quest. It may be for rocks or for snakes or for words; it may involve a house-wrecking search for some secret in chemistry. Whatever it is, let it develop.

For some adults, we must warn, discovering hidden gifts in children may demand a change in personal behavior patterns, for self-effacement in an adult is what draws the child out. Children think about the world and come to worthy conclusions — their own. They think about themselves and those around them and come to worthy conclusions — their own. The parent who values these judgments will need to restrain criticism if one wishes to have the enjoyment of seeing unsuspected gifts appear and grow. It is hard for us to listen in silence, even to one's own children, but the fascination of the game is worth every effort.

Slowly the interest of educators generally has turned to a serious consideration of discovering the gifted child. Superintendents of school, notably William Jansen of New York City and Theron Freese of Long Beach, California, have emphasized its importance; professors of education like Paul Witty of Northwestern University and Harvey Zorbaugh of New York University have contributed valuable studies; Joseph Justman, Irving Lorge, Dorothy W. Norris, Walter B. Barbe, Marion Scheifele, to pick names out of the day's educational news, are making revealing reports on the same theme; and Alice V. Keliher and Winifred Ward in their lively "workshops" are scattering the good news everywhere.

III

Some of the material of this chapter is adapted from an article which the editors of *The Reader's Digest* had invited me to prepare for them. Through the wide influence of *The Digest*, that message of unguessed gifts was translated into a dozen languages of the America's, Europe, and Asia, from

Canadian French to Brazilian Portuguese, from Finnish to Japanese. The hearty, approving returns that came from all parts of the world give me assurance that this book, our report on nearly fifty years of teaching children, youth, and adults, represents not just one individual's opinion but the long suppressed hopes and visions of multitudes everywhere.

A like reception, on a small scale, came unexpectedly from a few paragraphs in an article written on this same theme for *Childhood Education*. This particular bit, I noted, was continuously selected later for quoting or reprinting. Warm references were made to it in letters and upon meetings with those who had read the whole piece. That is another proof of the soundness of the really long observations and note takings that had brought those paragraphs forth.

This and many similar experiences have taught me that some arrangement of words has more power than others to stir up a keener observation of the creative possibilities of the ordinary events of daily living. This repeated quotation was obviously one of them. Besides, it seemed to have another effect; it caused teachers and parents, so they have told me, to be more watchful and more eager to search for the unguessed gifts not only of children but of adults as well, so once more I send them forth, this time as the conclusion of this book. Each one of us has a gift.

"There is the gift of courtesy often concealed in clumsy action, a gift of reticence when speech might hurt, a gift for withdrawal while the acquisitive are pushing into front place, a gift for dispassionate conclusions in the midst of partisan heat, a gift for the understanding of minorities, and a very special gift for the understanding of children.

"There is the gift of the quiet word that stills the anxious heartbeat, a gift of social grace that stoops to make life bearable for the awkward. For us, as well as for the young, there is the gift of living together, lost so often in the attachment to worthless possessions.

"There is the gift for raising the mass spirit to worthy endeavor, the gift for a fight and the gift for avoiding one, the gift of grit, the gift for patient suffering. There is also the tortoise gift of the plodder, the fox gift of cunning, the dog gift of faithfulness, the song-sparrow gift of cheerfulness, the swan gift of beauty in motion."

THE END

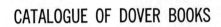

CATALOGUE OF DOVER BOOKS

Books Explaining Science and Mathematics

WHAT IS SCIENCE?, N. Campbell. The role of experiment and measurement, the function of mathematics, the nature of scientific laws, the difference between laws and theories, the limitations of science, and many similarly provocative topics are treated clearly and without technicalities by an eminent scientist. "Still an excellent introduction to scientific philosophy," H. Margenau in PHYSICS TODAY. "A first-rate primer . . . deserves a wide audience," SCIENTIFIC AMERICAN. 192pp. 5⅜ x 8. S43 Paperbound **$1.25**

THE NATURE OF PHYSICAL THEORY, P. W. Bridgman. A Nobel Laureate's clear, non-technical lectures on difficulties and paradoxes connected with frontier research on the physical sciences. Concerned with such central concepts as thought, logic, mathematics, relativity, probability, wave mechanics, etc. he analyzes the contributions of such men as Newton, Einstein, Bohr, Heisenberg, and many others. "Lucid and entertaining . . . recommended to anyone who wants to get some insight into current philosophies of science," THE NEW PHILOSOPHY. Index. xi + 138pp. 5⅜ x 8. S33 Paperbound **$1.25**

EXPERIMENT AND THEORY IN PHYSICS, Max Born. A Nobel Laureate examines the nature of experiment and theory in theoretical physics and analyzes the advances made by the great physicists of our day: Heisenberg, Einstein, Bohr, Planck, Dirac, and others. The actual process of creation is detailed step-by-step by one who participated. A fine examination of the scientific method at work. 44pp. 5⅜ x 8. S308 Paperbound **75¢**

THE PSYCHOLOGY OF INVENTION IN THE MATHEMATICAL FIELD, J. Hadamard. The reports of such men as Descartes, Pascal, Einstein, Poincaré, and others are considered in this investigation of the method of idea-creation in mathematics and other sciences and the thinking process in general. How do ideas originate? What is the role of the unconscious? What is Poincaré's forgetting hypothesis? are some of the fascinating questions treated. A penetrating analysis of Einstein's thought processes concludes the book. xiii + 145pp. 5⅜ x 8. T107 Paperbound **$1.25**

THE NATURE OF LIGHT AND COLOUR IN THE OPEN AIR, M. Minnaert. Why are shadows sometimes blue, sometimes green, or other colors depending on the light and surroundings? What causes mirages? Why do multiple suns and moons appear in the sky? Professor Minnaert explains these unusual phenomena and hundreds of others in simple, easy-to-understand terms based on optical laws and the properties of light and color. No mathematics is required but artists, scientists, students, and everyone fascinated by these "tricks" of nature will find thousands of useful and amazing pieces of information. Hundreds of observational experiments are suggested which require no special equipment. 200 illustrations; 42 photos. xvi + 362pp. 5⅜ x 8. T196 Paperbound **$2.00**

THE UNIVERSE OF LIGHT, W. Bragg. Sir William Bragg, Nobel Laureate and great modern physicist, is also well known for his powers of clear exposition. Here he analyzes all aspects of light for the layman: lenses, reflection, refraction, the optics of vision, x-rays, the photoelectric effect, etc. He tells you what causes the color of spectra, rainbows, and soap bubbles, how magic mirrors work, and much more. Dozens of simple experiments are described. Preface. Index. 199 line drawings and photographs, including 2 full-page color plates. x + 283pp. 5⅜ x 8. T538 Paperbound **$1.85**

SOAP-BUBBLES: THEIR COLOURS AND THE FORCES THAT MOULD THEM, C. V. Boys. For continuing popularity and validity as scientific primer, few books can match this volume of easily-followed experiments, explanations. Lucid exposition of complexities of liquid films, surface tension and related phenomena, bubbles' reaction to heat, motion, music, magnetic fields. Experiments with capillary attraction, soap bubbles on frames, composite bubbles, liquid cylinders and jets, bubbles other than soap, etc. Wonderful introduction to scientific method, natural laws that have many ramifications in areas of modern physics. Only complete edition in print. New Introduction by S. Z. Lewin, New York University. 83 illustrations; 1 full-page color plate. xii + 190pp. 5⅜ x 8½. T542 Paperbound **95¢**

CATALOGUE OF DOVER BOOKS

THE STORY OF X-RAYS FROM RONTGEN TO ISOTOPES, A. R. Bleich, M.D. This book, by a member of the American College of Radiology, gives the scientific explanation of x-rays, their applications in medicine, industry and art, and their danger (and that of atmospheric radiation) to the individual and the species. You learn how radiation therapy is applied against cancer, how x-rays diagnose heart disease and other ailments, how they are used to examine mummies for information on diseases of early societies, and industrial materials for hidden weaknesses. 54 illustrations show x-rays of flowers, bones, stomach, gears with flaws, etc. 1st publication. Index. xix + 186pp. 5⅜ x 8.   T622 Paperbound **$1.35**

SPINNING TOPS AND GYROSCOPIC MOTION, John Perry. A classic elementary text of the dynamics of rotation — the behavior and use of rotating bodies such as gyroscopes and tops. In simple, everyday English you are shown how quasi-rigidity is induced in discs of paper, smoke rings, chains, etc., by rapid motions; why a gyrostat falls and why a top rises; precession; how the earth's motion affects climate; and many other phenomena. Appendix on practical use of gyroscopes. 62 figures. 128pp. 5⅜ x 8.   T416 Paperbound **$1.00**

SNOW CRYSTALS, W. A. Bentley, M. J. Humphreys. For almost 50 years W. A. Bentley photographed snow flakes in his laboratory in Jericho, Vermont; in 1931 the American Meteorological Society gathered together the best of his work, some 2400 photographs of snow flakes, plus a few ice flowers, windowpane frosts, dew, frozen rain, and other ice formations. Pictures were selected for beauty and scientific value. A very valuable work to anyone in meteorology, cryology; most interesting to layman; extremely useful for artist who wants beautiful, crystalline designs. All copyright free. Unabridged reprint of 1931 edition. 2453 illustrations. 227pp. 8 x 10½.   T287 Paperbound **$3.00**

A DOVER SCIENCE SAMPLER, edited by George Barkin. A collection of brief, non-technical passages from 44 Dover Books Explaining Science for the enjoyment of the science-minded browser. Includes work of Bertrand Russell, Poincaré, Laplace, Max Born, Galileo, Newton; material on physics, mathematics, metallurgy, anatomy, astronomy, chemistry, etc. You will be fascinated by Martin Gardner's analysis of the sincere pseudo-scientist, Moritz's account of Newton's absentmindedness, Bernard's examples of human vivisection, etc. Illustrations from the Diderot Pictorial Encyclopedia and De Re Metallica. 64 pages.   **FREE**

THE STORY OF ATOMIC THEORY AND ATOMIC ENERGY, J. G. Feinberg. A broader approach to subject of nuclear energy and its cultural implications than any other similar source. Very readable, informal, completely non-technical text. Begins with first atomic theory, 600 B.C. and carries you through the work of Mendelejeff, Röntgen, Madame Curie, to Einstein's equation and the A-bomb. New chapter goes through thermonuclear fission, binding energy, other events up to 1959. Radioactive decay and radiation hazards, future benefits, work of Bohr, moderns, hundreds more topics. "Deserves special mention . . . not only authoritative but thoroughly popular in the best sense of the word," Saturday Review. Formerly, "The Atom Story." Expanded with new chapter. Three appendixes. Index. 34 illustrations. vii + 243pp. 5⅜ x 8.   T625 Paperbound **$1.45**

THE STRANGE STORY OF THE QUANTUM, AN ACCOUNT FOR THE GENERAL READER OF THE GROWTH OF IDEAS UNDERLYING OUR PRESENT ATOMIC KNOWLEDGE, B. Hoffmann. Presents lucidly and expertly, with barest amount of mathematics, the problems and theories which led to modern quantum physics. Dr. Hoffmann begins with the closing years of the 19th century, when certain trifling discrepancies were noticed, and with illuminating analogies and examples takes you through the brilliant concepts of Planck, Einstein, Pauli, Broglie, Bohr, Schroedinger, Heisenberg, Dirac, Sommerfeld, Feynman, etc. This edition includes a new, long postscript carrying the story through 1958. "Of the books attempting an account of the history and contents of our modern atomic physics which have come to my attention, this is the best," H. Margenau, Yale University, in "American Journal of Physics." 32 tables and line illustrations. Index. 275pp. 5⅜ x 8.   T518 Paperbound **$1.50**

SPACE AND TIME, E. Borel. Written by a versatile mathematician of world renown with his customary lucidity and precision, this introduction to relativity for the layman presents scores of examples, analogies, and illustrations that open up new ways of thinking about space and time. It covers abstract geometry and geographical maps, continuity and topology, the propagation of light, the special theory of relativity, the general theory of relativity, theoretical researches, and much more. Mathematical notes. 2 Indexes. 4 Appendices. 15 figures. xvi + 243pp. 5⅜ x 8.   T592 Paperbound **$1.45**

FROM EUCLID TO EDDINGTON: A STUDY OF THE CONCEPTIONS OF THE EXTERNAL WORLD, Sir Edmund Whittaker. A foremost British scientist traces the development of theories of natural philosophy from the western rediscovery of Euclid to Eddington, Einstein, Dirac, etc. The inadequacy of classical physics is contrasted with present day attempts to understand the physical world through relativity, non-Euclidean geometry, space curvature, wave mechanics, etc. 5 major divisions of examination: Space; Time and Movement; the Concepts of Classical Physics; the Concepts of Quantum Mechanics; the Eddington Universe. 212pp. 5⅜ x 8.   T491 Paperbound **$1.35**

Nature, Biology

NATURE RECREATION: Group Guidance for the Out-of-doors, William Gould Vinal. Intended for both the uninitiated nature instructor and the education student on the college level, this complete "how-to" program surveys the entire area of nature education for the young. Philosophy of nature recreation; requirements, responsibilities, important information for group leaders; nature games; suggested group projects; conducting meetings and getting discussions started; etc. Scores of immediately applicable teaching aids, plus completely updated sources of information, pamphlets, field guides, recordings, etc. Bibliography. 74 photographs. + 310pp. 5⅜ x 8½.   T1015 Paperbound **$1.75**

HOW TO KNOW THE WILD FLOWERS, Mrs. William Starr Dana. Classic nature book that has introduced thousands to wonders of American wild flowers. Color-season principle of organization is easy to use, even by those with no botanical training, and the genial, refreshing discussions of history, folklore, uses of over 1,000 native and escape flowers, foliage plants are informative as well as fun to read. Over 170 full-page plates, collected from several editions, may be colored in to make permanent records of finds. Revised to conform with 1950 edition of Gray's Manual of Botany. xlii + 438pp. 5⅜ x 8½.   T332 Paperbound **$1.85**

HOW TO KNOW THE FERNS, F. T. Parsons. Ferns, among our most lovely native plants, are all too little known. This classic of nature lore will enable the layman to identify almost any American fern he may come across. After an introduction on the structure and life of ferns, the 57 most important ferns are fully pictured and described (arranged upon a simple identification key). Index of Latin and English names. 61 illustrations and 42 full-page plates. xiv + 215pp. 5⅜ x 8.   T740 Paperbound **$1.35**

MANUAL OF THE TREES OF NORTH AMERICA, Charles Sprague Sargent. Still unsurpassed as most comprehensive, reliable study of North American tree characteristics, precise locations and distribution. By dean of American dendrologists. Every tree native to U.S., Canada, Alaska, 185 genera, 717 species, described in detail—leaves, flowers, fruit, winterbuds, bark, wood, growth habits etc. plus discussion of varieties and local variants, immaturity variations. Over 100 keys, including unusual 11-page analytical key to genera, aid in identification. 783 clear illustrations of flowers, fruit, leaves. An unmatched permanent reference work for all nature lovers. Second enlarged (1926) edition. Synopsis of families. Analytical key to genera. Glossary of technical terms. Index. 783 illustrations, 1 map. Two volumes. Total of 982pp. 5⅜ x 8.   T277 Vol. I Paperbound **$2.25**
                                                       T278 Vol. II Paperbound **$2.25**
                                                       The set **$4.50**

TREES OF THE EASTERN AND CENTRAL UNITED STATES AND CANADA, W. M. Harlow. A revised edition of a standard middle-level guide to native trees and important escapes. More than 140 trees are described in detail, and illustrated with more than 600 drawings and photographs. Supplementary keys will enable the careful reader to identify almost any tree he might encounter. xiii + 288pp. 5⅜ x 8.   T395 Paperbound **$1.35**

GUIDE TO SOUTHERN TREES, Ellwood S. Harrar and J. George Harrar. All the essential information about trees indigenous to the South, in an extremely handy format. Introductory essay on methods of tree classification and study, nomenclature, chief divisions of Southern trees, etc. Approximately 100 keys and synopses allow for swift, accurate identification of trees. Numerous excellent illustrations, non-technical text make this a useful book for teachers of biology or natural science, nature lovers, amateur naturalists. Revised 1962 edition. Index. Bibliography. Glossary of technical terms. 920 illustrations; 201 full-page plates. ix + 709pp. 4⅝ x 6⅜.   T945 Paperbound **$2.25**

FRUIT KEY AND TWIG KEY TO TREES AND SHRUBS, W. M. Harlow. Bound together in one volume for the first time, these handy and accurate keys to fruit and twig identification are the only guides of their sort with photographs (up to 3 times natural size). "Fruit Key": Key to over 120 different deciduous and evergreen fruits. 139 photographs and 11 line drawings. Synoptic summary of fruit types. Bibliography. 2 Indexes (common and scientific names). "Twig Key": Key to over 160 different twigs and buds. 173 photographs. Glossary of technical terms. Bibliography. 2 Indexes (common and scientific names). Two volumes bound as one. Total of xvii + 126pp. 5⅝ x 8⅜.   T511 Paperbound **$1.25**

INSECT LIFE AND INSECT NATURAL HISTORY, S. W. Frost. A work emphasizing habits, social life, and ecological relations of insects, rather than more academic aspects of classification and morphology. Prof. Frost's enthusiasm and knowledge are everywhere evident as he discusses insect associations and specialized habits like leaf-rolling, leaf-mining, and case-making, the gall insects, the boring insects, aquatic insects, etc. He examines all sorts of matters not usually covered in general works, such as: insects as human food, insect music and musicians, insect response to electric and radio waves, use of insects in art and literature. The admirably executed purpose of this book, which covers the middle ground between elementary treatment and scholarly monographs, is to excite the reader to observe for himself. Over 700 illustrations. Extensive bibliography. x + 524pp. 5⅜ x 8.   T517 Paperbound **$2.45**

CATALOGUE OF DOVER BOOKS

COMMON SPIDERS OF THE UNITED STATES, J. H. Emerton. Here is a nature hobby you can pursue right in your own cellar! Only non-technical, but thorough, reliable guide to spiders for the layman. Over 200 spiders from all parts of the country, arranged by scientific classification, are identified by shape and color, number of eyes, habitat and range, habits, etc. Full text, 501 line drawings and photographs, and valuable introduction explain webs, poisons, threads, capturing and preserving spiders, etc. Index. New synoptic key by S. W. Frost. xxiv + 225pp. 5⅜ x 8.   T223 Paperbound **$1.45**

THE LIFE STORY OF THE FISH: HIS MANNERS AND MORALS, Brian Curtis. A comprehensive, non-technical survey of just about everything worth knowing about fish. Written for the aquarist, the angler, and the layman with an inquisitive mind, the text covers such topics as evolution, external covering and protective coloration, physics and physiology of vision, maintenance of equilibrium, function of the lateral line canal for auditory and temperature senses, nervous system, function of the air bladder, reproductive system and methods—courtship, mating, spawning, care of young—and many more. Also sections on game fish, the problems of conservation and a fascinating chapter on fish curiosities. "Clear, simple language . . . excellent judgment in choice of subjects . . . delightful sense of humor," New York Times. Revised (1949) edition. Index. Bibliography of 72 items. 6 full-page photographic plates. xii + 284pp. 5⅜ x 8.   T929 Paperbound **$1.50**

BATS, Glover Morrill Allen. The most comprehensive study of bats as a life-form by the world's foremost authority. A thorough summary of just about everything known about this fascinating and mysterious flying mammal, including its unique location sense, hibernation and cycles, its habitats and distribution, its wing structure and flying habits, and its relationship to man in the long history of folklore and superstition. Written on a middle-level, the book can be profitably studied by a trained zoologist and thoroughly enjoyed by the layman. "An absorbing text with excellent illustrations. Bats should have more friends and fewer thoughtless detractors as a result of the publication of this volume," William Beebe, Books. Extensive bibliography. 57 photographs and illustrations. x + 368pp. 5⅜ x 8½.
T984 Paperbound **$2.00**

BIRDS AND THEIR ATTRIBUTES, Glover Morrill Allen. A fine general introduction to birds as living organisms, especially valuable because of emphasis on structure, physiology, habits, behavior. Discusses relationship of bird to man, early attempts at scientific ornithology, feathers and coloration, skeletal structure including bills, legs and feet, wings. Also food habits, evolution and present distribution, feeding and nest-building, still unsolved questions of migrations and location sense, many more similar topics. Final chapter on classification, nomenclature. A good popular-level summary for the biologist; a first-rate introduction for the layman. Reprint of 1925 edition. References and index. 51 illustrations. viii + 338pp. 5⅜ x 8½.   T957 Paperbound **$1.85**

LIFE HISTORIES OF NORTH AMERICAN BIRDS, Arthur Cleveland Bent. Bent's monumental series of books on North American birds, prepared and published under auspices of Smithsonian Institute, is the definitive coverage of the subject, the most-used single source of information. Now the entire set is to be made available by Dover in inexpensive editions. This encyclopedic collection of detailed, specific observations utilizes reports of hundreds of contemporary observers, writings of such naturalists as Audubon, Burroughs, William Brewster, as well as author's own extensive investigations. Contains literally everything known about life history of each bird considered: nesting, eggs, plumage, distribution and migration, voice, enemies, courtship, etc. These not over-technical works are musts for ornithologists, conservationists, amateur naturalists, anyone seriously interested in American birds.

BIRDS OF PREY. More than 100 subspecies of hawks, falcons, eagles, buzzards, condors and owls, from the common barn owl to the extinct caracara of Guadaloupe Island. 400 photographs. Two volume set. Index for each volume. Bibliographies of 403, 520 items. 197 full-page plates. Total of 907pp. 5⅜ x 8½.   Vol. I T931 Paperbound **$2.50**
Vol. II T932 Paperbound **$2.50**

WILD FOWL. Ducks, geese, swans, and tree ducks—73 different subspecies. Two volume set. Index for each volume. Bibliographies of 124, 144 items. 106 full-page plates. Total of 685pp. 5⅜ x 8½.   Vol. I T285 Paperbound **$2.50**
Vol. II T286 Paperbound **$2.50**

SHORE BIRDS. 81 varieties (sandpipers, woodcocks, plovers, snipes, phalaropes, curlews, oyster catchers, etc.). More than 200 photographs of eggs, nesting sites, adult and young of important species. Two volume set. Index for each volume. Bibliographies of 261, 188 items. 121 full-page plates. Total of 860pp. 5⅜ x 8½.   Vol. I T933 Paperbound **$2.35**
Vol. II T934 Paperbound **$2.35**

THE LIFE OF PASTEUR, R. Vallery-Radot. 13th edition of this definitive biography, cited in Encyclopaedia Britannica. Authoritative, scholarly, well-documented with contemporary quotes, observations; gives complete picture of Pasteur's personal life; especially thorough presentation of scientific activities with silkworms, fermentation, hydrophobia, inoculation, etc. Introduction by Sir William Osler. Index. 505pp. 5⅜ x 8.   T632 Paperbound **$2.00**

Puzzles, Mathematical Recreations

SYMBOLIC LOGIC and THE GAME OF LOGIC, Lewis Carroll. "Symbolic Logic" is not concerned with modern symbolic logic, but is instead a collection of over 380 problems posed with charm and imagination, using the syllogism, and a fascinating diagrammatic method of drawing conclusions. In "The Game of Logic" Carroll's whimsical imagination devises a logical game played with 2 diagrams and counters (included) to manipulate hundreds of tricky syllogisms. The final section, "Hit or Miss" is a lagniappe of 101 additional puzzles in the delightful Carroll manner. Until this reprint edition, both of these books were rarities costing up to $15 each. Symbolic Logic: Index. xxxi + 199pp. The Game of Logic: 96pp. 2 vols. bound as one. 5⅜ x 8. T492 Paperbound **$1.50**

PILLOW PROBLEMS and A TANGLED TALE, Lewis Carroll. One of the rarest of all Carroll's works, "Pillow Problems" contains 72 original math puzzles, all typically ingenious. Particularly fascinating are Carroll's answers which remain exactly as he thought them out, reflecting his actual mental process. The problems in "A Tangled Tale" are in story form, originally appearing as a monthly magazine serial. Carroll not only gives the solutions, but uses answers sent in by readers to discuss wrong approaches and misleading paths, and grades them for insight. Both of these books were rarities until this edition, "Pillow Problems" costing up to $25, and "A Tangled Tale" $15. Pillow Problems: Preface and Introduction by Lewis Carroll. xx + 109pp. A Tangled Tale: 6 illustrations. 152pp. Two vols. bound as one. 5⅜ x 8. T493 Paperbound **$1.50**

AMUSEMENTS IN MATHEMATICS, Henry Ernest Dudeney. The foremost British originator of mathematical puzzles is always intriguing, witty, and paradoxical in this classic, one of the largest collections of mathematical amusements. More than 430 puzzles, problems, and paradoxes. Mazes and games, problems on number manipulation, unicursal and other route problems, puzzles on measuring, weighing, packing, age, kinship, chessboards, joiners', crossing river, plane figure dissection, and many others. Solutions. More than 450 illustrations. vii + 258pp. 5⅜ x 8. T473 Paperbound **$1.25**

THE CANTERBURY PUZZLES, Henry Dudeney. Chaucer's pilgrims set one another problems in story form. Also Adventures of the Puzzle Club, the Strange Escape of the King's Jester, the Monks of Riddlewell, the Squire's Christmas Puzzle Party, and others. All puzzles are original, based on dissecting plane figures, arithmetic, algebra, elementary calculus and other branches of mathematics, and purely logical ingenuity. "The limit of ingenuity and intricacy," The Observer. Over 110 puzzles. Full Solutions. 150 illustrations. vii + 225pp. 5⅜ x 8. T474 Paperbound **$1.25**

MATHEMATICAL EXCURSIONS, H. A. Merrill. Even if you hardly remember your high school math, you'll enjoy the 90 stimulating problems contained in this book and you will come to understand a great many mathematical principles with surprisingly little effort. Many useful shortcuts and diversions not generally known are included: division by inspection, Russian peasant multiplication, memory systems for pi, building odd and even magic squares, square roots by geometry, dyadic systems, and many more. Solutions to difficult problems. 50 illustrations. 145pp. 5⅜ x 8. T350 Paperbound **$1.00**

MAGIC SQUARES AND CUBES, W. S. Andrews. Only book-length treatment in English, a thorough non-technical description and analysis. Here are nasik, overlapping, pandiagonal, serrated squares; magic circles, cubes, spheres, rhombuses. Try your hand at 4-dimensional magical figures! Much unusual folklore and tradition included. High school algebra is sufficient. 754 diagrams and illustrations. viii + 419pp. 5⅜ x 8. T658 Paperbound **$1.85**

CALIBAN'S PROBLEM BOOK: MATHEMATICAL, INFERENTIAL AND CRYPTOGRAPHIC PUZZLES, H. Phillips (Caliban), S. T. Shovelton, G. S. Marshall. 105 ingenious problems by the greatest living creator of puzzles based on logic and inference. Rigorous, modern, piquant; reflecting their author's unusual personality, these intermediate and advanced puzzles all involve the ability to reason clearly through complex situations; some call for mathematical knowledge, ranging from algebra to number theory. Solutions. xi + 180pp. 5⅜ x 8. T736 Paperbound **$1.25**

MATHEMATICAL PUZZLES FOR BEGINNERS AND ENTHUSIASTS, G. Mott-Smith. 188 mathematical puzzles based on algebra, dissection of plane figures, permutations, and probability, that will test and improve your powers of inference and interpretation. The Odic Force, The Spider's Cousin, Ellipse Drawing, theory and strategy of card and board games like tit-tat-toe, go moku, salvo, and many others. 100 pages of detailed mathematical explanations. Appendix of primes, square roots, etc. 135 illustrations. 2nd revised edition. 248pp. 5⅜ x 8. T198 Paperbound **$1.00**

MATHEMAGIC, MAGIC PUZZLES, AND GAMES WITH NUMBERS, R. V. Heath. More than 60 new puzzles and stunts based on the properties of numbers. Easy techniques for multiplying large numbers mentally, revealing hidden numbers magically, finding the date of any day in any year, and dozens more. Over 30 pages devoted to magic squares, triangles, cubes, circles, etc. Edited by J. S. Meyer. 76 illustrations. 128pp. 5⅜ x 8. T110 Paperbound **$1.00**

THE BOOK OF MODERN PUZZLES, G. L. Kaufman. A completely new series of puzzles as fascinating as crossword and deduction puzzles but based upon different principles and techniques. Simple 2-minute teasers, word labyrinths, design and pattern puzzles, logic and observation puzzles — over 150 braincrackers. Answers to all problems. 116 illustrations. 192pp. 5⅜ x 8.
T143 Paperbound **$1.00**

NEW WORD PUZZLES, G. L. Kaufman. 100 ENTIRELY NEW puzzles based on words and their combinations that will delight crossword puzzle, Scrabble and Jotto fans. Chess words, based on the moves of the chess king; design-onyms, symmetrical designs made of synonyms; rhymed double-crostics; syllable sentences; addle letter anagrams; alphagrams; linkograms; and many others all brand new. Full solutions. Space to work problems. 196 figures. vi + 122pp. 5⅜ x 8.
T344 Paperbound **$1.00**

MAZES AND LABYRINTHS: A BOOK OF PUZZLES, W. Shepherd. Mazes, formerly associated with mystery and ritual, are still among the most intriguing of intellectual puzzles. This is a novel and different collection of 50 amusements that embody the principle of the maze: mazes in the classical tradition; 3-dimensional, ribbon, and Möbius-strip mazes; hidden messages; spatial arrangements; etc.—almost all built on amusing story situations. 84 illustrations. Essay on maze psychology. Solutions. xv + 122pp. 5⅜ x 8.
T731 Paperbound **$1.00**

MAGIC TRICKS & CARD TRICKS, W. Jonson. Two books bound as one. 52 tricks with cards, 37 tricks with coins, bills, eggs, smoke, ribbons, slates, etc. Details on presentation, misdirection, and routining will help you master such famous tricks as the Changing Card, Card in the Pocket, Four Aces, Coin Through the Hand, Bill in the Egg, Afghan Bands, and over 75 others. If you follow the lucid exposition and key diagrams carefully, you will finish these two books with an astonishing mastery of magic. 106 figures. 224pp. 5⅜ x 8. T909 Paperbound **$1.00**

PANORAMA OF MAGIC, Milbourne Christopher. A profusely illustrated history of stage magic, a unique selection of prints and engravings from the author's private collection of magic memorabilia, the largest of its kind. Apparatus, stage settings and costumes; ingenious ads distributed by the performers and satiric broadsides passed around in the streets ridiculing pompous showmen; programs; decorative souvenirs. The lively text, by one of America's foremost professional magicians, is full of anecdotes about almost legendary wizards: Dede, the Egyptian; Philadelphia, the wonder-worker; Robert-Houdin, "the father of modern magic;" Harry Houdini; scores more. Altogether a pleasure package for anyone interested in magic, stage setting and design, ethnology, psychology, or simply in unusual people. A Dover original. 295 illustrations; 8 in full color. Index. viii + 216pp. 8⅜ x 11¼.
T774 Paperbound **$2.25**

HOUDINI ON MAGIC, Harry Houdini. One of the greatest magicians of modern times explains his most prized secrets. How locks are picked, with illustrated picks and skeleton keys; how a girl is sawed into twins; how to walk through a brick wall — Houdini's explanations of 44 stage tricks with many diagrams. Also included is a fascinating discussion of great magicians of the past and the story of his fight against fraudulent mediums and spiritualists. Edited by W.B. Gibson and M.N. Young. Bibliography. 155 figures, photos. xv + 280pp. 5⅜ x 8.
T384 Paperbound **$1.35**

MATHEMATICS, MAGIC AND MYSTERY, Martin Gardner. Why do card tricks work? How do magicians perform astonishing mathematical feats? How is stage mind-reading possible? This is the first book length study explaining the application of probability, set theory, theory of numbers, topology, etc., to achieve many startling tricks. Non-technical, accurate, detailed! 115 sections discuss tricks with cards, dice, coins, knots, geometrical vanishing illusions, how a Curry square "demonstrates" that the sum of the parts may be greater than the whole, and dozens of others. No sleight of hand necessary! 135 illustrations. xii + 174pp. 5⅜ x 8.
T335 Paperbound **$1.00**

EASY-TO-DO ENTERTAINMENTS AND DIVERSIONS WITH COINS, CARDS, STRING, PAPER AND MATCHES, R. M. Abraham. Over 300 tricks, games and puzzles will provide young readers with absorbing fun. Sections on card games; paper-folding; tricks with coins, matches and pieces of string; games for the agile; toy-making from common household objects; mathematical recreations; and 50 miscellaneous pastimes. Anyone in charge of groups of youngsters, including hard-pressed parents, and in need of suggestions on how to keep children sensibly amused and quietly content will find this book indispensable. Clear, simple text, copious number of delightful line drawings and illustrative diagrams. Originally titled "Winter Nights Entertainments." Introduction by Lord Baden Powell. 329 illustrations. v + 186pp. 5⅜ x 8½.
T921 Paperbound **$1.00**

STRING FIGURES AND HOW TO MAKE THEM, Caroline Furness Jayne. 107 string figures plus variations selected from the best primitive and modern examples developed by Navajo, Apache, pygmies of Africa, Eskimo, in Europe, Australia, China, etc. The most readily understandable, easy-to-follow book in English on perennially popular recreation. Crystal-clear exposition; step-by-step diagrams. Everyone from kindergarten children to adults looking for unusual diversion will be endlessly amused. Index. Bibliography. Introduction by A. C. Haddon. 17 full-page plates. 960 illustrations. xxiii + 401pp. 5⅜ x 8½.
T152 Paperbound **$2.00**

Entertainments, Humor

ODDITIES AND CURIOSITIES OF WORDS AND LITERATURE, C. Bombaugh, edited by M. Gardner. The largest collection of idiosyncratic prose and poetry techniques in English, a legendary work in the curious and amusing bypaths of literary recreations and the play technique in literature—so important in modern works. Contains alphabetic poetry, acrostics, palindromes, scissors verse, centos, emblematic poetry, famous literary puns, hoaxes, notorious slips of the press, hilarious mistranslations, and much more. Revised and enlarged with modern material by Martin Gardner. 368pp. 5⅜ x 8. **T759 Paperbound $1.50**

A NONSENSE ANTHOLOGY, collected by Carolyn Wells. 245 of the best nonsense verses ever written, including nonsense puns, absurd arguments, mock epics and sagas, nonsense ballads, odes, "sick" verses, dog-Latin verses, French nonsense verses, songs. By Edward Lear, Lewis Carroll, Gelett Burgess, W. S. Gilbert, Hilaire Belloc, Peter Newell, Oliver Herford, etc., 83 writers in all plus over four score anonymous nonsense verses. A special section of limericks, plus famous nonsense such as Carroll's "Jabberwocky" and Lear's "The Jumblies" and much excellent verse virtually impossible to locate elsewhere. For 50 years considered the best anthology available. Index of first lines specially prepared for this edition. Introduction by Carolyn Wells. 3 indexes: Title, Author, First lines. xxxiii + 279pp. **T499 Paperbound $1.35**

THE BAD CHILD'S BOOK OF BEASTS, MORE BEASTS FOR WORSE CHILDREN, and A MORAL ALPHABET, H. Belloc. Hardly an anthology of humorous verse has appeared in the last 50 years without at least a couple of these famous nonsense verses. But one must see the entire volumes—with all the delightful original illustrations by Sir Basil Blackwood—to appreciate fully Belloc's charming and witty verses that play so subacidly on the platitudes of life and morals that beset his day—and ours. A great humor classic. Three books in one. Total of 157pp. 5⅜ x 8. **T749 Paperbound $1.00**

THE DEVIL'S DICTIONARY, Ambrose Bierce. Sardonic and irreverent barbs puncturing the pomposities and absurdities of American politics, business, religion, literature, and arts, by the country's greatest satirist in the classic tradition. Epigrammatic as Shaw, piercing as Swift, American as Mark Twain, Will Rogers, and Fred Allen, Bierce will always remain the favorite of a small coterie of enthusiasts, and of writers and speakers whom he supplies with "some of the most gorgeous witticisms of the English language" (H. L. Mencken). Over 1000 entries in alphabetical order. 144pp. 5⅜ x 8. **T487 Paperbound $1.00**

THE PURPLE COW AND OTHER NONSENSE, Gelett Burgess. The best of Burgess's early nonsense, selected from the first edition of the "Burgess Nonsense Book." Contains many of his most unusual and truly awe-inspiring pieces: 36 nonsense quatrains, the Poems of Patagonia, Alphabet of Famous Goops, and the other hilarious (and rare) adult nonsense that place him in the forefront of American humorists. All pieces are accompanied by the original Burgess illustrations. 123 illustrations. xiii + 113pp. 5⅜ x 8. **T772 Paperbound $1.00**

MY PIOUS FRIENDS AND DRUNKEN COMPANIONS and MORE PIOUS FRIENDS AND DRUNKEN COMPANIONS, Frank Shay. Folksingers, amateur and professional, and everyone who loves singing: here, available for the first time in 30 years, is this valued collection of 132 ballads, blues, vaudeville numbers, drinking songs, sea chanties, comedy songs. Songs of pre-Beatnik Bohemia; songs from all over America, England, France, Australia; the great songs of the Naughty Nineties and early twentieth-century America. Over a third with music. Woodcuts by John Held, Jr. convey perfectly the brash insouciance of an era of rollicking unabashed song. 12 illustrations by John Held, Jr. Two indexes (Titles and First lines and Choruses). Introductions by the author. Two volumes bound as one. Total of xvi + 235pp. 5⅜ x 8½. **T946 Paperbound $1.25**

HOW TO TELL THE BIRDS FROM THE FLOWERS, R. W. Wood. How not to confuse a carrot with a parrot, a grape with an ape, a puffin with nuffin. Delightful drawings, clever puns, absurd little poems point out far-fetched resemblances in nature. The author was a leading physicist. Introduction by Margaret Wood White. 106 illus. 60pp. 5⅜ x 8. **T523 Paperbound 75¢**

PECK'S BAD BOY AND HIS PA, George W. Peck. The complete edition, containing both volumes, of one of the most widely read American humor books. The endless ingenious pranks played by bad boy "Hennery" on his pa and the grocery man, the outraged pomposity of Pa, the perpetual ridiculing of middle class institutions, are as entertaining today as they were in 1883. No pale sophistications or subtleties, but rather humor vigorous, raw, earthy, imaginative, and, as folk humor often is, sadistic. This peculiarly fascinating book is also valuable to historians and students of American culture as a portrait of an age. 100 original illustrations by True Williams. Introduction by E. F. Bleiler. 347pp. 5⅜ x 8. **T497 Paperbound $1.35**

THE HUMOROUS VERSE OF LEWIS CARROLL. Almost every poem Carroll ever wrote, the largest collection ever published, including much never published elsewhere: 150 parodies, burlesques, riddles, ballads, acrostics, etc., with 130 original illustrations by Tenniel, Carroll, and others. "Addicts will be grateful . . . there is nothing for the faithful to do but sit down and fall to the banquet," N. Y. Times. Index to first lines. xiv + 446pp. 5⅜ x 8.
T654 Paperbound **$2.00**

DIVERSIONS AND DIGRESSIONS OF LEWIS CARROLL. A major new treasure for Carroll fans! Rare privately published humor, fantasy, puzzles, and games by Carroll at his whimsical best, with a new vein of frank satire. Includes many new mathematical amusements and recreations, among them the fragmentary Part III of "Curiosa Mathematica." Contains "The Rectory Umbrella," "The New Belfry," "The Vision of the Three T's," and much more. New 32-page supplement of rare photographs taken by Carroll. x + 375pp. 5⅜ x 8.
T732 Paperbound **$1.65**

THE COMPLETE NONSENSE OF EDWARD LEAR. This is the only complete edition of this master of gentle madness available at a popular price. A BOOK OF NONSENSE, NONSENSE SONGS, MORE NONSENSE SONGS AND STORIES in their entirety with all the old favorites that have delighted children and adults for years. The Dong With A Luminous Nose, The Jumblies, The Owl and the Pussycat, and hundreds of other bits of wonderful nonsense. 214 limericks, 3 sets of Nonsense Botany, 5 Nonsense Alphabets, 546 drawings by Lear himself, and much more. 320pp. 5⅜ x 8.
T167 Paperbound **$1.00**

THE MELANCHOLY LUTE, The Humorous Verse of Franklin P. Adams ("FPA"). The author's own selection of light verse, drawn from thirty years of FPA's column, "The Conning Tower," syndicated all over the English-speaking world. Witty, perceptive, literate, these ninety-six poems range from parodies of other poets, Millay, Longfellow, Edgar Guest, Kipling, Masefield, etc., and free and hilarious translations of Horace and other Latin poets, to satiric comments on fabled American institutions—the New York Subways, preposterous ads, suburbanites, sensational journalism, etc. They reveal with vigor and clarity the humor, integrity and restraint of a wise and gentle American satirist. Introduction by Robert Hutchinson. vi + 122pp. 5⅜ x 8½.
T108 Paperbound **$1.00**

SINGULAR TRAVELS, CAMPAIGNS, AND ADVENTURES OF BARON MUNCHAUSEN, R. E. Raspe, with 90 illustrations by Gustave Doré. The first edition in over 150 years to reestablish the deeds of the Prince of Liars exactly as Raspe first recorded them in 1785—the genuine Baron Munchausen, one of the most popular personalities in English literature. Included also are the best of the many sequels, written by other hands. Introduction on Raspe by J. Carswell. Bibliography of early editions. xliv + 192pp. 5⅜ x 8.
T698 Paperbound **$1.00**

THE WIT AND HUMOR OF OSCAR WILDE, ed. by Alvin Redman. Wilde at his most brilliant, in 1000 epigrams exposing weaknesses and hypocrisies of "civilized" society. Divided into 49 categories—sin, wealth, women, America, etc.—to aid writers, speakers. Includes excerpts from his trials, books, plays, criticism. Formerly "The Epigrams of Oscar Wilde." Introduction by Vyvyan Holland, Wilde's only living son. Introductory essay by editor. 260pp. 5⅜ x 8.
T602 Paperbound **$1.00**

MAX AND MORITZ, Wilhelm Busch. Busch is one of the great humorists of all time, as well as the father of the modern comic strip. This volume, translated by H. A. Klein and other hands, contains the perennial favorite "Max and Moritz" (translated by C. T. Brooks), Plisch and Plum, Das Rabennest, Eispeter, and seven other whimsical, sardonic, jovial, diabolical cartoon and verse stories. Lively English translations parallel the original German. This work has delighted millions, since it first appeared in the 19th century, and is guaranteed to please almost anyone. Edited by H. A. Klein, with an afterword. x + 205pp. 5⅝ x 8½.
T181 Paperbound **$1.00**

HYPOCRITICAL HELENA, Wilhelm Busch. A companion volume to "Max and Moritz," with the title piece (Die Fromme Helena) and 10 other highly amusing cartoon and verse stories, all newly translated by H. A. Klein and M. C. Klein: Adventure on New Year's Eve (Abenteuer in der Neujahrsnacht), Hangover on the Morning after New Year's Eve (Der Katzenjammer am Neujahrsmorgen), etc. English and German in parallel columns. Hours of pleasure, also a fine language aid. x + 205pp. 5⅝ x 8½.
T184 Paperbound **$1.00**

THE BEAR THAT WASN'T, Frank Tashlin. What does it mean? Is it simply delightful wry humor, or a charming story of a bear who wakes up in the midst of a factory, or a satire on Big Business, or an existential cartoon-story of the human condition, or a symbolization of the struggle between conformity and the individual? New York Herald Tribune said of the first edition: ". . . a fable for grownups that will be fun for children. Sit down with the book and get your own bearings." Long an underground favorite with readers of all ages and opinions. v + 51pp. Illustrated. 5⅜ x 8½.
T939 Paperbound **75¢**

RUTHLESS RHYMES FOR HEARTLESS HOMES and MORE RUTHLESS RHYMES FOR HEARTLESS HOMES, Harry Graham ("Col. D. Streamer"). Two volumes of Little Willy and 48 other poetic disasters. A bright, new reprint of oft-quoted, never forgotten, devastating humor by a precursor of today's "sick" joke school. For connoisseurs of wicked, wacky humor and all who delight in the comedy of manners. Original drawings are a perfect complement. 61 illustrations. Index. vi + 69pp. Two vols. bound as one. 5⅜ x 8½.
T930 Paperbound **75¢**

Say It language phrase books

These handy phrase books (128 to 196 pages each) make grammatical drills unnecessary for an elementary knowledge of a spoken foreign language. Covering most matters of travel and everyday life each volume contains:

Over 1000 phrases and sentences in immediately useful forms — foreign language plus English.

Modern usage designed for Americans. Specific phrases like, "Give me small change," and "Please call a taxi."

Simplified phonetic transcription you will be able to read at sight.

The only completely indexed phrase books on the market.

Covers scores of important situations: — Greetings, restaurants, sightseeing, useful expressions, etc.

These books are prepared by native linguists who are professors at Columbia, N.Y.U., Fordham and other great universities. Use them independently or with any other book or record course. They provide a supplementary living element that most other courses lack. Individual volumes in:

Russian 75¢	Italian 75¢	Spanish 75¢	German 75¢
Hebrew 75¢	Danish 75¢	Japanese 75¢	Swedish 75¢
Dutch 75¢	Esperanto 75¢	Modern Greek 75¢	Portuguese 75¢
Norwegian 75¢	Polish 75¢	French 75¢	Yiddish 75¢
Turkish 75¢		English for German-speaking people 75¢	
English for Italian-speaking people 75¢		English for Spanish-speaking people 75¢	

Large clear type. 128-196 pages each. 3½ x 5¼. Sturdy paper binding.

Listen and Learn language records

LISTEN & LEARN is the only language record course designed especially to meet your travel and everyday needs. It is available in separate sets for FRENCH, SPANISH, GERMAN, JAPANESE, RUSSIAN, MODERN GREEK, PORTUGUESE, ITALIAN and HEBREW, and each set contains three 33⅓ rpm long-playing records—1½ hours of recorded speech by eminent native speakers who are professors at Columbia, New York University, Queens College.

Check the following special features found only in LISTEN & LEARN:

- **Dual-language recording. 812 selected phrases and sentences,** over 3200 words, spoken first in English, then in their foreign language equivalents. A suitable pause follows each foreign phrase, allowing you time to repeat the expression. You learn by unconscious assimilation.

- **128 to 206-page manual** contains everything on the records, plus a simple phonetic pronunciation guide.

- **Indexed for convenience. The only set on the market** that is completely indexed. No more puzzling over where to find the phrase you need. Just look in the rear of the manual.

- **Practical.** No time wasted on material you can find in any grammar. LISTEN & LEARN covers central core material with phrase approach. Ideal for the person with limited learning time.

- **Living, modern expressions,** not found in other courses. Hygienic products, modern equipment, shopping—expressions used every day, like "nylon" and "air-conditioned."

- **Limited objective.** Everything you learn, no matter where you stop, is immediately useful. You have to finish other courses, wade through grammar and vocabulary drill, before they help you.

- **High-fidelity recording.** LISTEN & LEARN records equal in clarity and surface-silence any record on the market costing up to $6.

"Excellent . . . the spoken records . . . impress me as being among the very best on the market," **Prof. Mario Pei,** Dept. of Romance Languages, Columbia University. "Inexpensive and well-done . . . it would make an ideal present," CHICAGO SUNDAY TRIBUNE. "More genuinely helpful than anything of its kind which I have previously encountered," **Sidney Clark,** well-known author of "ALL THE BEST" travel books.

UNCONDITIONAL GUARANTEE. Try LISTEN & LEARN, then return it within 10 days for full refund if you are not satisfied.

Each set contains three twelve-inch 33⅓ records, manual, and album.

SPANISH	the set $5.95	GERMAN		the set $5.95
FRENCH	the set $5.95	ITALIAN		the set $5.95
RUSSIAN	the set $5.95	JAPANESE		the set $5.95
PORTUGUESE	the set $5.95	MODERN GREEK		the set $5.95
MODERN HEBREW	the set $5.95			

Americana

THE EYES OF DISCOVERY, J. Bakeless. A vivid reconstruction of how unspoiled America appeared to the first white men. Authentic and enlightening accounts of Hudson's landing in New York, Coronado's trek through the Southwest; scores of explorers, settlers, trappers, soldiers. America's pristine flora, fauna, and Indians in every region and state in fresh and unusual new aspects. "A fascinating view of what the land was like before the first highway went through," Time. 68 contemporary illustrations, 39 newly added in this edition. Index. Bibliography. x + 500pp. 5⅜ x 8. T761 Paperbound **$2.00**

AUDUBON AND HIS JOURNALS, J. J. Audubon. A collection of fascinating accounts of Europe and America in the early 1800's through Audubon's own eyes. Includes the Missouri River Journals —an eventful trip through America's untouched heartland, the Labrador Journals, the European Journals, the famous "Episodes", and other rare Audubon material, including the descriptive chapters from the original letterpress edition of the "Ornithological Studies", omitted in all later editions. Indispensable for ornithologists, naturalists, and all lovers of Americana and adventure. 70-page biography by Audubon's granddaughter. 38 illustrations. Index. Total of 1106pp. 5⅜ x 8.
T675 Vol I Paperbound **$2.25**
T676 Vol II Paperbound **$2.25**
The set **$4.50**

TRAVELS OF WILLIAM BARTRAM, edited by Mark Van Doren. The first inexpensive illustrated edition of one of the 18th century's most delightful books is an excellent source of first-hand material on American geography, anthropology, and natural history. Many descriptions of early Indian tribes are our only source of information on them prior to the infiltration of the white man. "The mind of a scientist with the soul of a poet," John Livingston Lowes. 13 original illustrations and maps. Edited with an introduction by Mark Van Doren. 448pp. 5⅜ x 8. T13 Paperbound **$2.00**

GARRETS AND PRETENDERS: A HISTORY OF BOHEMIANISM IN AMERICA, A. Parry. The colorful and fantastic history of American Bohemianism from Poe to Kerouac. This is the only complete record of hoboes, cranks, starving poets, and suicides. Here are Pfaff, Whitman, Crane, Bierce, Pound, and many others. New chapters by the author and by H. T. Moore bring this thorough and well-documented history down to the Beatniks. "An excellent account," N. Y. Times. Scores of cartoons, drawings, and caricatures. Bibliography. Index. xxviii + 421pp. 5⅝ x 8⅜. T708 Paperbound **$1.95**

THE EXPLORATION OF THE COLORADO RIVER AND ITS CANYONS, J. W. Powell. The thrilling first-hand account of the expedition that filled in the last white space on the map of the United States. Rapids, famine, hostile Indians, and mutiny are among the perils encountered as the unknown Colorado Valley reveals its secrets. This is the only uncut version of Major Powell's classic of exploration that has been printed in the last 60 years. Includes later reflections and subsequent expedition. 250 illustrations, new map. 400pp. 5⅝ x 8⅜.
T94 Paperbound **$2.00**

THE JOURNAL OF HENRY D. THOREAU, Edited by Bradford Torrey and Francis H. Allen. Henry Thoreau is not only one of the most important figures in American literature and social thought; his voluminous journals (from which his books emerged as selections and crystallizations) constitute both the longest, most sensitive record of personal internal development and a most penetrating description of a historical moment in American culture. This present set, which was first issued in fourteen volumes, contains Thoreau's entire journals from 1837 to 1862, with the exception of the lost years which were found only recently. We are reissuing it, complete and unabridged, with a new introduction by Walter Harding, Secretary of the Thoreau Society. Fourteen volumes reissued in two volumes. Foreword by Henry Seidel Canby. Total of 1888pp. 8⅜ x 12¼. T312-3 Two volume set, Clothbound **$20.00**

GAMES AND SONGS OF AMERICAN CHILDREN, collected by William Wells Newell. A remarkable collection of 190 games with songs that accompany many of them; cross references to show similarities, differences among them; variations; musical notation for 38 songs. Textual discussions show relations with folk-drama and other aspects of folk tradition. Grouped into categories for ready comparative study: Love-games, histories, playing at work, human life, bird and beast, mythology, guessing-games, etc. New introduction covers relations of songs and dances to timeless heritage of folklore, biographical sketch of Newell, other pertinent data. A good source of inspiration for those in charge of groups of children and a valuable reference for anthropologists, sociologists, psychiatrists. Introduction by Carl Withers. New indexes of first lines, games. 5⅜ x 8½. xii + 242pp. T354 Paperbound **$1.75**

Art, History of Art, Antiques, Graphic Arts, Handcrafts

ART STUDENTS' ANATOMY, E. J. Farris. Outstanding art anatomy that uses chiefly living objects for its illustrations. 71 photos of undraped men, women, children are accompanied by carefully labeled matching sketches to illustrate the skeletal system, articulations and movements, bony landmarks, the muscular system, skin, fasciae, fat, etc. 9 x-ray photos show movement of joints. Undraped models are shown in such actions as serving in tennis, drawing a bow in archery, playing football, dancing, preparing to spring and to dive. Also discussed and illustrated are proportions, age and sex differences, the anatomy of the smile, etc. 8 plates by the great early 18th century anatomic illustrator Siegfried Albinus are also included. Glossary. 158 figures, 7 in color. x + 159pp. 5⅝ x 8⅜. T744 Paperbound **$1.50**

AN ATLAS OF ANATOMY FOR ARTISTS, F Schider. A new 3rd edition of this standard text enlarged by 52 new illustrations of hands, anatomical studies by Cloquet, and expressive life studies of the body by Barcsay. 189 clear, detailed plates offer you precise information of impeccable accuracy. 29 plates show all aspects of the skeleton, with closeups of special areas, while 54 full-page plates, mostly in two colors, give human musculature as seen from four different points of view, with cutaways for important portions of the body. 14 full-page plates provide photographs of hand forms, eyelids, female breasts, and indicate the location of muscles upon models. 59 additional plates show how great artists of the past utilized human anatomy. They reproduce sketches and finished work by such artists as Michelangelo, Leonardo da Vinci, Goya, and 15 others. This is a lifetime reference work which will be one of the most important books in any artist's library. "The standard reference tool," AMERICAN LIBRARY ASSOCIATION. "Excellent," AMERICAN ARTIST. Third enlarged edition. 189 plates, 647 illustrations. xxvi + 192pp. 7⅞ x 10⅝. T241 Clothbound **$6.00**

AN ATLAS OF ANIMAL ANATOMY FOR ARTISTS, W. Ellenberger, H. Baum, H. Dittrich. The largest, richest animal anatomy for artists available in English. 99 detailed anatomical plates of such animals as the horse, dog, cat, lion, deer, seal, kangaroo, flying squirrel, cow, bull, goat, monkey, hare, and bat. Surface features are clearly indicated, while progressive beneath-the-skin pictures show musculature, tendons, and bone structure. Rest and action are exhibited in terms of musculature and skeletal structure and detailed cross-sections are given for heads and important features. The animals chosen are representative of specific families so that a study of these anatomies will provide knowledge of hundreds of related species. "Highly recommended as one of the very few books on the subject worthy of being used as an authoritative guide," DESIGN. "Gives a fundamental knowledge," AMERICAN ARTIST. Second revised, enlarged edition with new plates from Cuvier, Stubbs, etc. 288 illustrations. 153pp. 11⅜ x 9. T82 Clothbound **$6.00**

THE HUMAN FIGURE IN MOTION, Eadweard Muybridge. The largest selection in print of Muybridge's famous high-speed action photos of the human figure in motion. 4789 photographs illustrate 162 different actions: men, women, children—mostly undraped—are shown walking, running, carrying various objects, sitting, lying down, climbing, throwing, arising, and performing over 150 other actions. Some actions are shown in as many as 150 photographs each. All in all there are more than 500 action strips in this enormous volume, series shots taken at shutter speeds as high as 1/6000th of a second! These are not posed shots, but true stopped motion. They show bone and muscle in situations that the human eye is not fast enough to capture. Earlier, smaller editions of these prints have brought $40 and more on the out-of-print market. "A must for artists," ART IN FOCUS. "An unparalleled dictionary of action for all artists," AMERICAN ARTIST. 390 full-page plates, with 4789 photographs. Printed on heavy glossy stock. Reinforced binding with headbands. xxi + 390pp. 7⅞ x 10⅝. T204 Clothbound **$10.00**

ANIMALS IN MOTION, Eadweard Muybridge. This is the largest collection of animal action photos in print. 34 different animals (horses, mules, oxen, goats, camels, pigs, cats, guanacos, lions, gnus, deer, monkeys, eagles—and 21 others) in 132 characteristic actions. The horse alone is shown in more than 40 different actions. All 3919 photographs are taken in series at speeds up to 1/6000th of a second. The secrets of leg motion, spinal patterns, head movements, strains and contortions shown nowhere else are captured. You will see exactly how a lion sets his foot down; how an elephant's knees are like a human's—and how they differ; the position of a kangaroo's legs in mid-leap; how an ostrich's head bobs; details of the flight of birds—and thousands of facets of motion only the fastest cameras can catch. Photographed from domestic animals and animals in the Philadelphia zoo, it contains neither semiposed artificial shots nor distorted telephoto shots taken under adverse conditions. Artists, biologists, decorators, cartoonists, will find this book indispensable for understanding animals in motion. "A really marvelous series of plates," NATURE (London). "The dry plate's most spectacular early use was by Eadweard Muybridge," LIFE. 3919 photographs; 380 full pages of plates. 440pp. Printed on heavy glossy paper. Deluxe binding with headbands. 7⅞ x 10⅝. T203 Clothbound **$10.00**

CATALOGUE OF DOVER BOOKS

THE AUTOBIOGRAPHY OF AN IDEA, Louis Sullivan. The pioneer architect whom Frank Lloyd Wright called "the master" reveals an acute sensitivity to social forces and values in this passionately honest account. He records the crystallization of his opinions and theories, the growth of his organic theory of architecture that still influences American designers and architects, contemporary ideas, etc. This volume contains the first appearance of 34 full-page plates of his finest architecture. Unabridged reissue of 1924 edition. New introduction by R. M. Line. Index. xiv + 335pp. 5⅜ x 8. T281 Paperbound **$2.00**

THE DRAWINGS OF HEINRICH KLEY. The first uncut republication of both of Kley's devastating sketchbooks, which first appeared in pre-World War I Germany. One of the greatest cartoonists and social satirists of modern times, his exuberant and iconoclastic fantasy and his extraordinary technique place him in the great tradition of Bosch, Breughel, and Goya, while his subject matter has all the immediacy and tension of our century. 200 drawings. viii + 128pp. 7¾ x 10¾. T24 Paperbound **$1.85**

MORE DRAWINGS BY HEINRICH KLEY. All the sketches from Leut' Und Viecher (1912) and Sammel-Album (1923) not included in the previous Dover edition of Drawings. More of the bizarre, mercilessly iconoclastic sketches that shocked and amused on their original publication. Nothing was too sacred, no one too eminent for satirization by this imaginative, individual and accomplished master cartoonist. A total of 158 illustrations. Iv + 104pp. 7¾ x 10¾. T41 Paperbound **$1.85**

PINE FURNITURE OF EARLY NEW ENGLAND, R. H. Kettell. A rich understanding of one of America's most original folk arts that collectors of antiques, interior decorators, craftsmen, woodworkers, and everyone interested in American history and art will find fascinating and immensely useful. 413 illustrations of more than 300 chairs, benches, racks, beds, cupboards, mirrors, shelves, tables, and other furniture will show all the simple beauty and character of early New England furniture. 55 detailed drawings carefully analyze outstanding pieces. "With its rich store of illustrations, this book emphasizes the individuality and varied design of early American pine furniture. It should be welcomed," ANTIQUES. 413 illustrations and 55 working drawings. 475. 8 x 10¾. T145 Clothbound **$10.00**

THE HUMAN FIGURE, J. H. Vanderpoel. Every important artistic element of the human figure is pointed out in minutely detailed word descriptions in this classic text and illustrated as well in 430 pencil and charcoal drawings. Thus the text of this book directs your attention to all the characteristic features and subtle differences of the male and female (adults, children, and aged persons), as though a master artist were telling you what to look for at each stage. 2nd edition, revised and enlarged by George Bridgman. Foreword. 430 illustrations. 143pp. 6⅛ x 9¼. T432 Paperbound **$1.50**

LETTERING AND ALPHABETS, J. A. Cavanagh. This unabridged reissue of LETTERING offers a full discussion, analysis, illustration of 89 basic hand lettering styles — styles derived from Caslons, Bodonis, Garamonds, Gothic, Black Letter, Oriental, and many others. Upper and lower cases, numerals and common signs pictured. Hundreds of technical hints on make-up, construction, artistic validity, strokes, pens, brushes, white areas, etc. May be reproduced without permission! 89 complete alphabets; 72 lettered specimens. 121pp. 9¾ x 8. T53 Paperbound **$1.35**

STICKS AND STONES, Lewis Mumford. A survey of the forces that have conditioned American architecture and altered its forms. The author discusses the medieval tradition in early New England villages; the Renaissance influence which developed with the rise of the merchant class; the classical influence of Jefferson's time; the "Mechanicsvilles" of Poe's generation; the Brown Decades; the philosophy of the Imperial facade; and finally the modern machine age. "A truly remarkable book," SAT. REV. OF LITERATURE. 2nd revised edition. 21 illustrations. xvii + 228pp. 5⅜ x 8. T202 Paperbound **$1.65**

THE STANDARD BOOK OF QUILT MAKING AND COLLECTING, Marguerite Ickis. A complete easy-to-follow guide with all the information you need to make beautiful, useful quilts. How to plan, design, cut, sew, appliqué, avoid sewing problems, use rag bag, make borders, tuft, every other aspect. Over 100 traditional quilts shown, including over 40 full-size patterns. At-home hobby for fun, profit. Index. 483 illus. 1 color plate. 287pp. 6¾ x 9½. T582 Paperbound **$2.00**

THE BOOK OF SIGNS, Rudolf Koch. Formerly $20 to $25 on the out-of-print market, now only $1.00 in this unabridged new edition! 493 symbols from ancient manuscripts, medieval cathedrals, coins, catacombs, pottery, etc. Crosses, monograms of Roman emperors, astrological, chemical, botanical, runes, housemarks, and 7 other categories. Invaluable for handicraft workers, illustrators, scholars, etc., this material may be reproduced without permission. 493 illustrations by Fritz Kredel. 104pp. 6½ x 9¼. T162 Paperbound **$1.00**

PRIMITIVE ART, Franz Boas. This authoritative and exhaustive work by a great American anthropologist covers the entire gamut of primitive art. Pottery, leatherwork, metal work, stone work, wood, basketry, are treated in detail. Theories of primitive art, historical depth in art history, technical virtuosity, unconscious levels of patterning, symbolism, styles, literature, music, dance, etc. A must book for the interested layman, the anthropologist, artist, handicrafter (hundreds of unusual motifs), and the historian. Over 900 illustrations (50 ceramic vessels, 12 totem poles, etc.). 376pp. 5⅜ x 8. T25 Paperbound **$2.00**

Fiction

FLATLAND, E. A. Abbott. A science-fiction classic of life in a 2-dimensional world that is also a first-rate introduction to such aspects of modern science as relativity and hyperspace. Political, moral, satirical, and humorous overtones have made FLATLAND fascinating reading for thousands. 7th edition. New introduction by Banesh Hoffmann. 16 illustrations. 128pp. 5⅜ x 8.
T1 Paperbound **$1.00**

THE WONDERFUL WIZARD OF OZ, L. F. Baum. Only edition in print with all the original W. W. Denslow illustrations in full color—as much a part of "The Wizard" as Tenniel's drawings are of "Alice in Wonderland." "The Wizard" is still America's best-loved fairy tale, in which, as the author expresses it, "The wonderment and joy are retained and the heartaches and nightmares left out." Now today's young readers can enjoy every word and wonderful picture of the original book. New introduction by Martin Gardner. A Baum bibliography. 23 full-page color plates. viii + 268pp. 5⅜ x 8.
T691 Paperbound **$1.50**

THE MARVELOUS LAND OF OZ, L. F. Baum. This is the equally enchanting sequel to the "Wizard," continuing the adventures of the Scarecrow and the Tin Woodman. The hero this time is a little boy named Tip, and all the delightful Oz magic is still present. This is the Oz book with the Animated Saw-Horse, the Woggle-Bug, and Jack Pumpkinhead. All the original John R. Neill illustrations, 10 in full color. 287 pp. 5⅜ x 8.
T692 Paperbound **$1.50**

FIVE GREAT DOG NOVELS, edited by Blanche Cirker. The complete original texts of five classic dog novels that have delighted and thrilled millions of children and adults throughout the world with their stories of loyalty, adventure, and courage. Full texts of Jack London's "The Call of the Wild"; John Brown's "Rab and His Friends"; Alfred Ollivant's "Bob, Son of Battle"; Marshall Saunders's "Beautiful Joe"; and Ouida's "A Dog of Flanders." 21 Illustrations from the original editions. 495pp. 5⅜ x 8.
T777 Paperbound **$1.75**

TO THE SUN? and OFF ON A COMET!, Jules Verne. Complete texts of two of the most imaginative flights into fancy in world literature display the high adventure that have kept Verne's novels read for nearly a century. Only unabridged edition of the best translation, by Edward Roth. Large, easily readable type. 50 illustrations selected from first editions. 462pp. 5⅜ x 8.
T634 Paperbound **$1.75**

FROM THE EARTH TO THE MOON and ALL AROUND THE MOON, Jules Verne. Complete editions of 2 of Vefne's most successful novels, in finest Edward Roth translations, now available after many years out of print. Verne's visions of submarines, airplanes, television, rockets, interplanetary travel; of scientific and not-so-scientific beliefs; of peculiarities of Americans; all delight and engross us today as much as when they first appeared. Large, easily readable type. 42 illus. from first French edition. 476pp. 5⅜ x 8.
T633 Paperbound **$1.75**

THE CRUISE OF THE CACHALOT, Frank T. Bullen. Out of the experiences of many years on the high-seas, First Mate Bullen created this novel of adventure aboard an American whaler, shipping out of New Bedford, Mass., when American whaling was at the height of its splendor. Originally published in 1899, the story of the round-the-world cruise of the "Cachalot" in pursuit of the sperm whale has thrilled generations of readers. A maritime classic that will fascinate anyone interested in reading about the sea or looking for a solid old-fashioned yarn, while the vivid recreation of a brief but important chapter of Americana and the British author's often biting commentary on nineteenth-century Yankee mores offer insights into the colorful era of America's coming of age. 8 plates. xiii + 271pp. 5⅜ x 8½.
T774 Paperbound **$1.00**

28 SCIENCE FICTION STORIES OF H. G. WELLS. Two full unabridged novels, MEN LIKE GODS and STAR BEGOTTEN, plus 26 short stories by the master science-fiction writer of all time! Stories of space, time, invention, exploration, future adventure—an indispensable part of the library of everyone interested in science and adventure. PARTIAL CONTENTS: Men Like Gods, The Country of the Blind, In the Abyss, The Crystal Egg, The Man Who Could Work Miracles, A Story of the Days to Come, The Valley of Spiders, and 21 more! 928pp. 5⅜ x 8.
T265 Clothbound **$4.50**

DAVID HARUM, E. N. Westcott. This novel of one of the most lovable, humorous characters in American literature is a prime example of regional humor. It continues to delight people who like their humor dry, their characters quaint, and their plots ingenuous. First book edition to contain complete novel plus chapter found after author's death. Illustrations from first illustrated edition. 192pp. 5⅜ x 8.
T580 Paperbound **$1.15**

GESTA ROMANORUM, trans. by Charles Swan, ed. by Wynnard Hooper. 181 tales of Greeks, Romans, Britons, Biblical characters, comprise one of greatest medieval story collections, source of plots for writers including Shakespeare, Chaucer, Gower, etc. Imaginative tales of wars, incest, thwarted love, magic, fantasy, allegory, humor, tell about kings, prostitutes, philosophers, fair damsels, knights, Noah, pirates, all walks, stations of life. Introduction. Notes. 500pp. 5⅜ x 8.
T535 Paperbound **$1.85**

Music

A GENERAL HISTORY OF MUSIC, Charles Burney. A detailed coverage of music from the Greeks up to 1789, with full information on all types of music: sacred and secular, vocal and instrumental, operatic and symphonic. Theory, notation, forms, instruments, innovators, composers, performers, typical and important works, and much more in an easy, entertaining style. Burney covered much of Europe and spoke with hundreds of authorities and composers so that this work is more than a compilation of records . . . it is a living work of careful and first-hand scholarship. Its account of thoroughbass (18th century) Italian music is probably still the best introduction on the subject. A recent NEW YORK TIMES review said, "Surprisingly few of Burney's statements have been invalidated by modern research . . . still of great value." Edited and corrected by Frank Mercer. 35 figures. Indices. 1915pp. 5⅜ x 8. 2 volumes. **T36 The Set, Clothbound $12.50**

A DICTIONARY OF HYMNOLOGY, John Julian. This exhaustive and scholarly work has become known as an invaluable source of hundreds of thousands of important and often difficult to obtain facts on the history and use of hymns in the western world. Everyone interested in hymns will be fascinated by the accounts of famous hymns and hymn writers and amazed by the amount of practical information he will find. More than 30,000 entries on individual hymns, giving authorship, date and circumstances of composition, publication, textual variations, translations, denominational and ritual usage, etc. Biographies of more than 9,000 hymn writers, and essays on important topics such as Christmas carols and children's hymns, and much other unusual and valuable information. A 200 page double-columned index of first lines — the largest in print. Total of 1786 pages in two reinforced clothbound volumes. 6¼ x 9¼. **The set, T333 Clothbound $17.50**

MUSIC IN MEDIEVAL BRITAIN, F. Ll. Harrison. The most thorough, up-to-date, and accurate treatment of the subject ever published, beautifully illustrated. Complete account of institutions and choirs; carols, masses, and motets; liturgy and plainsong; and polyphonic music from the Norman Conquest to the Reformation. Discusses the various schools of music and their reciprocal influences; the origin and development of new ritual forms; development and use of instruments; and new evidence on many problems of the period. Reproductions of scores, over 200 excerpts from medieval melodies. Rules of harmony and dissonance; influence of Continental styles; great composers (Dunstable, Cornysh, Fairfax, etc.); and much more. Register and index of more than 400 musicians. Index of titles. General Index. 225-item bibliography. 6 Appendices. xix + 491pp. 5⅝ x 8¾. **T705 Clothbound $10.00**

THE MUSIC OF SPAIN, Gilbert Chase. Only book in English to give concise, comprehensive account of Iberian music; new Chapter covers music since 1941. Victoria, Albéniz, Cabezón, Pedrell, Turina, hundreds of other composers; popular and folk music; the Gypsies; the guitar; dance, theatre, opera, with only extensive discussion in English of the Zarzuela; virtuosi such as Casals; much more. "Distinguished . . . readable," Saturday Review. 400-item bibliography. Index. 27 photos. 383pp. 5⅜ x 8. **T549 Paperbound $2.00**

ON STUDYING SINGING, Sergius Kagen. An intelligent method of voice-training, which leads you around pitfalls that waste your time, money, and effort. Exposes rigid, mechanical systems, baseless theories, deleterious exercises. "Logical, clear, convincing . . . dead right," Virgil Thomson, N.Y. Herald Tribune. "I recommend this volume highly," Maggie Teyte, Saturday Review. 119pp. 5⅜ x 8. **T622 Paperbound $1.25**

Prices subject to change without notice.

Dover publishes books on art, music, philosophy, literature, languages, history, social sciences, psychology, handcrafts, orientalia, puzzles and entertainments, chess, pets and gardens, books explaining science, intermediate and higher mathematics, mathematical physics, engineering, biological sciences, earth sciences, classics of science, etc. Write to:

Dept. catrr.
Dover Publications, Inc.
180 Varick Street, N.Y. 14, N.Y.